# Psychiatry
# for the
# House Officer
## Third Edition

Compliments of G. Mark Geiger
Sandoz Pharmaceuticals
(608) 825-6087

# BOOKS IN THE HOUSE OFFICER SERIES

Cardiology for the House Officer, Second Edition

Coronary Care for the House Officer

Critical Care Medicine for the House Officer

Dermatology for the House Officer, Second Edition

Diabetes Mellitus for the House Officer

Emergency Medicine for the House Officer

Endocrinology for the House Officer, Second Edition

Gastroenterology for the House Officer

Hematology for the House Officer, Second Edition

Infectious Disease for the House Officer

Nephrology for the House Officer

Neurology for the House Officer, Third Edition

Neurosurgical Management for the House Officer

Obstetrics for the House Officer

Oncology for the House Officer

Psychiatry for the House Officer, Second Edition

Respiratory Medicine for the House Officer, Second Edition

Rheumatology for the House Officer

Urology for the House Officer

Gynecologic Endocrinology and Infertility for the House Officer

# BOOKS IN THE CASE STUDIES FOR THE HOUSE OFFICER SERIES

Case Studies in Cardiology for the House Officer

Case Studies in Endocrinology for the House Officer

Case Studies in Neurology for the House Officer

Case Studies in Neurosurgery for the House Officer

Case Studies in Psychiatry for the House Officer

# BOOKS IN THE PEDIATRIC HOUSE OFFICER SERIES

Pediatric Cardiology for the House Officer

Pediatric Emergency Medicine for the House Officer

Pediatric Endocrinology for the House Officer

Pediatric Neurology for the House Officer

# Psychiatry
# for the
# House Officer
## Third Edition

**David A. Tomb, M.D.**
*Department of Psychiatry*
*University of Utah School of Medicine*
*Salt Lake City, Utah*

WILLIAMS & WILKINS
Baltimore • Hong Kong • London • Sydney

*Editor:* Nancy Collins
*Associate Editor:* Carol Eckhart
*Design:* Bob Och
*Copy Editor:* Stephen Siegforth
*Production:* Theda Harris

Copyright © 1988
Williams & Wilkins
428 East Preston Street
Baltimore, MD 21202, USA

Accurate indications, adverse reactions, and dosage schedules for drugs are provided in this book, but it is possible that they may change. The reader is urged to review the package information data of the manufacturers of the medications mentioned.

*Printed in the United States of America*

First Edition, 1981
  Reprinted 1982, 1983, 1984
Second Edition, 1984
  Reprinted 1984, 1985, 1986, 1987, 1988

**Library of Congress Cataloging in Publication Data**

Tomb, David A.
  Psychiatry for the house officer / David A. Tomb.—3rd ed.
    p. cm.
  Includes bibliographies and index.
  ISBN 0-683-08341-4
  1. Psychiatry—Handbooks, manuals, etc. 2. Mental illness—Handbooks, manuals, etc. 3. Psychological manifestations of general diseases—Handbooks, manuals, etc. I. Title.
  [DNLM: 1. Mental Disorders—handbooks. WM 34 T656p]
RC456.T65 1988
616.89—dc19
DNLM/DLC
for Library of Congress                                    88-5503
                                                              CIP

88  89  90  91  92
3  4  5  6  7  8  9  10

# *Dedication*

To my wife Jane and my daughter Collin
for time lost

# Preface to the Third Edition

The four years since the previous edition of this book have witnessed an explosion in psychiatric knowledge. In this new edition I have attempted to capture key advances, retain the best of previous practices, and keep the book's length short.

Of course, the real practice of psychiatry is far too complex to be completely contained between the pages of a book, however long. This book, thus, in only a place to start.

Best wishes.

David A. Tomb, MD

# Contents

# Chapter 1

# Psychiatric Classification

### DSM-III-R[1]

Psychiatric diagnosis has long been criticized as ambiguous and unreliable. Some diagnostic categories have been based on subjective, unverifiable intrapsychic phenomena, while others have been heterogeneously broad.[2]

Modern diagnosis attempts to avoid these pitfalls through the use of the revised version of the 3rd edition of the Diagnostic and Statistical Manual of Mental Disorders (DSM-III-R). This scheme asserts that there are a limited number of identifiable (though possibly overlapping) psychiatric disorders. DSM-III-R contains specific diagnostic criteria for each diagnosis. One matches facts from a particular patient's history and clinical presentation with those criteria from a likely diagnosis and if an adequate number are met, that diagnosis should be made. Each disorder has a unique set of diagnostic criteria. Multiple diagnoses are permitted, and there are several specific categories of disorders "not otherwise specified" (NOS) which allow for placement of the (often many) patients who have unusual presentations.

For example: A patient who (1) has been having auditory hallucinations which (2) have impaired his social relations and functioning at work (3) for at least 6 months and who is without evidence of (4) an Organic Mental Disorder or (5) prominent symptoms of a Major Affective Disorder <u>must</u> be given the diagnosis of schizophrenia. If the patient also has (6) a flat, incongruous, or silly affect and (7) frequent or constant incoherence, an additional diagnosis of Disorganized subtype must be made.

Conclusions about DSM-III-R at this point are that <u>reliability</u> (the likelihood that different professionals would make the same diagnosis on the same patient) is improved while <u>validity</u> (the certainty that the diagnoses identify unique, meaningful conditions) is less sure.[3,4]

MULTIAXIAL CLASSIFICATION:

In addition to the operationally defined criteria, DSM-III-R also introduces a multiaxial system of classification.[5] A patient is not fully classified until he is coded on each of five axes (although only the first three axes are needed for an official diagnosis):

- Axis    I:   The clinical syndrome (example above).
- Axis    II:  Personality disorders and/or developmental disorders (none may be present).
- Axis    III: Physical disorders (none may be present).
- Axis    IV:  A severity rating of psychosocial stress during the past year (scale of 1-6).[6,7]
- Axis    V:   The Global Assessment of Functioning Scale (GAF scale) - a measure of (1) current functioning and (2) the highest functioning over the preceding year (scale of 1-90).[8,9]

The specific rating scales for each axis are included in the text of DSM-III-R (pp 11-12).

## FUNDAMENTAL PSYCHIATRIC CONCEPTS

Psychiatric pathology is organized into several broad categories. Some (eg, organic mental disorders; mood disorders) are described in later chapters; others are described below.

Psychosis: A general term referring to a major mental disorder having a marked impairment of:

- a sense of reality, and
- the ability to communicate, and/or
- emotional awareness and control, and/or
- cognitive abilities

which lead (1) to an inability to maintain interpersonal relations and (2) to compromised daily functioning. The principle types of psychotic disorders are:

1. Schizophrenia, Paranoid and Schizoaffective Disorders;
2. Schizophreniform Disorder and Brief Reactive Psychosis;
3. Some Major Affective Disorders;
4. Severe Organic Mental Disorders.

Some of these have known organic causes; some do not (ie, the functional psychoses); most are suspected of having a biological etiology.

<u>Personality Disorder</u>:  A longstanding <u>maladaptive</u> personality trait of little concern to the patient but which causes impaired life adjustment.

<u>Neuroses</u>: A theoretical grouping of diverse, chronic, non-psychotic, uncomfortable psychiatric conditions based on presumed unresolved intrapsychic conflicts (eg, phobias, hypochondriasis, Hysterical Neurosis).   These conditions are scattered throughout DSM-III-R.

## REFERENCES

1. American Psychiatric Association Task Force on Nomenclature and Statistics: <u>Diagnostic and Statistical Manual of Mental Disorders, 3rd Ed. - Revised</u>, (DSM-III-R). Washington, D.C., American Psychiatric Association, 1987.
2. Bayer R, Spitzer RL: Neurosis, psychodynamics, and DSM-III. <u>Arch Gen Psychiatry</u> 42:187-196, 1985.
3. Fox HA: The DSM-III concept of organic brain syndrome. <u>Br J Psychiatry</u> 142:419-421, 1983.
4. Longabaugh R, Fowler DR, et al: Validation of a problem-focused nomenclature. <u>Arch Gen Psychiatry</u> 40:453, 1983.
5. Williams JBW: The multiaxial system of DSM-III: Where did it come from and where should it go. <u>Arch Gen Psychiatry</u> 42:175-186, 1985.
6. Zimmerman M, Pfohl B, et al: The Validity of DSM-III Axis IV. <u>Am J Psychiatry</u> 142:1437-1441, 1985.
7. Zimmerman M, Pfohl B, et al: The prognostic validity of DSM-III Axis IV in depressed inpatients. <u>Am J Psychiatry</u> 144:102-6, 1987.
8. Fernando T, Mellsop G, et al: The reliability of Axis V of DSM-III. <u>Am J Psychiatry</u> 143:752-755, 1986.
9. Schrader G, Gordon M, Harcourt R: The usefulness of DSM-III Axis IV and Axis V assessments. <u>Am J Psychiatr</u> 143:904-907, 1986.

# Chapter 2

## Assessment

A psychiatric evaluation helps (1) make a diagnosis, (2) estimate the severity of the patient's condition, (3) decide on an initial course of action, (4) develop a relationship with the patient, (5) assemble a dynamic understanding of the patient, and (6) engage the patient in psychotherapy.[1,2] Some (primarily analytically oriented) psychiatrists argue that the most reliable understanding of a patient results from an open-ended interview in which the course of the interview is directed by the patient's conscious and unconscious concerns. An alternate form of interview, and one encouraged by the requirements of DSM-III-R, requires a structured format that demands precise historical and descriptive information and the answers to specific questions. Which technique produces a fuller understanding of the patient remains unresolved, yet modern diagnosis requires the structured form described below.

A thorough evaluation of a psychiatric patient consists of a psychiatric history, mental status examination, complete physical examination, laboratory screening evaluation, and selected psychological and laboratory tests when indicated.[3] The history and mental status are usually obtained during the initial interview.

More is required in this process than merely collecting facts. The interviewer seeks useful information not only from the facts of the history and mental status examination, but also from the sequence in which the patient mentions things, the patient's interpersonal style, and the patient's non-verbal communication. Because there is so much information available from the patient outside the formal part of the interview, it is essential to avoid structuring the interview too early. Early on, allow the patient to express his concerns and find out his reason for coming for help (<u>Why now</u>?). Be supportive and encouraging - develop a rapport with the patient and try to get an empathic understanding of his distress. Help allay anxiety, if present.

Be patient, friendly, and receptive if the patient is quiet. If he rambles, you may have to impose a structure earlier. Develop a qualitative sense for the patient's impairment. Is he likely to be aggressive? Suicidal? In need of hospitalization?

If skillfully conducted, much of the information required by the history and mental status exam may be obtained unobtrusively during this period. Also, as the interview proceeds, it is possible to more clearly identify and narrow what is relevant so that the formal demand for specific information may be minimal. However, some such information is almost always required (eg, data to satisfy DSM-III-R diagnostic criteria, family psychiatric history, or mental status responses to rule out organicity or loss of abstracting ability), so at times during the interview mentally review what is missing and save time towards the end to pursue it by direct questioning. The transition to a more formal style of interviewing can be smooth if rapport has been developed beforehand.

## PSYCHIATRIC HISTORY

IDENTIFICATION OF THE PATIENT:

1. Name, age, birth date, marital status and children, race, religion, occupation, education, social class, handicaps, etc;
2. Identification of informants (if not the patient). Mood and apparent biases of informants;
3. Estimate of the reliability of the information.

CHIEF COMPLAINT:

Usually a verbatim statement of "what the problem is." Does it differ significantly from the reports of those who accompany the patient?

PRESENT ILLNESS:

Usually the focus of the interview. Get the patient's description of and feelings about his illness. Establish chronological order of symptoms and treatments. Has the patient noticed any other changes in himself? Major life changes during this time? Stresses and conflicts? Any secondary gain identifiable? Past psychiatric history—particularly diagnosis and severity of illness; types of treatment; drug use?

## PAST PERSONAL HISTORY:

Birth and early development: relatives may be a source of information: Mother's pregnancy and delivery; Prematurity? Planned pregnancy? Get estimate of temperament and behavior problems. Psychophysiological problems?

Childhood: Personality traits, behavior problems, social relationships, school adjustment, family relationships, and stability.

Social history: What kind of interpersonal relationships can the patient make? - Has he been a loner? follower? leader? What kind of group activities in the past and in the present? Who are the people important to him now? in the past? What was his premorbid personality? Military history?

Marriage: At what age? How many times? Relationship patterns within the marriage? Number of children and attitude toward them?

Education: Highest grade attained? Specific academic difficulties? Behavior problems? Social problems?

Occupational history: Should be fairly detailed with concentration on job changes, length of time jobs have been held, best job obtained and when. Social relations on job; with boss? with workers? How does job compare with ambition? with family expectations?

Sexual history: Sexual orientation? Psychosexual problems or deviant behavior? Feelings about sex?

## FAMILY HISTORY:

Who lives in the home? - patient should describe them and describe his relationship with them. Description of patient's family of origin and his role in it. Upwardly mobile family? Get detailed description of psychiatric (and medical) illnesses in family members.

## MEDICAL HISTORY:

Current and past medical problems and treatments.

## CURRENT SOCIAL SITUATION:

Personal living situation, income? Social environment? Estimated current marital and family stability and happiness?

## MENTAL STATUS EXAMINATION

A mental status examination is a systematic documentation of the quality of mental functioning at the time of interview.[4] It helps both with current diagnosis and treatment planning, and it serves as a baseline for future reference.  Although much of the information sought in a mental status exam is obtained informally during other parts of the interview, it is usually necessary for the patient to answer a few formal questions if the interviewer is to learn the patient's abilities in each of the categories of mental functioning listed below.  Upon concluding the mental status examination, estimate its reliability.

## GENERAL PRESENTATION:

Appearance: overall impression of the patient: attractive, unattractive, posture, clothes, grooming, healthy vs sickly, old looking vs young looking, angry, puzzled, frightened, ill-at-ease, apathetic, contemptuous, effeminate, masculine, etc.

General behavior: mannerisms, gestures, combative, psychomotor retardation, rigid, twitches, picking, clumsy, hand wringing, etc.

Attitude towards the examiner: cooperative, hostile, defensive, seductive, evasive, ingratiating, etc.

The psychotic patient may appear disheveled and bizarre with odd posturing (particularly catatonics) and grimacing. Some schizophrenics may stare and others look "blank." Paranoid patients may be hostile while hysterical patients often are seductive in manner and dress.  Depressed patients may be nearly mute and display psychomotor retardation. Restlessness may suggest anxiety, withdrawal, mania, etc.

## STATE OF CONSCIOUSNESS:

Is the patient alert (eg, normally aware of both internal and external stimuli) or is he hyperalert?  Is the patient lethargic - eg, does he "drift off" or do his thoughts wander?  The patient needs to be reasonably alert for the remainder of the exam to be reliable.  The causes for decreased alertness are usually organic.

## ATTENTION:

Can the patient pay attention for short periods of time (attend) without being distracted by minor stimuli?  Can he attend for lengths of time (concentrate)?  This ability is necessary if you are to assess higher level functions (ie, they may be intact, but the patient can't demonstrate it due to lack of attention).  Test attention by digit recall - eg, speak a series of numbers in a monotone and ask the patient to repeat them; begin with three and increase by one with each successful trial; a normal maximum response is 6 numbers repeated.  Test concentration by Random Letter Test

- eg, tell patient to note (by raising his finger) each time a certain letter is mentioned and then read a long string of letters; most people make very few errors. Defects in attention usually are due to organic causes but may be caused by marked anxiety or psychotic interruption of thoughts.

## SPEECH:

Listen to the patient's speech. Is it loud, soft, fast, slow, pressured, mute, etc? Does the patient speak spontaneously? with good vocabulary? Does the patient articulate with difficulty (dysarthria)?

Is there a deficiency in <u>language</u> - eg, aphasia? This speech is usually identifiable by the experienced listener (eg, patient tries to communicate but incorrect words are chosen and grammatical errors made) but may be confused with rambling psychotic speech. Manic patients often speak loudly and rapidly; depressed patients are soft and slow. Bizarre speech usually suggests a psychotic and/or organic state.

## ORIENTATION[5]:

Check for <u>person</u> (name? age? when born?), <u>place</u> (What place is this? What is your home address?), <u>time</u> (today's date? day of the week? time? season?), and <u>situation</u> (Why are you here?). Time sense is usually the first lost. Major disorientation suggests organicity. Minor loss may reflect temporary stress.

## MOOD AND AFFECT:

<u>Mood</u> is a sustained emotional state - eg, depressed, euphoric, elevated, anxious, angry, irritable.
<u>Affect</u> is the patient's current emotional state - it is the state the interviewer can <u>observe</u>. Common abnormal affects include flat, blunted, and inappropriate.

Note whether the affect you observe is consistent with the patient's expressed mood and congruent with his thought content. Distinguish a depressed mood from an organically caused apathy. The affective disorders most commonly display alterations in mood but so do psychotic, anxiety (eg, panic), and organic (eg, drug use) disorders.

## FORM OF THOUGHT:

Does the patient's thinking make sense? Does one thought follow another logically, or does the patient display circumstantiality (take forever to make his point; many unnecessary details - overinclusiveness), flight of ideas (rapidly jumping from idea to idea, but with understandable associations), evasiveness, loosening of associations (tangentiality - thoughts are unrelated, but the patient seems unaware of this), perseveration (needless repetition of the same thought or phrase), or blocking (speech and train of thought is interrupted and picked up again a few moments or minutes later). Are answers to questions relevant? Ask the patient for his impressions of his own thoughts.

These abnormalities in thought process are most commonly associated with schizophrenic or affective disorders. None are pathognomonic, but any major abnormality suggests a psychotic process.

THOUGHT CONTENT:

Check for: abnormal preoccupations and obsessions, excessive suspiciousness, phobias, rituals, hypochondriacal symptoms, deja vu experiences, depersonalization, delusions (fixed, false beliefs - characterize them as persecutory, of grandeur, of reference, of influence, unsystematized, etc). Always check for preoccupations about suicide or homicide.

Get at the presence of delusions by questions like: "Do you have any strong ideas other people don't share?" "Are there things you think about a lot?"

Delusions usually suggest a functional psychotic disorder (most commonly schizophrenia), but other conditions may display them (eg, poorly systematized delusions in OBS). Obsessions may occur with psychosis but also are typical of obsessive compulsive disorder. Phobias characterize phobic disorders.

Is the patient unaware that he is ill or has abnormal thinking (lacks insight)? Does he have a generalized loss of ability for abstractive thinking (ie, concreteness)? Test for abstractive ability by:

1. Similarities: "What do these things have in common?"

```
    baseball - orange
         car - train
        desk - bookcase
       happy - sad
       horse - apple
```

2. <u>Proverbs</u>: "What do people mean when they say ....?"

When the cat's away, the mice will play.
The proof of the pudding is in the eating.
A golden hammer breaks an iron door.
The tongue is the enemy of the neck.
The hot coal burns, the cold one blackens.

Always correlate abstractive thinking with intelligence. Concreteness in the face of normal intelligence is suggestive of a psychotic thought disorder (although this is questioned[6]). Note any bizarre responses to similarities or proverbs - Are the answers personalized? Are the answers vague because the patient is aware of failing (eg, OBS) and is obfuscating?

PERCEPTIONS:

Does the patient display <u>misperceptions</u> (draw wrong conclusions from self-evident information)? Are there <u>illusions</u> (misinterpretations of sensory stimuli - eg, a shadow becomes a person) or <u>hallucinations</u> (note whether auditory, visual, tactile, olfactory, etc)? <u>Always</u> determine if hallucinations are accusatory, threatening, or commanding. If not volunteered, get at the presence of hallucinations by questions like: "Have you had the experience of walking down the street, hearing your name called, and finding no one there?" "Have you had any mystical or psychic experiences?"

Illusions are most common in delirium but may also occur in functional psychoses. Hallucinations occur in a variety of conditions but most commonly in psychotic disorders. Schizophrenia usually has auditory hallucinations while visual hallucinations are more common in organic conditions. Tactile hallucinations are frequent in sedative-hypnotic and alcohol withdrawal states.

JUDGMENT:

An estimate of the patient's real life problem solving skills is often difficult to make. Judgement is a complex mental function which depends on maturation of the nervous system (poor in children). The best indicator is usually the patient's behavior, so history is very important. Some sense of the patient's judgment can be obtained through hypothetical examples: "What should you do if you find a stamped, addressed letter?" "What should you do if you lose a book belonging to a library?"

Judgement is regularly impaired in OBS, psychosis, and some retardation. Its assessment helps determine the patient's capacity for independent functioning.

## MEMORY:

Test all three types of memory: remote, recent, and immediate (retention and recall).

### Immediate:

1. Digit repetition
2. Ask patient to remember 3 objects and 3 words - ask for them after 5 minutes (they should be recalled).
3. Ask the patient to count - stop him at 27 - (wait 1 minute) - tell him to continue counting - stop at 42 (wait 3 minutes - then continue counting.

Recent: Ask questions about the past 24 hours - eg, "How did you travel here?" "What was on the news last night?"

Remote: Personal - born? school? work? etc.
        Historical - Name four presidents in this century; the dates of WW II; etc.

Recent and remote memory usually can be tested inconspicuously during the interview. Is the patient aware of his deficit? What is his attitude toward it? Loss of memory usually indicates an organic process unless it has some of the characteristics of the dissociative disorders (chapter 9).

Constructional ability is a sensitive test for early diffuse cortical damage. Draw a diamond and a 3-dimensional cube and have the patient copy them. Ask the patient to draw a flowerpot with a flower, or the face of a clock set at 2:45. Incomplete or very poorly done responses are suggestive of early organicity.

## INTELLECTUAL FUNCTIONING:

Intelligence is a global function which can be estimated from the general tone and content of the interview as well as by the patient's fund of information and ability to perform calculations.

### Fund of knowledge:

How many weeks in a year?
Name the last 6 Presidents.
What does the liver do?

How far is it from Chicago to LA?
Why are light colored clothes cool?
Who wrote <u>Remembrances of Things Past</u>?
What causes rust?

How many nickels in $1.15?

<u>Calculations</u>:

Serial 7's - "Take 100 and subtract 7 from it, then take
   7 from the answer, etc";
Serial 3's - eg, take 3 from 20, etc;
Simple calculations - 2x3, 5x3, 4x9.

Calculation relies on functions other than intelligence,
including concentration and memory.  If in doubt, ask for
formal IQ testing.  Organic conditions may produce a loss of
intellectual functioning, but psychoses seldom do (as long
as the patient can concentrate on the tests).

## PSYCHOLOGICAL TESTS

Psychological testing is requested for occasional psychiatric patients and may provide a useful enlargement of the
understanding of those patients.  Although not essential for
most patients, testing may:

1. Help identify organic syndromes;
2. Help localize organic pathology;
3. Contribute to the identification of borderline psychotic
   states;
4. Provide a baseline of general and specific functioning;
5. Generally help with differential diagnosis among psychiatric conditions.

Talk to the psychologist.  Describe what you are looking
for.  Ask for recommendations.  Although most patients receive a battery of tests, very specific questions may be
answered by only one test.  Carefully integrate the psychologist's report with your own evaluation but do not allow
test results to supersede clinical judgement.  Commonly used
tests for adults include:

<u>Wechsler Adult Intelligence Scale (WAIS)</u>: A very useful
test.  Although it does yield three separate IQ scores
(full-scale, verbal, and performance), a careful evaluation
of how the patient answered the 11 different subtests within
the WAIS provides clues to the presence of a thought disorder, an attention or memory deficit, visual-motor impairment, etc.

Minnesota Multiphasic Personality Inventory (MMPI): This is a self-administered personality test which takes little of the therapist's time, produces a general description of the patient's personality characteristics, and can even be computer-scored. Although a useful global description of the patient, do not stretch it too far diagnostically.

Bender-Gestalt Test: This test is easily administered - the patient draws nine specific geometric figures on a blank sheet of paper. Its greatest application is in detecting visual-motor impairment and organic deficits.

Rorschach Test: This is an unstructured projective test which asks the patient to "describe what he sees" in a series of ten standardized ink blots. Elaborate scoring systems exist which allow a skilled examiner to infer elements of the patient's personality functioning. It is used diagnostically to help identify psychoses and personality disorders. Its diagnostic validity has not been assured.

Thematic Apperception Test (TAT): This is a projective test similar to the Rorschach which draws conclusions from the patient's responses to a series of suggestive and ambiguous human figure drawings.

Draw-a-Person Test: The patient is asked to draw a picture of a "person" and then a picture of a person of the opposite sex. The results are then interpreted by the examiner.

## EEG

The EEG plays a useful supportive role in psychiatry.[7] It is not definitive in any psychiatric condition, but it does help rule in or out a diversity of conditions. Its primary use is in the differentiation between organic and functional conditions.

1. Epileptics (particularly temporal lobe epilepsy) often mimic psychiatric patients - the EEG helps differentiate (although 30% of epileptics have a normal tracing between attacks).
2. The patient who is confused and disoriented (delirium) due to organic factors usually has diffuse EEG slowing. A major exception is Alcohol Withdrawal Delirium (delirium tremens) which shows increased fast activity.
3. The patient who has Primary Degenerative Dementia of the Alzheimer Type (50% of demented patients) usually has a normal EEG. Most reversible forms of dementia produce abnormal tracings. The EEG of a person with pseudodementia (eg, depression which mimics dementia) is usually normal.

4. Drugs often alter the EEG - eg, sedative-hypnotics increase fast activity; major tranquilizers increase slow activity.
5. A variety of organic causes can produce bizarre behavior (eg, brain tumor, cerebral infarcts, cerebral trauma). A normal EEG does not rule out organic pathology, but an abnormal tracing is suspicious.

Several populations of psychiatric patients have a slightly increased frequency of nonspecific abnormalities on the EEG - eg, schizophrenics (particularly catatonics) and manic-depressives. Patients with antisocial personality disorder have perhaps the highest frequency of abnormal tracings - look for but don't overread organic pathology in these patients. On the other hand, some patients with borderline personality disorder show a slowing of the EEG.[8]

Brain electrical activity mapping (computed EEG; "brain mapping;" "BEAM;" EEG frequency analysis with topographic mapping) represents new technology which appears to increase the usefulness of EEG data. Although demanding further research, it may be useful in the diagnosis of several conditions including stroke,[9] dementia,[10] schizophrenia,[11,12] alcoholism, and depression. Many other biological measures also may be helpful in assessment, including CT scan, CBF measures, a variety of laboratory tests, and PET scan (in research settings).

## THE AMYTAL INTERVIEW

The administration of amobarbital (Amytal), thiopental (Pentothal), or pentobarbital (Nembutal) during an interview to produce a sedated state has been used for many years both diagnostically (Amytal interview) and therapeutically (narcoanalysis).[13] In spite of a long history of use, the indications for and value of this technique are unclear.

The technique usually consists of administering a total of 200-500 mg (occasionally more) of sodium amobarbital IV at a rate of 25-50 mg/min. The interviewer talks with the patient throughout administration and halts the drug temporarily when the desired level of sedation is attained (eg, appearance of lateral nystagmus for light sedation; development of slurred speech for a deeper state). Additional Amytal may be given if the interview is lengthy.

In this sedated state some patients present a markedly altered clinical picture which may be of diagnostic value.[14] Although opinion varies,[15] diagnostic uses for the Amytal interview may include:

1. Evaluation of mute patients - Patients with <u>catatonic schizophrenia</u> often recover dramatically when sedated (although a thought disorder usually remains) but return to the full catatonic state when the amytal wears off. This is very useful in differentiating catatonia from marked psychomotor retardation in the depressed patient (they show little improvement).
   Patients mute for other reasons (eg, hysterical, acute stress) may begin to talk under sedation.
2. Acute panic states - Patients immobilized by severe stress may talk about their concerns when sedated.
3. <u>Organic vs functional differentiation</u> - Patients who are confused, disoriented, or demented due to organic factors usually worsen with Amytal while clinically similar functional patients often clear temporarily.
4. Hysterical phenomena - <u>Amnesias</u>, <u>fugues</u>, and <u>conversion disorders</u> often are temporarily relieved by Amytal. Useful information may be obtained during this time- eg, the patient's name and address; the cause of the patient's anger.
5. The interview is less reliably useful with psychotic states (except for catatonic schizophrenia), although some patients may contribute information they wouldn't have otherwise.

Although helpful in confirming some diagnoses, the Amytal interview also may contribute to the treatment of a few patients by allowing them to confront and deal with stressful or troubling experiences which they previously had been reluctant or unable to face.

## REFERENCES

1. MacKinnon RA, Michels R: <u>The Psychiatric Interview in Clinical Practice</u>. Philadelphia, WB Saunders, 1971.
2. Sullivan HS: <u>The Psychiatric Interview</u>. New York, WW Norton Co, 1954.
3. MacKinnon RA, Yudofsky SC: <u>The Psychiatric Evaluation in Clinical Practice</u>. Philadelphia, JB Lippincott Co, 1986.
4. Strub RL, Black FW: <u>The Mental Status Examination in Neurology</u>. Philadelphia, FA Davis Co, 1977.
5. Katzman R, Brown T, Fuld P, et al: Validation of a short orientation-memory-concentration test of cognitive impairment. <u>Am J Psychiatry</u> 140:734, 1983.
6. Andreasen NC: Reliability and validity of proverb interpretation to assess mental status. <u>Compr Psychiatry</u> 18: 465, 1977.
7. Shagass C, Roemer RA, Straumanis JJ: Relationships between psychiatric diagnosis and some quantitative EEG variables. <u>Arch Gen Psychiatry</u> 39:1423, 1982.

8.  Snyder S, Pitts WM: Electroencephalography of DSM-III borderline personality disorder. _Acta Psychiatr Scand_ 69:129-134, 1984.
9.  Nuwer MR, Jordan SE, Ahn SE: Evaluation of stroke using EEG frequency analysis and topographic mapping. _Neurology_ 37:1153-1159, 1987.
10. Duffy FH, Albert MS, McAnulty G: Brain electrical activity in patients with presenile and senile dementia of the Alzheimer type. _Ann Neurol_ 16:439-48, 1984.
11. Guenther W, Breitling D, et al: EEG mapping of left hemisphere dysfunction during motor performance in schizophrenia. _Biol Psychiatry_ 21:249-62, 1986.
12. Mukundan CR: Computed EEG in schizophrenics. _Biol Psychiatry_ 21:1221-5, 1986.
13. Naples M, Hackett RP: The Amytal interview: history and current uses. _Psychosomatics_ 19:98, 1978.
14. Perry JC, Jacobs D: Overview: clinical applications of the Amytal interview in psychiatric emergency settings. _Am J Psychiatry_ 139:552, 1982.
15. Dysken MW, Kooser JA, et al: Clinical usefulness of sodium amobarbital interviewing. _Arch Gen Psychiatry_ 36:789, 1979.

# Chapter 3

# Psychotic Disorders

"Psychosis" describes a degree of severity, not a specific disorder (see p 2). A psychotic patient has a grossly impaired sense of reality, often coupled with emotional and cognitive disabilities, which severely compromises his ability to function. He is likely to talk and act in a bizarre fashion, have hallucinations, or strongly hold ideas that are contrary to fact (delusions). He may be confused and disoriented.

This chapter covers all the major psychotic disorders - ie, conditions which <u>must</u> reach psychotic proportions at some time during their course (although the patients may be nonpsychotic most of the time). Recognize that these are primarily descriptive groupings of clinical syndromes - <u>not</u> discrete diseases.

Schizophrenia:

Disorganized type
Catatonic type
Paranoid type
Undifferentiated type
Residual type

Schizophreniform Disorder

Brief Reactive Psychosis

Schizoaffective Disorder

Induced Psychotic Disorder

Delusional (Paranoid) Disorder

Atypical Psychosis

DIFFERENTIAL DIAGNOSIS:

There are a variety of other conditions (psychiatric, medical, neurological) which occasionally can present with psychosis. Look for a basic dichotomy: some psychoses, like the conditions above, are functional (no certain organic, medical cause) while others are caused by physical factors (fever, trauma, infection, drugs, medical diseases, etc). Most of the functional conditions present with emotional and thinking disturbances in a patient with a clear sensorium while most of the organic psychoses have a degree of delirium (eg, clouding of consciousness, confusion, disorientation). Unfortunately, exceptions to either of these characterizations are frequent.

Since it is always important to identify organic conditions when they are present (the Organic Mental Disorders, DSM-III-R p 162), obtain a complete history and physical on all psychotic patients. Possible organic causes of psychosis include almost any type of serious medical illness or drug abuse (see Chapters 5, 6, 14, 15). Suspect an organic etiology if:

- The patient presents with significant memory loss, confusion, disorientation, or clouding of consciousness.
- There is no personal or family history of serious psychiatric illness.
- The patient has a serious medical illness or a chronic medical condition with periodic relapses.
- The psychosis has developed rapidly (eg, days) in a patient who previously had been functioning well.

Psychiatric conditions which may (but don't necessarily) reach psychotic proportions include:

1. Major Affective Disorder (see chapter 4)[1] - look for the psychosis to coexist with and be dominated by an affective component (either manic or depressed) which preceded the development of the psychosis.
2. Brief reactive psychoses may occur with stress in patients with personality disorders of the histrionic, borderline, paranoid, and schizotypal types. Some obsessive-compulsive persons at times may develop a psychosis if they fail to control their environment.
3. Some acute panic or rage attacks may be of psychotic intensity - eg, acute homosexual panic; rage in the patient with an explosive disorder (see chapter 7).
4. A few psychotic conditions develop in childhood and continue into the adult years - AUTISTIC DISORDER (DSM-III-R p 38, 299.00) and PERVASIVE DEVELOPMENTAL DISORDER NOS (DSM-III-R p 39, 299.80).

5. Psychotic states occasionally may be mimicked unconsciously or even "faked" - Factitious Disorder with
   Psychological Symptoms; Malingering.


## SCHIZOPHRENIA

Schizophrenia is the most common psychotic disorder -
almost 1% of people worldwide develop it during their lifetime; over 2 million persons are affected in the USA. It
occurs more frequently in urban populations and in lower
socioeconomic groups - probably due to a "downward drift"
(ie, poorly functional, unemployable persons end up in mar-
ginal settings). Poor environments do not "cause" the
disorder, although they make it more intractable.

The diagnosis of schizophrenia has had a checkered history. There have been numerous different ways to make the
diagnosis, which have thus represented numerous different
populations of patients. The current diagnostic scheme
(DSM-III-R) uses specific objective criteria to define
several forms of schizophrenia. Because there are no pathognomonic findings, "schizophrenia" is a <u>clinical</u> diagnosis
which may represent a nonspecific syndrome of heterogeneous
etiologies. However, biological, genetic, and phenomenological information suggest that it is a valid disorder(s).
The five identified subtypes are also based on clinical
variables.


## CLINICAL PRESENTATION:

While the nature of schizophrenia is uncertain, the
current clinical description and method of making the
diagnosis are more clear (DSM-III-R).

Most schizophrenics are psychotic for only a small part
of their lives. Typically they spend many years in a <u>resid-
ual phase</u> during which time they display more minor features
of their illness. During these residual periods the patients may be withdrawn, isolated, and "peculiar." They
usually are noticeable to others and may lose their jobs or
friends both because of their own lack of interest and
ability to perform and because they are behaving oddly.
Their thinking and speech are vague and are felt by others
to be odd and to "not quite make sense." They may be convinced that they are different from others, feel that they
have special powers and sensitivities, and have "mystical"
or "psychic" experiences. Their personal appearance and
manners deteriorate, and they may display affect which is
blunted, flat, or inappropriate. They are frequently anhe-

donic (unable to experience pleasure). Often this deterioration merely represents a gradual worsening of a condition the patient has displayed for many years - the first psychotic episode may have been preceded by a similar period of eccentric thinking and behavior (prodromal phase).

A "prepsychotic personality" is seen in some chronic schizophrenics and is characterized by social withdrawal, social awkwardness, and marked shyness in a youth who has difficulty in school in spite of a normal IQ. An equally common pattern is involvement in minor antisocial activities in the year or two prior to the initial psychotic episode. Many of these patients have been diagnosed previously as having a schizoid, borderline, antisocial, or schizotypal personality disorder. It is only when they develop their first psychotic episode (normally in their teens or early 20's (men) or 20's and early 30's (women); a first "breakdown" after age 40 is unusual) that the diagnosis is changed to schizophrenia. Often a presumed precipitating stress can be identified. The typical acute psychosis displays a variable mixture of several of the following symptoms.

**Disturbance of Thought Form**: These patients usually have a formal thought disorder - ie, their thinking is frequently incomprehensible to others and appears illogical. Characteristics include:

Loosening of associations (tangential associations) - Patient's ideas are disconnected. He may jump obliviously from topic to unconnected topic, confusing the listener. When this occurs frequently (eg, in midsentence), the speech is often incoherent.

Overinclusiveness - Patient continually may disrupt the flow of his thoughts by including irrelevant information

Neologisms - Patient coins new words (may have a symbolic meaning for him).

Blocking - Speech is halted (often in midsentence) and then picked up a moment (or minutes) later, usually at another place. This may represent the patient's ideas being interrupted by intrusive thoughts (eg, hallucinations). These patients are often very distractible and have a short attention span.

Clanging - The patient chooses his next words and themes based on the sound of the words he is using rather than the thought content. Usually he rhymes a primary word in one sentence with a word in the preceding sentence.

Echolalia - Patient repeats words or phrases in a musical or singsong fashion but without an apparent effort to communicate.

Concreteness - Patient of normal or above average IQ thinks in abstract terms poorly.

<u>Poverty of speech content</u> - Patient may talk a lot and say very little.

**Disturbance of Thought Content:**   <u>Delusions</u> (fixed, false beliefs - particularly ideas that are beyond credibility and are not modified in spite of clear evidence to the contrary) are common in most serious mental disorders, but some specific forms of delusional thought are particularly frequent in schizophrenia.   The more acute the psychosis, the more likely the delusion is to be disorganized and nonsystematized.

<u>Bizarre, confused delusions</u>
<u>Persecutory delusions</u> - particularly nonsystematic types.
<u>Delusions of grandeur</u>
<u>Delusions of influence</u> - patient believes that he can control events through telepathy.
<u>Delusions of reference</u> - patient is convinced that there are "meanings" behind events and people's actions which are directed specifically toward himself.

Many schizophrenic patients display <u>lack of insight</u> - ie, the patient is unaware of his own illness or of his need for treatment, even though his disorder is evident to others.

**Disturbance of Perception:**   Most common are <u>hallucinations</u>,[2] usually auditory but also visual, olfactory, and tactile. The auditory hallucinations (most often voices - one or several) may include a running commentary about the patient and events, derogatory or threatening comments made to the patient, or direct orders to the patient (command hallucinations).[3]   The voices may be perceived as coming from outside or inside the patient's head and occasionally the patient may hear his own thoughts spoken aloud (often to his shame or embarrassment).   The voices are quite "real" to the patient, except in the early phases of the psychosis.

These patients may also have illusions, depersonalizations, derealizations, and a hallucinatory sense of bodily change.

**Disturbance of Emotions:**   Acutely psychotic patients may display any emotion and may switch from one to another in a surprisingly short span of time.   Two frequent (but not pathognomonic) underlying affects are:

<u>Blunted or flat affect</u> - The patient expresses very little emotion, even when it is appropriate to do so.   He appears to be without warmth.

Inappropriate Affect - The affect may be intense, but it is inconsistent with the patient's thoughts or speech.

Disturbance of Behavior: Many different bizarre and inappropriate behaviors may be seen including strange grimacing and posturing, ritual behavior, excessive silliness, aggressiveness, and some sexual inappropriateness.

An acute psychotic attack can last weeks or months (occasionally years). Many patients have recurrences of the active phase periodically throughout their lives, typically separated by months or years. During the intervening periods, patients usually present residual symptoms (often with the degree of impairment gradually increasing over the years); however, a few patients are symptom-free between acute episodes. Many schizophrenic patients in remission display early signs of a developing relapse - always look for them. These early signs include increasing restlessness and nervousness, loss of appetite, mild depression and anhedonia, insomnia, and trouble concentrating.

## CLASSIFICATION:

To be considered schizophrenic, a patient must (DSM-III-R, p 194)

1. have had at least 6 months of
2. sufficiently deteriorated occupational, interpersonal, and self-supportive functioning,
3. must have been actively psychotic in a characteristic fashion during at least part of that period, and
4. must not be able to account for the symptoms by the presence of a Major Affective Disorder, Autism, or Organic Mental Disorder.

The course of the illness should be classed as subchronic, chronic, subchronic with acute exacerbation, chronic with acute exacerbation, or in remission. Moreover, all schizophrenic patients should be classed as one of five recognized subtypes which describe the most frequently occurring behavioral manifestations of the illness. There have been numerous subclassifications of schizophrenia in the past, all unsatisfactory, and the current divisions share some of those deficiencies. Although genetic data suggests that schizophrenia is a stable diagnosis, there is no comparable information for the subtypes.[4] Symptomatically, they tend to overlap, and the diagnosis can shift from one to another with time (either during one episode or in a subsequent episode). Finally, over the years, the clinical presentations of many patients tend to converge towards a common picture of interpersonal withdrawal, flattened affect, idiosyncratic thinking, and impaired social and personal functioning. (At the same time, the course becomes more stable, with few acute symptoms or episodes.)

DISORGANIZED TYPE (DSM-III-R p 197, 295.1x): The patient has (1) blunted, silly, or inappropriate affect, (2) frequent incoherence, and (3) no systematized delusions. Grimacing and bizarre mannerisms are common.

CATATONIC TYPE (DSM-III-R p 196, 295.2x): The patient may have any one (or a combination) of several forms of catatonia.

1. Catatonic stupor or mutism - Patient does not appreciably respond to his environment or to the people in it. In spite of appearances, these patients are often thoroughly aware of what is going on around them.
2. Catatonic negativism - Patient resists all directions or physical attempts to move him.
3. Catatonic rigidity - Patient is physically rigid.
4. Catatonic posturing - Patient assumes bizarre or unusual postures.
5. Catatonic excitement - Patient is extremely (eg, wildly) active and excited. May be life-threatening (eg, due to exhaustion).

PARANOID TYPE (DSM-III-R p 197, 295.3x): This is the most stable subtype over time and usually develops later than other forms of schizophrenia. The patient must display consistent, often paranoid, delusions which he may or may not act on. These patients are often uncooperative and difficult to deal with and may be aggressive, angry, or fearful, but they rarely display disorganized, incoherent behavior.

UNDIFFERENTIATED TYPE (DSM-III-R p 198, 295.9x): The patient has prominent hallucinations, delusions, and other evidences of active psychosis (eg, confusion, incoherence) but without the more specific features of the preceding three categories.

RESIDUAL TYPE (DSM-III-R p 198, 295.6x): The patient is in remission from active psychosis but displays symptoms of the residual phase (eg, social withdrawal, flat or inappropriate affect, eccentric behavior, loosening of associations, and illogical thinking).

PROGNOSIS:

Schizophrenia is a chronic disorder. A person gradually may become more withdrawn, "eccentric," and nonfunctional over many years. Some patients may experience low-level delusions and hallucinations indefinitely. Many of the more dramatic and acute symptoms disappear with time, but the patient ends up chronically needing sheltered living or spending years in mental hospitals. Involvement with the law for misdemeanors is common (eg, vagrancy, disturbing the peace). A few patients become markedly demented. Overall life expectancy is shortened - primarily due to accidents, suicide, and an inability of the patients to care for themselves.

This pattern has exceptions. Psychiatrists have long distinguished between process schizophrenia (slowly developing; chronic, deteriorating course) and reactive schizophrenia (rapid onset; somewhat better prognosis). Clinical characteristics associated with an improved prognosis include:

1. A rapid onset of the active psychotic symptoms.
2. An onset after age 30.
3. Good premorbid social and occupational functioning. Past performance remains the best predictor of future performance.
4. Marked confusion and emotional features during the acute episode (some question this).
5. A probable precipitating stress to the acute psychosis.
6. No family history of schizophrenia.

It may be that these are two etiologically (and biologically?) distinct disorders. Although there is great variability, Disorganized Type generally has the worst prognosis while Paranoid Type (and some catatonics) have the best. The patient's prognosis is worsened if he abuses drugs or if he lives in a family setting overtly hostile to him.

25-50% of patients recovering from an acute episode develop a major depression during the months following improvement (postpsychotic depression).[5] Although treatment-resistant, psychotherapy and antidepressant medication may be useful (lithium may also help). Watch for it-suicide rate is increased in this population. Don't overdiagnose - some of these patients may have a medication-induced akinesia mimicking depression.[6]

## BIOLOGY OF SCHIZOPHRENIA:

No pathognomonic structural or functional abnormality has been found in schizophrenics; however, numerous intriguing abnormalities exist (and have been replicated, as well as contested) in subpopulations of patients[7]: frontal concentrations of neuropeptides, increased platelet MAO activity, CSF cytomegalovirus antibody, P-type (stimulated) atypical lymphocytes, cerebral ventricular enlargements,[8] abnormal left hemisphere function, impaired transmission in the corpus callosum, a thickened corpus callosum, a small cerebellar vermis, decreased cerebral blood flow[9] and glucose metabolism (by PET scan) in the frontal lobes[10], EEG and EP abnormalities (by BEAM), and pathologically demonstrated fibrillary gliosis in the basal forebrain, to name a few. Moreover, some of these measures can be correlated with the specific symptoms and severity of the schizophrenia[11]. Also, there is an increased incidence of birth complications and minor neurological abnormalities[12] among individuals who develop schizophrenia[13]. Each of these changes are real in some patients, but their significance is unknown. However, taken together, they underscore (1) the biological nature and (2) the heterogeneity of schizophrenia.


## BIOCHEMISTRY OF SCHIZOPHRENIA:

The biochemical etiology of schizophrenia is unknown. Most of the major hypotheses implicate an abnormality of central neurotransmitters. The current predominant theory postulates excessive central dopamine (DA) activity[14] (the Dopamine Hypothesis) and is based on two key findings.

1. The antipsychotic activity of neuroleptic medications (eg, phenothiazines) is derived in major part from their blockade of postsynaptic dopamine receptors.
2. Amphetamine psychosis often is clinically indistinguishable from an acute paranoid schizophrenic psychosis. Amphetamines release central dopamine. Also, amphetamines worsen schizophrenia.

These findings could reflect (1) a hypersensitivity of postsynaptic dopamine receptors, (2) an increased number of receptors, (3) an overactivity of presynaptic dopamine neurons, or (4) a relative deficiency of dopamine-beta-hydroxylase (the enzyme which converts DA to NE, forcing DA to become the transmitter in the absence of NE).

Other theories include:

1. <u>Transmethylation hypothesis</u> - Two of the major classes of central transmitters, catecholamines (DA, NE, epinephrine) and indoleamines (serotonin), both produce small amounts of methylated derivatives which are inherently hallucinogenic (eg, mescaline, psilocybin, bufotenine, DMT). Do schizophrenics produce excesses? Are they unable to detoxify those produced? Megavitamin therapy is based on the rationale that certain compounds (eg, nicotinamide) are methyl acceptors and thus, given in large amounts, can "detoxify" the schizophrenic.
2. Excessive central NE (limbic forebrain) occurs in some schizophrenics and decreases with medication and improved clinical state. Thus, NE may be the transmitter to watch, rather than DA.[15]


<u>GENETICS OF SCHIZOPHRENIA</u>:

Schizophrenia has a significant inherited component - possibly polygenic.[16]

Consanguinity studies: Schizophrenia is a familial disorder; ie, it "runs in families." The closer the relative, the greater the risk.
Twin studies: Monozygotic twins are 4-6 times more likely to develop illness than dizygotes.
Adoption studies: Children of schizophrenic parents adopted away at birth into normal families have the same increased rate of illness as if they had been raised by their natural parents.

<u>Genetic Counseling</u> - Lifetime risk of developing schizophrenia:

| | |
|---|---|
| General population | 1% |
| Monozygotic twins | 40-50% |
| Dizygotic twins | 10% |
| Sibling of a schizophrenic | 10% |
| Parent of a schizophrenic | 5% |
| Child of one schizophrenic parent | 10-15% |
| Child of two schizophrenic parents | 30-40% |

Note that 50% of monozygotic twins do <u>not</u> both develop schizophrenia - thus clearly environment plays a role. Development of illness reflects nature <u>and</u> nurture.

Although inadequately studied, several nonschizophrenic disorders occur with increased frequency in the families of schizophrenics and may be related genetically: schizotypal and borderline personality disorders (the <u>Schizophrenia Spectrum Disorders</u>); obsessive compulsive disorder; possibly antisocial and paranoid personality disorders.[17]

## FAMILY PROCESSES:

Family dynamics and family turbulence play a major role in producing a relapse or maintaining a remission. Patients who are discharged to home are more likely to relapse over the following year than are those who are placed in a residential setting. Most at risk are patients from hostile families or families which display excessive anxiety, over-concern, or overprotectiveness toward the patient (called <u>expressed emotion</u>, or EE).[18] Schizophrenic patients often do not "emancipate" from their families.

Some researchers have identified peculiar and patholog-ical styles of communication in these families - typically, communications are vague and subtly illogical. Bateson (1956)[19] described a characteristic "<u>double bind</u>" in which the patient is frequently required by a key family member to respond to an overt message which contradicts a covert message. The significance of this unpleasant bind in either maintaining or causing (as Bateson suggests) schizophrenia is unclear. Recent work suggests that these family communi-cation patterns may be the effect of having a schizophrenic child, not the cause of it.

## DIFFERENTIAL DIAGNOSIS:

Schizophrenia must be differentiated from all of those conditions which produce active psychoses (see above). Of all the possibilities, be particularly careful to eliminate schizoaffective disorder, the major affective disorders, and several organic conditions which may closely mimic schizo-phrenia[20] - eg, early Huntington's chorea, early Wilson's disease, temporal lobe epilepsy, frontal or temporal lobe tumors, early MS, early SLE, porphyria, general paresis, chronic drug use, chronic alcoholic hallucinosis, and the adult form of metachromatic leukodystrophy. Carefully evaluate catatonia for medical/neurological conditions.

## TREATMENT:

<u>Biological methods</u> (**see chapter** 23): Treat acute psy-choses with antipsychotics (equivalent dose range = chlor-promazine 300-1200 mg/day, or more). Relapsing schizophren-ics should be considered for antipsychotic drug maintenance

(long-acting depot fluphenazine may be the medication of choice). Medication is primarily useful in controlling the "active" symptoms (eg, hallucinations, emotional lability, delusions, etc) and not the "passive" symptoms (eg, anhedonia, social withdrawal), so don't expect too much long-term benefit from meds (except in preventing relapse). Be aware that a chronically excessive dose may chronically hinder patient functioning. A subgroup of schizophrenics may benefit from lithium.

ECT may be useful for rapid control of a few acute psychotics. A very few chronic schizophrenics who respond poorly to medication may improve with ECT - unpredictable.

Psychosocial methods: The primary mode of treatment of schizophrenia is pharmacological. Long-term insight psychotherapy has a limited place.[21] On the other hand, supportive, reality-oriented psychosocial methods are particularly useful in the long-term treatment of schizophrenia.[22,23]

The acutely psychotic patient should be approached cautiously, but he should be approached. Keep a comfortable distance from the patient if he appears disturbed by your presence. It is essential to establish some communication with these patients.

1. Talk to the patient. Be relaxed, interested, and supportive. Give the impression that you believe the patient can respond appropriately to you.
2. Be specific. Ask pointed, factual questions. Try to identify the patient's major current fears and concerns but don't be led into a lengthy discussion of complex delusions and hallucinations.
3. Take your time during the interview. Don't rush the patient to respond to each question but do maintain some control over the direction of the conversation.
4. Make some specific observations of the patient's behavior (eg, "you look frightened; you look angry") but don't become involved in lengthy "interpretations." Don't draw incorrect conclusions about the patient's emotional state from inappropriate affect.
5. Explain to the patient what is being done to him, and why.
6. If the conversation is going nowhere (eg, the patient refuses to talk), break off the interview with a positive expectation - eg, "I'll be back to see you in a little while when you are feeling better and able to talk."

If the acutely psychotic patient is delirious, suicidal, homicidal, and/or has no community support - hospitalize. It is usually better to avoid long-term hospitalization if alternate outpatient arrangements are possible: the deleterious effects of chronic hospitalization are real (regression and marked withdrawal, loss of skills, etc). The recent trend has been towards short hospital stays during acute episodes with maintenance as outpatients in between.

When hospitalized, allow the patient as much independence as his behavior permits within the limits of a safe environment. Therapeutic milieus (eg, therapeutic community, token economy, etc) all depend upon community support (staff and patients) - be aware of the patient's behavior and provide helpful "corrective feedback" to him. The milieu is a place for the patient to develop skills in maintaining interpersonal relationships and to learn new methods of coping. Behavior modification has been found clearly effective at eliminating specific unacceptable behaviors and in teaching low-level personal skills with some regressed, poorly functioning inpatients.

Most schizophrenics can be treated as outpatients. Several principles should be kept in mind.

- See the patient frequently enough to safely monitor medication and detect early deterioration (eg, weekly, monthly, or even every several months - dependent upon the patient's course and reliability).

- Communicate with the patient clearly and unambiguously. Be factual and goal-oriented. Avoid extensive discussion of hallucinations and delusions. Help the patient with reality issues - eg, living arrangements, work. Help the patient avoid excessive stress. Recognize that the more productive and skillful the patient, the more likely he is to maintain a recovery - encourage the patient to hold an appropriate job. Provide social skills training.

- Talk about medication - eg, the need for it; the patient's feelings about taking it; etc.

- Develop a consistent, trusting relationship (often difficult). Be empathic over time, even when the patient is being "unreasonable," but also maintain a "professional distance." Be a constant presence.

- Learn the patient's strengths and weaknesses. Teach him to identify an impending decompensation.[24] What are the precipitants, if any? If the patient misses appointments, investigate (he may be relapsing). If the patient is decompensating, be ready to insist on hospitalization. Recognize that overstimulation and overindependence can precipitate a decompensation. These patients are at risk for suicide at times during their illnesses (particularly if they have self-destructive command hallucinations).

- Always evaluate the family. Have they contributed to the patient's decompensation? Can the members deal appropriately with the patient's illness? Are they hostile? Suspicious? Overprotective? Consider <u>family therapy</u>. Family members often need considerable support and understanding themselves. When worked with well, they can be a (the?) major help to the patient.

- Consider <u>group therapy</u>.[25] The usual orientation is toward support and reality testing. It helps with resocialization, forces interpersonal interactions, and provides support. Several studies have shown it to be effective (in combination with medication) in preventing relapse in outpatients.

- Know and use community resources. Be alert to the devastating effect on the patient of a poor quality of life[26] (eg, Does he live in a "psychiatric ghetto" or "on the street?").

- Do not expect too much. Many patients have chronic disability.


## SCHIZOPHRENIFORM DISORDER

(DSM-III-R p 207, 295.40)

This disorder is clinically indistinguishable from brief reactive psychosis and schizophrenia except that the symptoms last more than 1 month but less than 6 months. This population of patients seems to differ from schizophrenic in several important ways:

1. Symptoms begin and end more abruptly.
2. Symptoms are usually more turbulent and "acute."
3. There is good premorbid adjustment and higher functioning after recovery.
4. There is only a slightly increased prevalence of schizophrenia in the family. There may be a higher prevalence of affective disorder.

Thus, schizophreniform disorder appears to be a separate disease from schizophrenia. Recognize, however, that many schizophrenic patients pass through a period (ie, the first 6 months) when their diagnosis needs to be schizophreniform disorder. Don't miss an organic psychosis.

Treatment is similar to that of an acute schizophrenic episode, but the prognosis is better.

## BRIEF REACTIVE PSYCHOSIS

(DSM-III-R p 205, 298.80)

This condition describes those patients who experience an acute psychotic episode lasting less than 1 month which immediately follows an important life stress. The illness comes as a surprise - there is usually no suggestion before the stress that the person is likely to "break down," although this disorder is more common in people with a pre-existing personality disorder (particularly histrionic and borderline types).

The psychosis is typically very turbulent and dramatic with marked emotional lability, bizarre behavior, confused and incoherent speech, transient disorientation and memory loss, and/or brief but striking hallucinations and delusions. Thus, it mimics the acute psychotic onset of a major affective disorder, schizophreniform disorder, atypical psychosis, or organic psychosis - the diagnosis must be changed to one of these if the illness extends beyond 1 month. Always carefully rule out OBS and, particularly, drug-related problems. The validity of this diagnosis as a separate category is debated.[27]

Treat the acutely psychotic patient with understanding, a secure environment, and antipsychotic medication, if needed. The patient usually recovers completely in several days, and the long-term prognosis is good, although the patient may be at risk for future brief episodes when equivalently stressed

## SCHIZOAFFECTIVE DISORDER

(DSM-III-R p 208, 295.70)

This is a vague and poorly defined disorder meant for patients who have evidence of both schizophrenia and major affective disorder. There are no specific diagnostic criteria - the diagnosis is made by exclusion. These patients may present with an affective disturbance which grades into a purely schizophrenic picture or may display symptoms of both conditions simultaneously.[28] It is a genetically heterogeneous disorder - both schizophrenia and mood disorders occur with increased frequency in family members. Much work remains to be done to better define these patients.[29]

Treat as one would the equivalent schizophrenic or affective patient. Antipsychotics are generally most useful but lithium has benefited some patients. These patients seem to have a better prognosis than schizophrenics but a poorer outcome than manic-depressives.

## DELUSIONAL DISORDER

(DSM-III-R p 199, 297.10)

These patients <u>do not</u> display the pervasive disturbances of mood and thought found in other psychotic conditions. They do not have flat or inappropriate affect, prominent hallucinations, or markedly bizarre delusions. They <u>do</u> have one or more delusions, often of persecution but also of infidelity, grandiosity, somatic change, or erotomania which are:

1. Usually specific - eg, involve a certain person or group, a given place or time, or a particular activity.
2. Usually well organized - eg, the "culprits" have elaborate reasons for what they are doing, which the patient can detail.
3. Usually grandiose - eg, a powerful group is interested just in <u>him</u>.
4. Not bizarre enough to suggest schizophrenia.

These patients (who tend to be in their 40's) may be unrecognizable until their delusional system is pointed out by family or friends. Even then the diagnosis may be difficult because they may be too mistrustful to confide in the examiner and don't voluntarily seek treatment. They are frequently hypersensitive, argumentative, and litigious, and come to attention through ill-founded legal activities. Although they may perform well occupationally and in areas distant from their delusions, they tend to be social isolates either by preference or as a result of their interpersonal inhospitality (eg, spouses frequently abandon them).

These conditions appear to form a clinical continuum with conditions like paranoid personality disorder and paranoid schizophrenia; delineation of the limits of each syndrome awaits further research. Rule out an affective disorder - morbid jealousy and paranoid ideas are common in depression. Paranoia is common among the elderly (see chapter 24) and among stimulant drug abusers. Acute paranoid reactions frequently are seen in patients with mild delirium and in patients who are bedridden (and sensory-deprived).

Etiology is unknown. No genetic or biological factors have been identified. There is a higher incidence among refugee and minority groups and among those with impaired hearing. There is a tendency for their family relationships to be characterized by turbulence, callousness, and coldness yet the significance of this pattern is unclear. Typical defense mechanisms seen in these patients include denial, projection, and regression.

TREATMENT:

Treatment is notoriously difficult. Individual psychotherapy is useful. Emphasis should be on developing a trusting relationship, with the patient seeing the therapist as neutral and accepting. Interfere with the patient's freedom of choice as little as possible. Gradually help the patient see his world from your perspective. These patients are _very_ sensitive to criticism (overt or implied), so this kind of a relationship is extremely difficult to develop and maintain.

Antipsychotic medication may help a few - it may at least take the "energy" out of the delusion. Recent use of antidepressants appears promising - consider it.

### INDUCED PSYCHOTIC DISORDER

(DSM-III-R p 210, 297.30)

An otherwise normal person may adopt the delusional system of someone else. Most commonly, a dependent, isolated wife will accept the delusional ideas of her (dominant) spouse (eg, both may come to believe that their children are attempting to murder them with poison gas). When _two_ people share the same delusion, it is _folie a deux_. Separation of the partners with shared delusions often results in disappearance of the delusions in the healthier member.

## ATYPICAL PSYCHOSIS

(DSM-III-R p 211, 298.90)

If a psychotic patient does not have an affective disorder, OBS, or one of the disorders in this chapter and is not malingering, he has PSYCHOTIC DISORDER NOS. The most common use of this classification is for patients for whom there is insufficient information to make a more specific diagnosis.

## REFERENCES

1. Glazer WM, Pino CD, Quinlan D: The reassessment of chronic patients previously diagnosed as schizophrenic. J Clin Psychiatry 48:430-434, 1987.
2. Asaad G, Shapiro B: Hallucinations: Theoretical and clinical overview. Am J Psychiatry 143:1088-1097, 1986.
3. Hellerstein D, Frosch W, Koenigsberg HW: The clinical significance of command hallucinations. Am J Psychiatry 144:219-221, 1987.
4. Kendler KS, Gruenberg AM, Tsuang MT: A family study of the subtypes of schizophrenia. Am J Psychiatry 145:57-62, 1988.
5. Becker RE, Singh MM, Meisler N, Shillcutt S: Clinical significance, evaluation and management or secondary depression in schizophrenia. J Clin Psychiatry 46 (11, Sec.2):26-32, 1985.
6. Siris SG: Akinesia and postpsychotic depression. J Clin Psychiatry 48:240-243, 1987.
7. Nasrallah HA, Weinberger DR: The Neurology of Schizophrenia. Amsterdam, Elsevier, 1986.
8. Shelton RC, Karson CN, Doran AR, et al: Cerebral structured pathology in schizophrenia: Evidence for a selective prefrontal cortical defect. Am J Psychiatry 145:154-163, 1988.
9. Berman KF, Weinberger DR, Shelton RC, Zec RF: A relationship between anatomical and physiological brain pathology in schizophrenia. Am J Psychiatry 144:1277-1282, 1987.
10. Wolkin A, Angrist B, Wolf A, et al: Low frontal glucose utilization in chronic schizophrenia: A replication study. Am J Psychiatry 145:251-253, 1988.
11. Volkow ND, Wolf AP, Van Gelder P, et al: Phenomenological correlates of metabolic activity in 18 patients chronic schizophrenia. Am J Psychiatry 144:151-158, 1987.
12. Heinricks DW, Buchanan RW: Significance and meaning of neurological signs in schizophrenia. Am J Psychiatry 145:11-18, 1988.

13. DeLisi LE, Goldin LR, Maxwell E, et al: Clinical features of illness in siblings with schizophrenia or schizoaffective disorder. Arch Gen Psychiatry 44:891-896, 1987.
14. Wong DF, Wagner HN, Tune LE, et al: Positron emission tomography reveals elevated $D_2$ dopamine receptors in drug-naive schizophrenics. Science 234:1558-1563, 1986.
15. Glazer WM, Charney DS, Heninger GR: Noradrenergic function in schizophrenia. Arch Gen Psychiatry 44:898-904, 1987.
16. Baron M: Genetics of schizophrenia. Biol Psychiatry 21:1051-1066, 1986.
17. Baron M, Gruen R, Rainer JD, et al: A family study of schizophrenic and normal control probands. Am J Psychiatry 142:447-455, 1985.
18. Kanter J, Lamb HR, Loeper C: Expressed emotion in families: A critical review. Hosp Community Psychiatry 38:374-380, 1987.
19. Bateson G, Jackson DD, Haley J, Weakland JH: Towards a theory of schizophrenia. Behav Sci 1:251, 1956.
20. Cummings JL: Organic psychosis. Psychosomatics 29:16-26, 1988.
21. Sjostrom R: Effects of psychotherapy in schizophrenia. Acta Psychiatr Scand 71:513-522, 1985.
22. Drake RE, Sederer LI: Inpatient psychosocial treatment of chronic schizophrenia. Hosp Community Psychiatry 37:897-901, 1986.
23. Liberman RP, Mueser KT, Wallace CJ: Social skills training for schizophrenic individuals at risk for relapse. Am J Psychiatry 143:523-526, 1986.
24. Heinrichs DW, Carpenter WT: Prospective study of prodromal symptoms in schizophrenic relapse. Am J Psychiatry 142:371-373, 1985.
25. Kanas N: Inpatient and outpatient group therapy for schizophrenic patients. Am J Psychother 39:431, 1985.
26. Gelberg L, Linn LS, Leake BD: Mental health, alcohol and drug use, and criminal history among homeless adults. Am J Psychiatry 145:191-196, 1988.
27. Munoz RA, Amado H, Hyatt S: Brief reactive psychosis. J Clin Psychiatry 48:324-327, 1987.
28. Levinson DF, Levitt MEM: Schizoaffective mania reconsidered. Am J Psychiatry 144:415-425, 1987.
29. Breslau N, Meltzer HY: Validity of subtyping psychotic depression: Examination of phenomenology and demographic characteristics. Am J Psychiatry 145:35-40, 1988.

# Chapter 4

# Mood
# Disorders

Patients with disorders of mood are common (3-5% of the population at any one time) and are seen by all medical specialists. It is essential to identify them and either treat or refer appropriately.

Two basic abnormalities of mood are recognized: depression and mania. Both occur on a continuum from normal to the clearly pathological - symptoms in a few patients reach psychotic proportions. Although minor symptoms may be an extension of normal sadness or elation, more severe symptoms are associated with discrete syndromes (affective disorders) which appear to differ qualitatively from normal processes and which require specific therapies.

## CLASSIFICATION

DSM-III-R has defined several different mood disorders which differ, among other things, in their clinical presentation, course, genetics, and treatment response. These conditions are distinguished from one another by (1) the presence or absence of mania (bipolar vs unipolar), (2) the severity of the illness (major vs minor), and (3) the role of medical or other psychiatric conditions in causing the disorder ($1^0$ vs $2^0$).[1]

MOOD DISORDERS - <u>major</u> depressive and/or manic signs and symptoms.

<u>Bipolar Disorder</u> (Manic-Depression) - mania in past or present (with or without presence or history of depression).

<u>Unipolar Disorder</u> (Major Depression) - depression alone.

OTHER SPECIFIC MOOD DISORDER - <u>minor</u> depressive and/or manic signs and symptoms.

<u>Dysthymia</u> - depression alone.

<u>Cyclothymia</u> - depressive, <u>and</u> hypomanic symptoms in past or present.

ORGANIC MOOD DISORDER - may be depressed, manic, or mixed; these are the $2^O$ mood disorders.

ADJUSTMENT DISORDER WITH DEPRESSED MOOD - depression caused by stress.

The DSM-III-R classification also requires the examiner to specify whether the current bipolar episode is manic, depressed, or mixed; whether the unipolar disorder is a single episode or recurrent; whether either disorder shows psychotic features; and whether a major depressive episode is <u>chronic</u> (present at least 2 yrs) or meets the criteria for <u>melancholia</u> (profound vegetative and cognitive symptoms including psychomotor retardation or agitation, sleep disturbance, anorexia or weight loss, and/or excessive guilt-see DSM-III-R p 224). These characteristics are felt to be important in determining treatment and prognosis.

## CLINICAL PRESENTATION OF MOOD DISORDERS

Of the core clinical features common to affective disturbances, the Major Affective Disorders have the greater number and severity of symptoms and signs while dysthymia and cyclothymia have less. The most common symptoms and signs of mood disorders include:

<u>Symptoms</u> of depression:

Emotional features
  <u>depressed</u> mood, "blue"
  <u>irritability</u>, anxiety
  <u>anhedonia</u>, <u>loss of interest</u>
  loss of zest
  diminished emotional bonds
  interpersonal withdrawal
  preoccupation with death

Cognitive features
  self-criticism, <u>sense of worthlessness</u>, guilt
  pessimism, <u>hopelessness</u>, despair
  distractible, <u>poor concentration</u>
  uncertain and indecisive

variable obsessions
somatic complaints (<u>particularly in the elderly</u>)
memory impairment
delusions and hallucinations

Vegetative features
<u>fatigability</u>, no energy
<u>insomnia</u> or hypersomnia
anorexia or hyperrexia
weight loss or gain
psychomotor retardation
psychomotor agitation
impaired libido
frequent diurnal variation

<u>Signs</u> of depression:

stooped and slow moving
tearful, sad facies
dry mouth and skin
constipation

<u>Symptoms</u> of mania: (when mild = <u>hypomania</u>)

Emotional features
excited, elevated mood, euphoria
emotional <u>lability</u>
rapid, temporary shifts to acute depression
<u>irritability</u>, low frustration tolerance
demanding, egocentric

Cognitive features
elevated self-esteem, <u>grandiosity</u>
speech disturbances
loud, word rhyming (clanging)
pressure of speech
flight of ideas
progression to incoherence
<u>poor judgement</u>, disorganization
paranoia
delusions and hallucinations

Physiological features
boundless energy
insomnia, <u>little need for sleep</u>
decreased appetite

<u>Signs</u> of mania:

psychomotor agitation

A sufficient combination of these symptoms often clinches the diagnosis. However, particularly when the symptoms are mild, disorders of mood are frequently missed.

Although many depressed patients complain of depression, some do not. Moreover, other problems may obscure the diagnosis. Some patients present with alcohol or drug abuse or acting-out behavior. Others, particularly early on, present primarily with anxiety or agitation. Still others, instead of feeling sad, complain of <u>fatigue</u>, <u>insomnia</u>, dyspnea, tachycardia, and vague and/or chronic pains (usually GI, cardiac, headaches, or backaches - all unrelieved by analgesics). People with such presentations (known as masked depressions) often have a personal or family history of depression and frequently respond to antidepressants. Suspect depression in the unimproved patient who has atypical medical symptoms.

Patients with mania often do not complain of their symptoms. A few feel too good and elated to complain; others feel agitated and unpleasant but fail to notice that their behavior is outrageous.

Patient rating tests can help determine the severity of a depression and can be used to measure change over time: eg, the Beck Depression Inventory (21 questions - patient self-rates) and the Hamilton Rating Scale for Depression (17-21 questions - therapist rates).

## NORMAL AFFECTIVE PROCESSES

<u>Sadness</u> or simple unhappiness affect us all from time to time. The cause is often obvious, the reaction understandable, and improvement follows the disappearance of the cause. However, prolonged unhappiness in response to a chronic stress may be indistinguishable from a minor affective disorder and require treatment. Support and altered life circumstances are the keys to recovery.

<u>Grief</u> or <u>UNCOMPLICATED BEREAVEMENT</u> (DSM-III-R p 361, V62.82) is a more profound sense of dysphoria which follows a severe loss or trauma and which may produce a full depressive syndrome but, as time distances the precipitating event, the symptoms disappear. This process often takes weeks or months and requires a "working through" which often includes disbelief, anger, intense mourning, and eventual resolution (see chapter 10). Some bereavement grades into and, with time, becomes a major depressive disorder.

There is no generally accepted equivalent nonpathological manic process, although some people do react to stress with hypomania.

## MINOR AFFECTIVE DISORDERS

DEPRESSION:

The common <u>chronic</u> nonpsychotic disorder of lowered mood and/or anhedonia is <u>DYSTHYMIA (Depressive Neurosis)</u> (DSM-III-R p 230, 300.40). These patients feel depressed, have difficulty falling asleep, characteristically feel best in the morning and despondent in the afternoon and evening, and can display any of the nonpsychotic symptoms and signs of depression. Symptoms must have been present, at least intermittently, for two or more years. It is more common in women (W:M = 3-4:1), often develops for the first time in the late 20's or 30's, and begins insidiously, frequently in a person predisposed to depression by:

- major loss in childhood; eg, parent (maybe[2,3])
- recent loss; eg, health, job, spouse.
- chronic stress; eg, medical disorder.
- psychiatric susceptibility; eg, personality disorders of histrionic, compulsive, and dependent types; alcohol and drug abuse; major depression in partial remission; obsessive compulsive disorder. It frequently coexists with these conditions.

It is similar to but less severe than a Major Depression. However, 10-15% of patients who experience major depression will clear incompletely, and chronically suffer a residue of dysthymia ("double depression").[4]

Dysthymia must be differentiated from <u>ADJUSTMENT DISORDER WITH DEPRESSED MOOD</u> (DSM-III-R p 331, 309.00). This disorder occurs in an adequately functioning individual shortly after a readily identifiable, causative stress, results in impaired functioning and resolves as the stress disappears. These patients present a depressive syndrome midway between normal sadness and major depression. If social withdrawal predominates without strong feelings of depression, the patient may have <u>ADJUSTMENT DISORDER WITH WITHDRAWAL</u> (DSM-III-R p 331, 309.83).

MANIA:

<u>CYCLOTHYMIA</u> (DSM-III-R p 226, 301.13) requires the presence of mild depression <u>and</u> hypomania, separately or intermixed, continuously or intermittently over at least a 2-year

period. It usually begins in the 20's in patients (females 2:1) with a family history of major affective disorder and forms a chronically disabling pattern which yields troubled interpersonal relationships, job instability, occasional suicide attempts and short hospitalizations, and a markedly increased risk of drug and alcohol abuse.

## MAJOR AFFECTIVE DISORDERS

Patients with major affective disorders are profoundly depressed or excited. Clinical presentations and genetic studies support two distinct groups, MAJOR DEPRESSION (unipolar) (DSM-III-R p 228, 296.2x-.3x) and BIPOLAR DISORDER (DSM-III-R p 225, 296.4x-.6x), yet some question this dichotomy (eg, bipolar disorder may be a more severe form of recurrent unipolar disorder). The lifetime risk in the general population for a major depression is about 5-7$^{+}$%[5]: 8-10 times the frequency of bipolar disorder. 15% of patients kill themselves eventually.

MAJOR DEPRESSION:

These patients have many serious symptoms and signs of depression, yet their clinical presentations can vary markedly - from profound retardation and withdrawal to irritable, unrelieved agitation. A presumed precipitating event occurs in 25% (50% among the elderly). A diurnal variation is common, with the most severe symptoms early in the day. Some fail to recognize their depression, complaining instead of their "insides rotting out" or their "minds going crazy," yet the profound affective disturbance is usually recognizable to the observer.

A thought disorder is occasionally present. Delusions are usually affect-laden and mood congruent, but need not be. Hallucinations are uncommon, auditory, and usually have a self-condemning or paranoid content. These "psychotic depressions" may represent a separate disorder or may simply be a more severe form of depression (M.D., or B.D., WITH PSYCHOTIC FEATURES).[6] Depressed elderly may present primarily with retardation, memory impairment, and mild disorientation (pseudodementia).

The disorder can occur at any age (median age of onset is 37; 10% occur after age 60) with the majority of cases spread evenly throughout the adult years and with females affected 2:1. (However, increasing numbers of teenagers and young adults seem to be afflicted.) Unlike schizophrenia, it occurs frequently in the higher social strata. Family and twin studies strongly suggest a genetic factor - increased incidence of major depression, alcoholism, and possibly antisocial personality disorder in relatives (the "depressive spectrum" disorders). The prevalence of affective illness in first-degree relatives is 13% contrasted with 1-3% in the general population. 30-40% of identical twins are concordant for unipolar depression. Alcoholism and chronic stress may predispose to the development of the illness.

A few patients will have only one episode (M.D., SINGLE EPISODE, 296.2x); most have two or more attacks (M.D., RECURRENT, 296.3x). Some patients clear between episodes; others remain mildly depressed (10-15%); and some are chronically, severely depressed. Most attacks begin gradually over 1-3 weeks and, untreated, last from 3-8 months or longer. Relapse shortly after recovery from an acute episode is common[7] but may be partly avoidable.[8] These patients are often incapacitated during an episode and are at great risk of suicide. About half of patients with recurrent illness will recover over 1-2 decades, while the other half will be chronically affected.

Postpartum depression is a severe depression beginning 1-2 weeks after delivery, usually of the second or third child. Affected women are at risk for repeated episodes with future births.

Seasonal affective disorder (SAD) is characterized by the development of major depression with a seasonal pattern: symptoms appear each fall/winter and return to normal (or even hypomania) during the spring/summer.[9] It afflicts predominantly women (F:M = 3-4:1), displays many features of "atypical" depression (hypersomnia, wt gain, hyperphagia), and is often treated successfully with bright, artificial light (2-6 hrs/day - response in 2-3 days[10]). Its relationship to more classical major depression is unclear.

The apparent biological nature of many serious depressions is reflected in the recent development of several putative biological tests for depression: the dexamethasone suppression test[11] (DST - positive test is the failure of normal suppression of plasma cortisol 6-24 hours after an oral dose of dexamethasone); urinary MHPG (3-methoxy-4-hydroxyphenyleneglycol - a catabolite of norepinephrine, low in some depressions); CSF 5-HIAA (a metabolite of serotonin, low in some depression); TRH stimulation test (blunted TSH and GH responses to exogenous TRH suggest unipolar depression); sleep abnormalities (short REM latency - time from falling asleep to start of REM sleep; frequent awakenings; increased REM density - frequency of rapid eye movements in REM sleep); and the stimulant challenge tests (some depressed patients briefly improve when given 10 mg of amphetamine). Unfortunately, these tests have little routine clinical utility. They all suffer from inadequate sensitivity and specificity (too many false positives and negatives). However, each further emphasizes that biology plays a role in many depressions.

BIPOLAR DISORDER:

Mania, at some time severe enough to produce compromised functioning, is necessary for this diagnosis, but 80-90% of patients also have periods of depression (B.D., DEPRESSED, 296.5x). The manic episode typically develops over days and may become uncontrolled and psychotic (B.D., MANIC, 296.4x). 20%[+] of manics have hallucinations and/or delusions. A severe mania may be indistinguishable from an organic delirium (sudden onset, anorexia, insomnia, disorientation, paranoia, hallucinations, and delusions) or schizophrenia. When the bipolar pt is depressed, the depression is usually profound but may present as a mild depressive syndrome. Attacks are usually separated by months or years but the patient occasionally may cycle from one to the other over days or weeks ("rapid cyclers" - 15% of pts[12]) or actually present contrasting symptoms simultaneously (eg, spirited singing intermixed with crying) (B.D., MIXED, 296.6x). This is a recurrent illness - single attacks are rare. Pure manic syndromes (patients who have had only mania - unipolar mania) occur clinically but are unusual and are probably not a separate entity.

The lifetime risk for developing bipolar disorder is approximately 0.6-1.0%.[5] This is a genetic disorder. First-degree relatives are at risk for bipolar disorder (5-10% develop it), major depression (10%[+]), and cyclothymia. There is a 70%[+] concordance for bipolar illness in identical twins. In contrast with major depression, male:female is 1:1. The type of inheritance is uncertain - probably polygenic, although there is controversial data suggesting an X-linked dominance with incomplete penetrance, linked to color blindness and Xg blood group. Recent linkage studies are beginning to identify possibly aberrant genes (eg, on chromosome 11, in one large Amish family[13]).

The first manic episode is often before age 30, begins quickly, and resolves in 2-4 months if untreated. One or more episodes of depression usually have already occurred. Most patients go on to have a majority of depressive episodes. Suicide is the major risk during periods of depression. Legal difficulties and drug and alcohol abuse (as well as suicide) occur with manic periods.

## ATYPICAL AFFECTIVE DISORDER

BIPOLAR DISORDER NOS (DSM-III-R p 228, 296.70) and DEPRESSIVE DISORDER NOS (DSM-III-R p 233, 311.00) include the remaining (unusual) affective presentations.[14]

## DIFFERENTIAL DIAGNOSIS

DEPRESSION:[1]

Psychiatric Syndromes:

Schizophrenic Disorders - particularly catatonics, but any type can look or be depressed during or after an episode. Poor premorbid adjustment, formal thought disorder with well-formed delusions and complex hallucinations, lack of cyclic history, and no family history for affective disorder all suggest schizophrenia.

Schizoaffective Disorder - a psychotic disorder that does not meet the criteria for an affective or schizophrenic disorder but which contains features of both.

Generalized Anxiety Disorder - anxiety appears first and predominates. With the anxious patient, always consider depression.

Alcoholism and Drug Abuse - alcoholism and depression are both often present ("dual diagnosis" patients).

Obsessive Compulsive Neurosis; Histrionic and Compulsive Personality Disorders: Are the full syndromes present?

Dementia - "pseudodepression" is common and differentiation is tricky, particularly in the elderly. Check for memory impairment and disorientation.

Physical Syndromes (Organic Mood Disorders)[15]:

Tumors - particularly of brain and lung, carcinoma of panacreas (50% develop psychiatric symptoms before the diagnosis is made).

Infections - influenza, mononucleosis, "flu-fatigue" syndrome (EB virus?), encephalitis, hepatitis.

Medication - oral contraceptives, corticosteroids, reserpine (6% of patients), alphamethyldopa, guanethidine, levodopa, indomethacin, benzodiazepines, opiates, cimetidine, propranolol, anticholinesterases, amphetamine withdrawal.

Endocrine disorders - Cushing's disease (or exogenous steroids), hypothyroidism (some experts recommend a careful thyroid evaluation in most (all?)) depressed patients[16]), apathetic hyperthyroidism, hyperparathyroidism (symptoms parallel levels of serum $Ca^{++}$), diabetes, Turner's syndrome.

Blood - anemia (particularly Pernicious Anemia).
Nutrition and electrolytes - pellagra, hyponatremia, hypokalemia, hypercalcemia, inappropriate ADH.
Misc. - MS, heavy metal poisoning, Parkinson's disease, head trauma, stroke (post-stroke depression; particularly L-frontal),[17] early Huntingtons disease, post-MI, PMS (?), menopause (relieved by estrogens).

## MANIA:

### Psychiatric Syndromes:

Schizophrenic Disorders - often indistinguishable in acute cases. Check past personal and family history.
Schizoaffective Disorder
Borderline Personality Disorder

### Organic Affective Syndromes[18]:

Tumors - of brain.
Infections - encephalitis, influenza, syphilis (20% of patients with general paresis).
Medication - steroids, amphetamines, cocaine, L-dopa, hallucinogens, various toxic deliriums.
Misc. - MS, Wilson's disease, head trauma, psychomotor epilepsy, hyperthyroidism.

## PSYCHOBIOLOGICAL THEORIES

Psychoanalytic theory (Freud) postulates that a depressed patient has suffered a real or imagined loss of an ambivalently loved object, has reacted with unconscious rage which has been then turned against the self, and this has resulted in a lowered self-esteem and depression. Cognitive Theory postulates a "cognitive triad" of distorted perceptions in which (1) a person's negative interpretation of his own life experiences (2) causes a devaluation of himself which (3) causes depression.

Promising but unproven biological theories focus on brain norepinephrine (NE) and serotonin (5-HT) abnormalities. Biological and psychological theories need not be mutually exclusive. The catecholamine hypothesis suggests that low brain NE levels cause depression and elevated levels cause mania; however, urinary MHPG levels (a major metabolite of NE) are low in only some depressions. The indoleamine hypothesis holds that low cerebral 5-HT (or the primary metabolite, 5-HIAA) causes depression and elevation causes mania, yet exceptions occur. The permissive hypothesis postulates that lowered NE produces depression and raised NE causes mania only if 5-HT levels are low. The known mechanisms of action of antidepressants support these theories - tricyclics block NE and 5-HT reuptake and MAOIs block oxidation of NE. In addition, recent research suggests that there may be some fundamental abnormality of the circadian rhythms of depressed patients.[19]

## TREATMENT OF DEPRESSION

Evaluate medically and psychiatrically to rule out secondary depression and to attempt to identify an affective syndrome. Always ask about vegetative features and evaluate suicidal potential (see chapter 7). If the patient is (1) incapacitated by the disorder, (2) has a destructive home environment or limited environmental support, (3) is a suicide risk, or (4) has an associated medical illness requiring treatment - hospitalize. All depressed patients should receive psychotherapy - some must receive physical therapies in addition. The specific treatments used depend on the diagnosis, severity, patient's age, and past responses to therapy.

PSYCHOLOGICAL THERAPIES:

Supportive psychotherapy is always indicated. Be warm, empathic, understanding, and optimistic. Help the patient to identify and express concerns and to ventilate. Identify precipitating factors and help correct. Help solve external problems (eg, rent, job) - be directive, particularly during the acute episode and if the patient is immobilized. Train the patient to recognize signs of future decompensation. See the patient frequently (1-3X/wk initially) and regularly, but not interminably - be available. Recognize that some depressed patients can provoke anger in you (via anger, hostility, unreasonable demands, etc) - watch for it. Long-term insight-oriented psychotherapy may be of value in selected chronic minor depressions and some conflicted patients with a major depression in remission.

Behavior therapy may help mild to moderately severe depressives. Felt to be "learned helplessness," depressions are treated by giving patients skill training and providing success experiences. Cognitive therapy is clearly effective with many patients.[20] The patient is trained to recognize and eliminate negative expectations.

Partial sleep deprivation (awaken midway through the night and keep up until the next evening) helps lessen the symptoms of a major depression. Physical exercise (running, swimming) may produce improvement in depression, for poorly understood biological reasons.

PHYSICAL THERAPIES (see **Chapter 23**):

All major and most chronic or unimproved minor depressions require a trial of antidepressants (70-80% of patients respond), even though an apparent precipitant of the depression is identified. Begin with a <u>tricyclic antidepressant</u> but consider a trial with a different antidepressant, an <u>MAOI</u> (particularly in "atypical" depressions), or a drug combination if the first drug fails. Be alert to side effects and be aware that antidepressants may precipitate a manic episode in a few bipolar patients[21]. Maintain for several months after remission (longer in chronic cases), then taper slowly.

<u>Lithium</u> is moderately effective at maintaining remission in bipolar and some unipolar patients.[22] Antidepressants and lithium may be started concurrently, and the lithium continued after remission. Lithium <u>may</u> be useful in treating acute bipolar depressions and a few unipolar depressions, but it can exacerbate symptoms in some patients. Psychotic, paranoid, or very agitated patients may require an <u>antipsychotic</u>, alone or with an antidepressant, lithium, or ECT - an antidepressant alone usually is not sufficient.

Electroconvulsive therapy (ECT) may be the treatment of choice (1) if medication fails after one or more 6-week trials, (2) if the patient's condition demands an immediate remission (eg, <u>acutely</u> suicidal), (3) in some psychotic depressions, or (4) in patients who can't tolerate medication (eg, some elderly cardiac patients). Up to 90% of patients respond.

TREATMENT OF MANIA

Evaluate carefully but quickly. Is the patient medically ill or taking drugs? Has he been manic before? Is he taking lithium? What is the blood level?

<u>If hypomanic</u>, consider outpatient treatment. Send home with family. Sedate with antipsychotic medication; eg, haloperidol 3-20 mg daily. Begin lithium carbonate.

<u>If manic</u>, hospitalize. Is the patient debilitated? Seriously sleep deprived?

1. Medicate acutely with antipsychotics (large doses are often required; eg, haloperidol 10-40 mg or more, during the first 24 hrs). Consider adjunctive use of a benzodiazepine early on.[23]

2. Be relaxed, reasonable, and controlled.  Treat in quiet setting with minimal stimuli.  Set firm limits.
3. Begin lithium carbonate; however, as many as 30% of manics stay partially symptomatic in spite of lithium. If lithium fails, consider <u>carbamazepine</u>.  Other, (unproven) drugs that look promising for mania include clonazepam,[24] lorazepam,[25] clonidine,[26] and sodium valproate.[27]

## REFERENCES

1. Winokur G, Black DW, Nasrallah A: Depressions secondary to other psychiatric disorders and medical illnesses. <u>Am J Psychiatry</u> 145:233-237, 1988.
2. Ragan PV, McGlashan TH: Childhood parental death and adult psychopathology. <u>Am J Psychiatry</u> 143:153-157, 1986.
3. Sklar AD, Harris RF: Effects of parent loss: Interaction with family size and sibling order. <u>Am J Psychiatry</u> 142: 708-714, 1985.
4. Keller MB, Lavori PW, Endicott J, et al: "Double depression": two-year follow-up. <u>Am J Psychiatry</u> 140:689, 1983.
5. Robins LN, Helzer JE, Weissman M, et al: Lifetime prevalence of specific psychiatric disorders in three sites. <u>Arch Gen Psychiatry</u> 41:949-958, 1984.
6. Coryell W, Lavori P, Endicott J, et al: Outcome in schizoaffective, psychotic, and nonpsychotic depression. <u>Arch Gen Psychiatry</u> 41:787-791, 1984.
7. Faravelli C, Ambonetti A, Pallanti S, Pazzagli A: Depressive relapses and incomplete recovery from index episode. <u>Am J Psychiatry</u> 143:888-891,1986.
8. Kupfer DJ, Frank E: Relapse in recurrent unipolar depression. <u>Am J Psychiatry</u> 144:86-88, 1987.
9. Rosenthal NE, Wehr TA: Seasonal affective disorders. <u>Psychiatr Ann</u> 17:670-674, 1987.
10. Wehr RA, Skwerer RG, Jacobsen FM, et al: Eye versus skin phototherapy of seasonal affective disorder. <u>Am J Psychiatry</u> 144:753-757, 1987.
11. Task Force on Laboratory Tests in Psychiatry: The dexamethasone suppression test: an overview of its current status in psychiatry. An APA Task Force Report. <u>Am J Psychiatry</u> 144:1253-1262, 1987.
12. Wehr TA, Sack DA, Rosenthal NE, Cowdry RW: Rapid cycling affective disorder: Contributing factors and treatment responses in 51 patients. <u>Am J Psychiatry</u> 145:179-184, 1988.
13. Egeland JA, Gerhard DS, Pauls DL, et al: Bipolar affective disorders linked to DNA markers on chromosome 11. <u>Nature</u> 325:783-787, 1987.

14. Akiskal HS: The clinical significance of the "soft" bipolar spectrum. Psychiatr Ann 16:667-671, 1986.
15. Cameron OG: Presentations of Depression. New York, John Wiley & Sons, 1987.
16. Gold MS, Herridge P, Hapworth WE: Depression and "symptomless" autoimmune thyroiditis. Psychiatr Ann 17: 750-757, 1987.
17. Robinson RG: Depression and stroke. Psychiatr Ann 17: 731-740, 1987.
18. Stasiek C, Zetin M: Organic manic disorders. Psychosomatics 26:394-402, 1985.
19. Sack DA, Nurnberger J, Rosenthal NE, et al: Potentiation of antidepressant medications by phase advance of the sleep-wake cycle. Am J Psychiatry 142:606-608, 1985.
20. Beck AT, Hollon SD, Young JE, et al: Treatment of depression with cognitive therapy and amitriptyline. Arch Gen Psychiatry 42:142-148, 1985.
21. Wehr TA, Goodwin FK: Can antidepressants cause mania and worsen the course of affective illness? Am J Psychiatry 144:1403-1411, 1987.
22. Goodnick PJ, Fieve RR, Schlegel A, Baxter N: Predictors of interepisode symptoms and relapse in affective disorder patients treated with lithium carbonate. Am J Psychiatry 144:367-369, 1987.
23. Cohen S, Khan A, Johnson S: Pharmacological management of manic psychosis in an unlocked setting. J Clin Psychopharmacol 7:261-264, 1987.
24. Chouinard G: Antimanic effects of clonazepam. Psychosomatics 26, No 12 (Supplement):7-12, 1985.
25. Modell JG, Lenox RH, Weiner S: Inpatient clinical trial of lorazepam for the management of manic agitation. J Clin Psychopharmacol 5:109-113, 1985.
26. Hardy M, Lecrubier Y, Widlocher D: Efficacy of clonidine in 24 patients with acute mania. Am J Psychiatry 143: 1450-1453, 1986.
27. McElroy SL, Keck PE, Pope HG: Sodium valproate: Its use in primary psychiatric disorders. J Clin Psychopharmacol 7:16-24, 1987.

# Chapter 5

# Delirium and Other Organic Brain Syndromes

Organic brain syndromes (OBS) are mental disorders of various types caused by a wide range of organic pathology. The most common types are delirium (see below), dementia (see chapter 6), and intoxication and withdrawal (see chapters 16 and 17).

These syndromes are common, particularly among the elderly (10-15% of all acute medical inpatients develop a degree of OBS - usually delirium). Delirium is usually brief and reversible, and dementia is longer-lasting and more likely to be irreversible, yet none of these characterizations is completely true (eg, 15-20% of dementias are reversible). These conditions are clinically defined, and their course and characteristics are dependent upon the nature, severity, course, and location of the causative organic pathology. First identify the syndrome, then determine the likely organic cause.

## DELIRIUM

### (DSM-III-R p 100, 293.00)

This is a common condition, particularly among persons who are physically ill.[1,2] These patients may be confused, bizarre, or even "wild," and thus can be mistakenly thought to be suffering from other psychotic illnesses. Other delirious patients may appear somnolent or perfectly normal during the day but decompensate dramatically in the evening or night. Still other patients may have increasing difficulty functioning due to a mild delirium which is only revealed by specific mental status testing. Synonyms include acute brain syndrome, toxic psychosis, acute confusional state, and metabolic encephalopathy.

DIAGNOSIS:

Delirium is a rapidly developing disorder of disturbed attention which fluctuates with time. Although the clinical presentation of delirium differs considerably from patient to patient, there are several characteristic features which help make the diagnosis.

- Clouding of consciousness: The patient is not normally alert and may appear bewildered and confused. He may have noticeably decreased alertness (grading into stupor) or he may be hyperalert. Observe the patient.

- Attention deficit: The patient usually is very distractible and unable to focus his attention sufficiently or for a long enough time to follow a train of thought or to understand what is occurring around him. Have the patient do serial 7's and/or a Random Letter Test.

- Perceptual disturbances: These are common and include misinterpretations of environmental events, illusions (eg, the curtain blows and the patient believes someone is climbing in the window), and hallucinations (usually visual). The patient may or may not recognize these misperceptions as unreal.

- Sleep-wake alteration: Insomnia is almost always present (all symptoms are usually worse at night and in the dark) while marked drowsiness may also occur.

- Disorientation: Most frequently to time but also to place, situation, and (lastly) person. Ask for the date, time, and day of the week. "What place is this?" etc.

- Memory impairment: The patient typically has a recent memory deficit and usually denies it (he may confabulate and may want to talk about the distant past). Ask about the recent past - eg, "Who brought you to the hospital? Did you have any tests yesterday? What did you have for breakfast?" etc. Name four objects and two words and ask the patient for them in 5 minutes. Does he remember your name?

- Incoherence: The patient may attempt to communicate but the speech may be confused or even unintelligible. Verbal perseveration may occur.

- Altered psychomotor activity: Most delirious patients are restless and agitated and may display perseveration of motion; some may be excessively somnolent; and some may fluctuate from one to the other (usually restless at night and sleepy during the day).

- <u>Fluctuations</u>: Most of the characteristics listed above vary in severity over hours and days.

A delirium usually develops over days and <u>may</u> precede signs of the organic condition causing it. Usually it lasts less than a week (depending on the cause). Many of these patients are significantly anxious or frightened by their experiences, may become combative, and may develop some delusional ideas based on their misperceptions. A few patients become dangerously suicidal - watch for it. Environmental conditions can significantly alter the presentation of a delirium. Change of setting (eg, moving out of familiar surroundings), overstimulation, and understimulation (eg, darkness, sensory deprivation) can all worsen the symptoms, as can stress of any kind.

It is necessary to have a high index of suspicion and to ask specific mental status questions if you are going to identify delirium early. Ask tactfully since many patients defensively resist this probing. The early, prodromal symptoms which should alert you to a developing delirium include[3,4]:

Restlessness (particularly at night), anxiety
Daytime somnolence
Insomnia, vivid dreams and nightmares
Hypersensitivity to light and sound
Fleeting illusions and hallucinations
Distractibility; difficulty in thinking clearly

The EEG (although usually not necessary to make the diagnosis) has a characteristic pattern of <u>diffuse slowing</u> that is proportional to the severity of the delirium. It can help if there is a question of the presence of a functional psychosis, drug use, or a dissociative state. Delirium may also be accompanied by a tremor, asterixis, diaphoresis, tachycardia, elevated BP, tachypnea, and flushing.

<u>ETIOLOGY AND DIFFERENTIAL DIAGNOSIS</u>:

The presence of a delirium usually means that the patient is seriously medically ill.[5,6] Delirium is a diagnosis that immediately demands a search for causes. Most causes produce diffuse cerebral impairment and lie <u>outside</u> the CNS - usually due to some form of deranged metabolism (eg, infection, fever, hypoxia, hypoglycemia, medication side effects, drug withdrawal states, hepatic encephalopathy, postoperative changes) - but also include CNS trauma and postictal states. The specific potential etiologies are too numerous to list (consult a more complete source[3]), although usually the cause is evident. These patients all deserve a thorough physical and laboratory examination.

The major problem in differential diagnosis is in distinguishing a delirium from an acute functional psychosis.[7] The delirious patient is usually more acute and confused, and the hallucinations are usually more disorganized and are more likely to be visual. Patients with functional psychoses usually don't have confusion, disorientation, and illusions, and they are more likely to have a formal thought disorder. Always check the personal and family history for serious psychiatric illness.

TREATMENT:

- Provide adequate medical care for an identified cause of the delirium. Patients with delirium have an increased mortality rate.[6]
- Provide for the patient's safety. Maintain around-the-clock observation (particularly at night). This may require someone in the room constantly - preferably someone with whom the patient is familiar. Use restraints only if absolutely necessary (they frequently increase agitation).
- Keep the patient in a quiet, well-lighted room. Keep familiar objects around and use the same treatment personnel, if possible.
- Frequently (and tactfully) re-orient the patient. Introduce yourself again and describe what you are doing and why.
- Anticipate the patient's anxiety and reassure him. Be calm and sympathetic.
- Medication should be used cautiously. Use low doses. If psychotic features are prevalent, consider haloperidol or chlorpromazine. If sedation is called for (usually for marked agitation), consider the benzodiazepines (eg, diazepam, clonazepam[8]).

---

The following organic brain syndromes are considerably less common than delirium, dementia, and the substance abuse syndromes of intoxication and withdrawal. They are also more likely to be associated with focal organic pathology and with a few specific medical or neurological diseases.

## AMNESTIC SYNDROME

(DSM-III-R p 108, 294.00)

These patients have severe memory deficits which usually appear suddenly following a CNS insult and which may be chronic.  The deficits are <u>both</u> retrograde (old memories-ask about childhood, schooling, etc) and anterograde (new memory - ask the patient to remember several facts for 5-10 minutes).  The patients are often unaware that their memory is impaired.  Unlike delirium, the sensorium is usually clear, although there may be disorientation.  Unlike dementia, serious memory loss occurs without intellectual or other associated changes.

There are numerous potential causes which include CNS trauma, hypoxia, herpes simplex encephalitis, and some substance abuse (particularly alcohol and sedative-hypnotic abuse - see chapters 16 and 17).  Bilateral lesions of the medial temporal and/or diencephalic regions appear to be required.  Treatment consists of correcting any medical/ organic causes and waiting.

## ORGANIC HALLUCINOSIS

(DSM-III-R p 110, 293.82)

The only characteristic symptom is the presence of hallucinations (of any type but usually visual or auditory), although they may be accompanied by concern or anxiety.  The patient is usually (but not always) aware of the symptom's unreality.  The most common etiology is drug abuse (usually hallucinogens) or sensory deprivation (eg, deafness).  It is easily distinguished from delirium and the psychotic disorders by the absence of other related symptoms.

## ORGANIC PERSONALITY SYNDROME

(DSM-III-R p 114, 310.10)

These patients display a personality <u>change</u> or a marked exacerbation of previous personality characteristics.  Often this takes the form of a loss of control over impulses and emotions or the development of apathy, irritability, or indifference.  Impairment of social judgement is common. The usual cause is frontal lobe damage (the frontal lobe syndrome) due to stroke, tumor, CNS trauma, normal pressure hydrocephalus, general paresis, Huntington's chorea, or MS. Be careful not to mistake it for mild delirium or the early changes of dementia, schizophrenia, or Major Affective Disorder.

## ORGANIC DELUSIONAL SYNDROME

### (DSM-III-R p 109, 293.81)

This syndrome may mimic schizophrenia - the presence of delusions (usually paranoid) in a clear sensorium is the predominant symptom, but almost any psychotic-like symptom can occur. The most common cause is amphetamine abuse but it may also be due to abuse of other drugs (eg, cocaine, cannabis), encephalitis, psychomotor epilepsy, and occasionally other CNS pathology. Without good evidence of organic pathology, it is very difficult to differentiate this syndrome from a functional psychosis.

## ORGANIC MOOD SYNDROME

### (DSM-III-R p 111, 293.83)

This syndrome typically mimics a depression or mania. To make the diagnosis, it is necessary to identify a likely organic factor as causative. Numerous drugs and medical conditions can cause this syndrome (see chapters 13, 14, and 15).

## ORGANIC ANXIETY SYNDROME

### (DSM-III-R p 113, 294.80)

These patients suffer from generalized anxiety, panic attacks, or both - due to organic pathology. Likely causes include hyper- and hypothyroidism and other endocrine disorders, stimulant use, drug withdrawal, and a number of other medical conditions (see chapters 13, 14, and 15).

### REFERENCES

1. Lipowski ZJ: Delirium (acute confusional state). In JAM Frederiks (Ed.) Handbook of Clinical Neurology, Vol. 2, Neurobehavioural Disorders. New York, Elsevier Science Pub., 1985.
2. Zisook S, Braff DL: Delirium: Recognition and management in the older patient. Geriatrics 41:67-78, 1986.
3. Lipowski ZJ: Delirium. Springfield, IL, Charles C Thomas Pub., 1980.
4. Lipowski ZJ: Transient cognitive disorders (delirium, acute confusional states) in the elderly. Am J Psychiatry 140:1426, 1983.
5. Jacob JW, Bernhad MR, Delgado A, Strain JJ: Screening for organic mental syndromes in the medically ill. Ann Intern Med 86:40, 1977.

6.  Weddington WW: The mortality of delirium: an underappreciated problem? _Psychosomatics_ 23:1232, 1982.
7.  Dubin WR, Weiss KJ, Zeccardi JA: Organic brain syndrome: the psychiatric imposter. _JAMA_ 249:60, 1983.
8.  Freinhar JP, Alvarez WA: Clonazepam treatment of organic brain syndromes in three elderly patients. _J Clin Psychiatry_ 47:525-526, 1986.

# Chapter 6

# Dementia

<u>DEMENTIA</u> (DSM-III-R p 103, 294.10) results from a broad loss of intellectual functions due to diffuse organic disease of the cerebral hemispheres which is of sufficient severity to impair social and/or occupational functioning. Dementia is a clinical presentation demanding a diagnosis - <u>not</u> a diagnosis itself. Causes are numerous, but clinical presentations are remarkably similar. 60% of dementias are irreversible, but, since 25% are controllable and 15% are reversible, treatable causes must be identified.

## MAKING THE DIAGNOSIS

Dementia usually develops slowly and is easily overlooked. A rapid onset suggests a recent (and possibly treatable) insult although frequently a mild, unrecognized dementia is made worse and obvious by a medical illness (eg, pneumonia, CHF). <u>Always</u> interview the family - they frequently notice changes (in personality, memory, etc) of which the patient is unaware. Unlike Delirium, there is <u>no</u> clouding of consciousness - make sure the patient is alert.

EARLY - Effects include: subtle changes in personality, impaired social skills, a decrease in the range of interests and enthusiasms, lability and shallowness of affect, agitation, numerous somatic complaints, vague psychiatric symptoms, and a gradual loss of intellectual skills and acuity. These are often first noticed in work settings where high performance is required. Patients may recognize a loss of abilities initially but vigorously deny it. Early dementia often precipitates a depression.[1] Remember: early dementia may present primarily with emotional (usually depressive) rather than cognitive symptoms, <u>but also</u> emotional disorders may mimic early dementia - don't under- or overdiagnose it.

LATE - Parts of the full picture emerge:

Memory loss - Usually immediate and recent memory loss but
gradually involves remote recall (medial temporal and
diencephalic regions involved). Does patient forget
appointments, the news, people he has just met, or
places he has just been? Patient may confabulate, so
check his information.

Ask patient to (1) repeat digits (normal - remember
6 forward, 4 backward) and (2) recall 2 words and 3
objects after 5 minutes. Does he know your name? the
nurse? this place? the names of his visitors? last
night's meal? Does he know his birth date? his home-
town? the name of his high school?

Changes in mood and personality - Often exaggeration of
previous personality (eg, more compulsive or more
excitable). Depression, anxiety, and/or irritability
early on - later, withdrawal and apathy. Has the
patient become sloppy, belligerent, thoughtless of
others, paranoid, socially inappropriate, fearful? Does
he lack initiative or interest? Use vulgar language or
jokes?

Loss of orientation - Particularly time (of day, day of
week, date, season) but also place ("What place is
this?") and , when severe, person. Has he been getting
lost - in new places? in old neighborhood? at home?
Does he know why he is here (situation)? He may not
sleep well, wander around at night, and get lost.

Intellectual impairment - Patient is "less sharp" than he
used to be. Does he have trouble doing things he could
previously do easily? General information (last 5
Presidents, 6 large U.S. cities)? calculations
(multiplication tables, serial 7's, make change)?
similarities (How are a ball and an orange alike? a
mouse and an elephant? a fly and a tree?).

Compromised judgement - Doesn't anticipate consequences.
Does he act impulsively? "What should you do if you
found a stamped, addressed envelope?" "If you noticed a
fire in a theater?"

Psychotic symptoms - Hallucinations (usually simple),
illusions, delusions, unshakable preoccupations, ideas
of reference.

Language impairment - Often vague and imprecise; occasionally almost mute. Is there perseveration, blocking, or
aphasia? (With early aphasia, suspect focal pathology.)

Ask about history of chronic medical or psychiatric disease, family psychiatric illness, drug or alcohol abuse, head injury, exposure to toxins.

## PHYSICAL EXAMINATION:

Examine for the numerous medical causes of dementia - eg, endocrine, heart, kidney, lung, liver, infection (see below). Always perform a careful neurologic exam - identify any focal CNS causes of dementia. Always test for sense of smell (1st cranial nerve) - may identify a large, unrecognized frontal lobe lesion. Always test hearing. Advanced diffuse disease displays ataxia, facial grimaces, agnosias, apraxias, motor impersistence, and/or perseveration, and pathological reflexes (grasp, snout, suck, glabella tap, tonic foot, etc). Recognize that all types of physical illnesses occur more frequently in the demented (reasons for this are unclear). Survival time is reduced.

## LABORATORY EXAMINATION:

Select tests based on suspected etiology. Consider screening with: ESR, CBC, STS, SMA-12, $T_3$ & $T_4$, vitamin $B_{12}$ and folate assays, UA, chest X-ray, and CT scan. Other tests based on likely causes include drug levels, EEG (20% of all elderly have an abnormal EEG), LP (rarely[2,3]), arteriography, etc. The EEG is useful for identifying pathology in the usually silent CNS areas (frontal and temporal lobes) - investigate further if the dementia is mild but the EEG is grossly abnormal.

## PSYCHOLOGICAL TESTING:

These can (1) help identify a focal lesion, (2) provide a baseline, (3) help with the diagnosis, and (4) identify strengths to be used in planning treatment. Useful tests include: WAIS, Bender-Gestalt Test, the Luria test, and the Halstead and Reitan Batteries (very time-consuming). Don't use routinely. A brief but useful screening test is the Mini-Mental State Exam.[4,5] Patients with even mild dementia often will show impaired constructional ability; thus, have them draw simple figures (eg, a diamond, a cross, and cube - can be done on initial interview).

## CAUSES

### Major Untreatable Dementias

PRIMARY DEGENERATIVE DEMENTIA OF THE ALZHEIMER TYPE
(DSM-III-R p 119, 290.xx)(Alzheimer's and Pick's
Diseases): Approx. 50% of all dementias (5% of people over
65), but - usually a diagnosis by exclusion. It is frequently overdiagnosed. Usually begins insidiously in the
50's, 60's, or 70's and progresses to death in 6-10 years.
Ceaseless pacing and a shuffling gait are common; social
responses often remain intact until very late. Look for
cortical atrophy and enlarged ventricles by CT scan. EEG
is often normal for age early on[6] - a good screening test
since it is often abnormal with reversible causes of
dementia (except for general paresis and NPH). Histo-
logically there are senile plaques, neurofibrillary tan-
gles, and neuronal granulovacuolar degeneration. Recent
evidence implicates primary degeneration of cholinergic
neurons of the basal forebrain, particularly the nucleus
basalis.[7,8] There is an increased incidence in women
(1.5:1), first-degree relatives, and Down's syndrome.[9]

Huntington's Chorea: Psychiatric symptoms, ranging from
neurotic to psychotic (including dementia), may precede
the chorea.[10] Dementia always occurs terminally. Auto-
somal dominant - so check family history.

Parkinson's Disease: Depression (40%)[11] and/or dementia in
some patients. L-Dopa relieves temporarily only.

Others: Progressive Supranuclear Palsy, spinocerebellar
degenerations, Parkinsonism-Dementia Complex of Guam,
SSPE, Creutzfeldt-Jakob disease, herpes simplex
encephalitis, MS.

### Treatable Forms of Dementia

MULTI-INFARCT DEMENTIA (DSM-III-R p 121, 290.4x):    10% of
dementias. Differentiate from Primary Degenerative
Dementia by history of rapid onset and stepwise
deterioration in a patient in his 50's or early 60's and
by presence of focal neurological impairment. EEG may
show focal abnormalities. Caused by multiple
thromboembolic episodes (numerous small cerebral infarcts
pathologically) in a patient with atherosclerotic disease
of the major vessels or valvular disease of the heart.
Hypertension is usually present. Pseudobulbar phenomena
are common: emotional lability, dysarthria, and dysphagia.
Controlling BP may help.

<u>Normal Pressure Hydrocephalus</u> (NPH): A "classic triad" of gait ataxia, incontinence, and progressive dementia - either idiopathic or following cerebral trauma, hemorrhage, or infection. There is normal CSF pressure but dilated ventricles by CT scan and pneumoencephalography. Confirm with isotope cisternography. Treat with a lumboperitoneal or ventriculoatrial shunt - 55% show improvement.

<u>DEMENTIA ASSOCIATED WITH ALCOHOLISM</u> (DSM-III-R p 133, 291.20): A diagnosis by exclusion - following many years of heavy drinking. May be partly reversible with good nutrition and abstinence.

<u>Drug Intoxication</u>: Common, particularly in the elderly (too many meds, misunderstood instructions, etc). Watch for major and minor tranquilizers, analgesics (particularly phenacetin), digoxin, primidone, diphenylhydantoin, methyldopa, and bromides. Reevaluate and stop, if possible.

<u>Brain Tumors</u>: Primarily metastatic tumors (from lung and breast) and meningiomas. Focal signs are usually present except in frontal lobe. Get CSF pressure and protein, EEG, and CT scan. EEG may be localizing.

<u>Brain Trauma</u>: Dementia is unusual except for <u>subdural hematoma</u> in the elderly - dementia, headache, and drowsiness developing over weeks or months with or without a history of trauma. Don't do LP. Get CT scan, then arteriography (diagnostic). <u>May</u> be reversible.

<u>Infection</u>: Any significant infection (eg, pneumonia, UTI) can produce delirium and worsen a dementia in the elderly. Dementia can be caused by brain abscess, CNS syphilis (general paresis - serologic tests of blood and CSF usually positive), and tuberculosis and cryptococcal meningitis.

<u>Metabolic Disorders</u>: Most common are thyroid disorders - <u>hypothyroidism</u> (Dementia even with near normal hormone levels; may be reversible; look for diffuse slowing on EEG) and also hyperthyroidism ("apathetic thyrotoxicosis" - particularly in the elderly). Electrolyte imbalances are also common causes in the elderly - eg, hypo- and hypernatremia and hypercalcemia. Suspect Wilson's Disease if there are signs of liver failure, tremor, rigidity, and convulsions in a person under 40. Also consider Cushing's syndrome, hypoglycemia, and hyper- and hypoparathyroidism.

<u>Disorders of heart, lung, liver, kidney</u>:  Particularly CHF,
   arrhythmias, SBE, chronic hypoxia and hypercapnia (eg,
   emphysema), hepatic encephalopathy, uremia, dialysis
   dementia.

<u>Other</u>:  Malnutrition (particularly vitamin $B_{12}$ and folate
   deficiencies - check for pernicious anemia and combined
   system disease), toxins (eg, lead, mercury, nitrobenzenes,
   organophosphates), remote effects of carcinoma, SLE,
   epilepsy.

### DIFFERENTIAL DIAGNOSIS

   <u>Normal aging</u> may mimic mild dementia, particularly if
the patient is stressed by <u>environmental changes</u>, <u>social
isolation</u>, <u>fatigue</u>, or <u>visual and hearing disorders</u> (sensory
deprivation).    Many elderly will develop mild <u>anxiety</u>,
<u>depressive</u>,   or   <u>hypochondriacal</u>   disorders  which  mimic
dementia, but with persistent questioning and encouragement
normal memory, orientation, etc. can be seen.   Intellectual
deterioration  with  schizophrenia  is  differentiated  from
dementia by a history of psychosis and social withdrawal and
by the presence of a characteristic thought disorder.    An
amytal  interview  may  help  distinguish  dementia  from
<u>catatonic schizophrenia</u>.   In <u>delirium</u> there is an altered
and  fluctuating  level  of  consciousness.    Delirium  and
dementia frequently coexist, but the delirium must clear
before the diagnosis of dementia can be made.

   A <u>Major Depression</u> is the most common cause of
<u>pseudodementia</u>.  Unlike the demented patient, these patients
have a rapid, recent onset (family can usually date it),
<u>complain</u> of a severe memory loss (usually mild when tested),
have marked affective changes, emphasize their inabilities
and failings, and frequently answer simple questions with "I
don't know" (the demented patient usually attempts an
answer).  A temporary clearing during an interview and the
lack of a deteriorating course helps identify these
patients.  Consider a $DST^{12}$ and CT scan.  These patients
usually improve with antidepressants or ECT.

   Don't mistake an aphasia due to a focal lesion for a
dementia (although perhaps 10% of severely demented patients
have a related aphasia).

## TREATMENT

Supportive Treatment[13]:

- Provide good physical care - eg, good nutrition, eye glasses, hearing aids, protection (eg, stairs, stoves, medication), etc.
- Keep in familiar settings, if possible. Surround with familiar objects; keep old friends engaged. Encourage the family's participation and understanding.[14]
- Keep the patient involved - through personal contact, frequent orientation (remind him of the day, of the time). Discuss the news with him. Use calendars, radio, TV. Structure daily activities - make them predictable.
- Help maintain patient's self-esteem. Treat him like an adult. Plan towards his strengths. Be accepting, tolerant.
- Avoid dark, isolated settings; avoid overstimulation.

Symptomatic Treatment:

Psychiatric conditions require small doses of appropriate medication.

- Acute anxiety, restlessness, aggression: eg, haloperidol 0.5 mg PO tid (or lower[15]); thioridazine, 25 mg PO tid-qid.
- Nonpsychotic anxiety: eg, diazepam 2 mg PO bid-tid; oxazepam 10 mg PO bid-tid.
- Depression: begin slowly and work up to - eg, desipramine 75-150 mg PO daily.
- Insomnia: for short periods only; use (eg) temazepam 15 mg PO HS.

Specific Treatment:

- Identify and correct any treatable condition.
- No specific drug treatment for dementia has been found to be consistently useful, although many are being investigated - eg, cerebral vasodilators, anti-coagulants, cerebral metabolic stimulants, stimulants, hyperbaric oxygen. Increasing central cholinergic activity may relieve some symptoms in a few patients with Primary Degenerative Dementia temporarily. Acetyl-choline precursors (choline, lecithin) are of little value,[16] but anticholinesterases (physostigmine - short-acting; THA - tetrahydroaminoacridine[17] - withdrawn (temporarily?) due to hepatotoxicity) show promise. Hydergine (3.0-6.0 mg/day for 6 months) may improve mood and functioning modestly, but significant improvement is unlikely.

## REFERENCES

1.  Reifler BV, Larson E, Hanley R: Coexistence of cognitive impairment and depression in geriatric outpatients. Am J Psychiatry 139:623, 1982.
2.  Becker PM, Feussner JR, Mulrow CD, et al: The role of lumbar puncture in the evaluation of dementia. J Am Geriatr Soc 33:392-396, 1985.
3.  Hammerstrom DC, Zimmer B: The role of lumbar puncture in the evaluation of dementia. J Am Geriatr Soc 33:397-400, 1985.
4.  Folstein MF, Folstein SE, McHugh PR: "Mini-mental state" - a practical method for grading the mental state of patients for the clinician. J Psychiatr Res 12:189, 1975.
5.  Teng EL, Chui HC: The modified mini-mental state (3MS) examination. J Clin Psychiatry 48:314-318, 1987.
6.  Rae-Grant A, Blume W, Lau C, et al: The electroencephalogram in Alzheimer-type dementia. Arch Neurol 44:50-54, 1987.
7.  Plotkin DA, Jarvik LF: Cholinergic dysfunction in Alzheimer disease: Cause or effect? In, Van Ree JM, Matthysse S (Eds), Progress in Brain Research, Vol 65. New York, Elsevier, 1986.
8.  Davies P, Wolozin BL: Recent advances in the neurochemistry of Alzheimer's disease. J Clin Psychiatry 48 (5, Suppl):23-30, 1987.
9.  Karlinsky H: Alzheimer's disease in Down's syndrome. J Am Geriatr Soc 34:728-734, 1986.
10. Caine ED, Shoulson I: Psychiatric syndromes in Huntington's disease. Am J Psychiatry 140:728-733, 1983.
11. Mayeux R, Stern Y, Williams JBW, et al: Clinical and biochemical features of depression in Parkinson's disease. Am J Psychiatry 143:756-759, 1986.
12. Jenike MA, Albert MS: The dexamethasone suppression test in patients with presenile and senile dementia of the Alzheimer's type. J Am Geriatr Soc 32:441-444, 1984.
13. Reisberg B: Dementia: A systematic approach to identifying reversible causes. Geriatrics 41:30-46, 1986.
14. Mace NL, Rabins PV: The 36-Hour Day. Baltimore, Johns Hopkins Univ Press, 1981.
15. Risse SC, Lampe TH, Cubberley L: Very low-dose neuroleptic treatment in two patients with agitation associated with Alzheimer's disease. J Clin Psychiatry 48:207-208, 1987.
16. Dysken M: A review of recent clinical trials in the treatment of Alzheimer's dementia. Psychiatr Ann 17:178-191, 1987.
17. Summers WK, Majovski LV, Marsh GM, et al: Oral tetrahydroaminoacridine in long-term treatment of senile dementia, Alzheimer type. NEJM 315:1241-1245, 1986.

*Chapter 7*

# Suicidal and Assaultive Behaviors

THE SUICIDAL PATIENT

EPIDEMIOLOGY:

-Reported suicides in the USA - 30,000/yr (12/100,000).
-Suicide is under-reported - often listed as accidental.
-Attempted suicide:successful suicide ratio is 20:1.
-Suicide increases with age; 2nd leading cause of death in male adolescents and college students.
-Completers 3:1 (M:F); attempters 3:1 (F:M).
-Most common attempt is by drug ingestion; most likely to be fatal is by shooting.
-Most patients are <u>not</u> "psychotic or incompetent."

All clinicians will encounter suicidal patients. Many will not recognize them. Some of those patients will kill themselves.

IDENTIFYING THE POTENTIALLY SUICIDAL PATIENT

One fifth of suicides are unsuspected; accurate prediction is difficult, if not impossible.[1] Entertain the possibility when:

1. Suicide attempt: Patient seen in ER, medical ward, etc.
2. Overt or indirect suicide talk or threats: "You won't be bothered by me much longer" (most often made to family members).
3. Depressed or anxious mood due to a depression.
4. Significant recent loss: eg, spouse, job, self-esteem.
5. Unexpected change in behavior: making a will, intense talks with friends, giving away possessions.
6. Unexpected change in attitude: Suddenly cheerful, angry, or withdrawn.

## ASSESSING SUICIDAL RISK[2,3]

ASSESSMENT PROCEDURE:

First, build rapport during a supportive, nonjudgemental interview. If not volunteered, investigate suicidal thoughts by asking questions of increasing specificity: eg, "Have you been feeling sad?"; "Have you thought of doing away with yourself?"; "How?"; etc. Asking about suicide does not precipitate it. After a serious attempt, wait until the patient is alert enough to cooperate.

The following must be learned about all suicidal pts:

1. The patient's intention - Why does he want to die?
2. Is a suicide plan made? - the more specific the plan, the more likely the act.
3. Method - the more lethal the technique, the more serious the plan.
4. Presence of psychiatric or organic factors - eg, psychotic depression, thought disorder, sedative self-medication, organicity.
5. Determine the role of impulsivity vs premeditation.
6. Is the precipitating crisis resolving?
7. Take an "inventory of loss."
8. Does the patient have plans for the future?
9. Does the patient have caring family or other supports?
10. Does the patient think he is going to commit suicide?

Population Risk Factors: Males, elderly, isolated, whites, American Indians, policemen.

Individual Risk Factors:
- Sense of hopelessness,[4] helplessness, loneliness, exhaustion, "unbearable" psychological pain.
- Psychiatric illness (in 90% of suicide pts),[5,6] mainly:
    1. Major affective disorder (either $1^\circ$ or $2^\circ$; 50% of all suicides), particularly with vegetative signs or constriction of thought; 15% lifetime suicide risk.
    2. Alcoholism (suicide rate 50X norm - 25% of all suicides) - mostly chronic pts; mostly men; often following interpersonal loss; 15% lifetime risk. Drug addiction (10% die by suicide).
    3. Schizophrenia, particularly when lonely, depressed, chronic, or with persecutory delusions or self-destructive command hallucinations;[7] 10% life risk.
    4. Other: Psychoses due to organic brain syndromes; personality disorders (borderline, antisocial).
- Failing health, particularly if previously independent (5% of all suicides).
- Intoxication; active use (abuse) of alcohol and drugs.

- Impaired impulse control for any reason; hostility.
- <u>Past history of suicide attempts</u>, particularly serious attempts.
- Nature of past or present suicide attempts: eg, shooting or jumping more lethal than most ingestions or wrist cutting. Warning given? Help available at the time?
- Family history of suicide;[8] personal exposure to suicide; suicide itself may run in families genetically.
- Widowed, divorced, separated, <u>single</u>, <u>unemployed</u>, retired.
- Medical patients on renal dialysis.
- Family stresses or instability; few external supports.
- A change in status - <u>up</u> or down.
- Recent loss or rejection.
- Parental loss during childhood.

Other Risk Factors:
- Holidays, spring, anniversaries.
- Possible biochemical measures of suicide potential[9]: decreased CSF 5-HIAA[10] and HVA[11] and increased MHPG;[12] decreased urine NE/E ratio;[13] increased adrenal wt;[14] positive DST.[15]

## INITIATING APPROPRIATE TREATMENT

The first question often is: "Should you hospitalize?" If the patient has pressing suicidal thoughts and/or decreased impulse control coupled with several risk factors, hospitalize, if only overnight. Be conservative. Don't write off patients as "just manipulative" - all statements of suicide intent initially should be taken seriously (particularly from adolescents[16]). Manipulative suicide patients have "accidentally" killed themselves after being denied admission - 60% of successful suicides have had previous suicide attempts. The most emotionally upset patient is not necessarily the most suicidal. The suicidal state is episodic; a patient may be "safe" just hours after a serious suicide attempt. Be very cautious of the patient who has trouble considering any alternative to suicide.

The decision <u>to</u> hospitalize should be communicated to the patient decisively but optimistically. Hospitalization should be involuntary if necessary. Assure the patient's physical safety in the hospital through appropriate "suicide precautions," eg, close supervision, no isolation, no dangerous objects.

A patient of lesser risk may be followed as an outpatient if there is a reliable family to help monitor him-assess that support. If the patient is <u>not</u> to be hospitalized, specific plans for follow-up must be made with the patient. Be absolutely clear about this with him.

TREATMENT PRINCIPLES:

1. Identify and treat psychiatric or medical conditions. Treat depression vigorously. Treat psychotic depressions with an antidepressant <u>and</u> antipsychotic. If the patient is determinedly suicidal, use ECT rather than wait for a medication response. Phenothiazines and benzodiazepines may be briefly useful with the agitated patient.
2. Develop a therapeutic alliance with the patient. Be concerned and accepting. Attempt to understand why the patient wants to die. Allow him to express anger, "unacceptable" thoughts, and feelings of rejection and hopelessness. These patients often feel misunderstood and trapped but unable to ask for help. Reduce the psychological pain anyway you can.
3. Suicidal patients are usually <u>ambivalent about death</u> and may not know why they are trying to kill themselves. Point out that ambivalence to them - show them evidence of their desire to live. Be hopeful. Be definite. Make specific plans with and for the patient. Appeal to his mature rather than his regressive side.
4. The patients are often bewildered and have a narrowed focus of thought - deal with reality issues.
5. Don't minimize the seriousness of a suicide attempt to the patient.
6. Never agree to hold a suicide plan in confidence.
7. Help the patient to grieve over losses.
8. Do not explain away the patient's symptoms - eg, "I'd feel the same way myself."
9. Suicide potential can change rapidly. Reassess the patient's state of mind frequently.
10. Use community resources. Involve the family and significant others in treatment; use family therapy when appropriate. Actively try to reduce social isolation and withdrawal. Help make changes in the patient's environment where it is pathological.
11. Many suicides in depressives occur during the first 3-6 months after hospital discharge. <u>Don't lose contact</u> with the patient. Monitor closely during holidays.
12. Be active but insist that the patient ultimately take responsibility for his own life.
13. Tricyclics, MAO inhibitors, and many sedative-hypnotics have serious overdose potential. Some depressed outpatients store medication, so track drugs prescribed.

Theoretical explanations of suicide include the loss of a sense of identity with the social group (Durkheim), hostility turned against the self (Freud), a "cry for help," and a reflection of biologic, psychiatric conditions.

## THE VIOLENT PATIENT

Human aggression has complex and uncertain biological, psychosocial, and cultural roots. Implicated in violent behavior are lesions of the prefrontal cortex (Frontal Lobe Syndrome) and stimulation of the amygdala and limbic system. Also, elevated androgens and CSF norepinephrine or decreased CSF serotonin (similar to "violent" suicide) and GABA.[17]

Prediction of violence is difficult. Anyone can become violent, yet some <u>groups</u> are at risk: young males 15-25; urban, black, violent cultural subgroups, alcoholics. Key <u>individual</u> predictors of violent behavior are:

1. A past history of violence.
2. Active use of alcohol.
3. Physical abuse as a child.
4. Some form of brain injury.

### MENTAL DISORDERS WITH ASSOCIATED VIOLENT BEHAVIOR

Although most mentally ill are not dangerous, some patients present an increased risk. (NOTE: Serious medical illness can first present with violent behavior.)

1. Organic brain syndromes - particularly with confusion or decreased impulse control; eg, the demented, drugs in the elderly, hypoglycemia, CNS infections, anoxia, metabolic acidosis.
2. Alcohol and drug abuse - particularly with intoxication, delirium, or delusional states of Etoh, amphetamines, cocaine, or PCP; also with intoxication from inhalants or "downers."
3. Schizophrenia, paranoid and catatonic types - particularly with command hallucinations or patients who drink.
4. Acute psychotic states of any origin.
5. Certain mentally retarded; XYY karyotype - possibly.
6. Attention deficit disorder with hyperactivity, in adults.

### SEVERAL RECOGNIZABLE PATTERNS OF VIOLENCE

1. <u>Chronic, aggressive, self-aggrandizing life style</u> - seen with ANTISOCIAL PERSONALITY DISORDER and thus associated with drug and alcohol abuse, onset in youth, delinquency and adult crime, truancy and school failure. Patients fight frequently and are "constantly in trouble."

2. <u>Episodic violence</u> - explosive rages with little provocation, daily to several times/yr, brief, occasional amnesia for event and remorse about it. A mixed group of clinical presentations; CNS abnormalities in most.

If violence is <u>directed</u>: consider (1) <u>INTERMITTENT EXPLOSIVE DISORDER</u> (DSM-III-R p 321, 312.34) - usually males with history of violent outbursts, family history of violence, neurological soft signs, abnormal EEGs, normal between episodes; (2) <u>ORGANIC PERSONALITY SYNDROME, EXPLOSIVE TYPE</u> (DSM-III-R p 114, 310.10)- neurologic origin (encephalitis, epilepsy, MS, tumor, poststroke, etc), disturbed personality between episodes; or (3) rages in borderline or histrionic personality disorders; or with intoxication.

If violence <u>poorly directed</u>: consider temporal lobe epilepsy (get NP leads), alcohol idiosyncratic intoxication, or other neurologic syndromes.[18]

## EVALUATING THREATS OF VIOLENCE

Take all ideas or threats of violence seriously. Assess risk factors.[19]

What is the patient's current mental state? Can he control his impulses and rage? Does he feel under great tension and fear losing control? Is there an intended victim? Is the victim covertly provoking the attack? Specific plans made? Sadistic fantasies present? Weapons available? Patient armed (always check)? Family support system present?

## MANAGEMENT OF THE VIOLENT PATIENT

1. First decide if patient is acutely out of control. If so, treat immediately with restraint and medication, not talk. See immediately - don't keep him waiting.
2. Approach an unfamiliar patient cautiously and from a position of strength (help available, open door). Be alert to warning signs: eg, restlessness, demandingness. If talking appears useful, try, but set clear limits during interview. Use physical controls if patient can't maintain but emphasize their temporary, helping nature. If patient arrives in restraints, <u>don't remove</u> until rapport established and some evaluation done- however, many patients do better without restraints. Restraints may increase agitation and cause hyper- thermia. If force is needed to subdue, use overwhelm- ing force - 1 person to each limb. Don't take chances.
3. Medication:
   For the majority of acutely agitated patients: <u>haloperi- dol</u> 5-10 mg IM every 45 minutes until calm (max. 40 mg/24 hr - occasionally more). Has patient taken CNS depressants, is he delirious, or is a medical condition responsible for behavior? - If so, hold meds and observe. ECT can control psychotic violence.
4. If patient is threatening and agitated but not wild, treat with respect - be civil, direct, confident, calm,

reassuring. Don't challenge, provoke, or openly dis-
agree with the patient. Eliminate red tape. <u>Always</u>
explain what you are doing, and why. Violent patients
are often frightened - find out why and of what.
5. Determine etiology of violence. Is a mental illness
present? A brain injury? Drugs involved (get urine
screen)? Are there identifiable environmental precipitants? Expect to intervene directly with the psychotic
patient.
6. Most patients can be "talked down" with support, understanding (and medication) - however, hospitalize involuntarily if necessary. Is this really a criminal
matter, and should the police be involved instead?

## ONGOING CARE

1. The chronically violent should receive medication trials.
Treat psychosis with antipsychotics, seizures with anticonvulsants. For continued outbursts, consider[20,21]:

> propranolol (200-800 mg/day, divided doses), may
> take 4-6 weeks for effect
> carbamazepine (600-1200 mg/day, divided doses)
> lithium (blood level 0.6-1.2 meq/l)
> stimulants in hyperactive adults

Benzodiazepines can be useful during times of stress,
but paradoxical rages occur in some patients.
2. Teach patient to recognize early signs of increasing
anger and to develop ways to discharge tension. The
severely brain damaged may need a structured environment
and behavioral techniques.[22]
3. Help patient to develop a support system and to learn to
control environmental stresses. Maintain a channel of
communication with the potentially violent patient - be
available by phone. Also, you have some legal responsibility.[23]

## REFERENCES

1. Pokorny AD: Prediction of suicide in psychiatric
patients. <u>Arch Gen Psychiatry</u> 40:249, 1983.
2. Motto JA, Heilbron DC, Juster RP: Development of a
clinical instrument to estimate suicide risk. <u>Am J
Psychiatry</u> 142:680-686, 1985.
3. Clark DC, Young MA, et al: A field test of Motto's risk
estimator for suicide. <u>Am J Psychiatry</u> 144:923-926,
1987.
4. Beck AT, Steer RA, et al: Hopelessness and eventual
suicide. <u>Am J Psychiatry</u> 142:559-563, 1985.
5. Robins E: <u>The Final Months: a Study of the Lives of 134</u>

_Persons Who Committed Suicide_. New York, Oxford University Press, 1981.

6.  Black DW, Warrack G, Winokur G: The Iowa record-linkage study. _Arch Gen Psychiatry_ 42:71-75, 1985.

7.  Drake RE, Gates C, Cotton PG: Suicide among schizophrenics. _Br J Psychiatry_ 149:784-787, 1986.

8.  Roy A: Family history of suicide in affective disorder patients. _J Clin Psychiatry_ 46:317-319, 1985.

9.  Mann JJ, Stanley M: _Psychobiology of Suicidal Behavior_. New York, The New York Academy of Sciences, 1986.

10. Edman G, Asberg M, et al: Skin conductance habituation and cerebrospinal fluid 5-hydroxyindoleacetic acid in suicidal patients. _Arch Gen Psychiatry_ 43:587-592, 1986.

11. Roy A, Agren H, et al: Reduced CSF concentrations of homovanillic acid and homovanillic acid to 5-hydroxyindoleacetic acid ratios in depressed patients. _Am J Psychiatry_ 143:1539-1545, 1986.

12. Brown GL, Ebert MH, et al: Aggression, suicide, and serotonin. _Am J Psychiatry_ 139:741, 1982.

13. Ostroff RB, Giller E, et al: The norepinephrine-to-epinephrine ratio in patients with a history of suicide attempts. _Am J Psychiatry_ 142:224-227, 1985.

14. Dorovini-Zis K, Zis AP: Increased adrenal weight in victims of violent suicide. _Am J Psychiatry_ 144:1214-5, 1987.

15. Targum SD, Rosen L, Capodanno AE: The dexamethasone suppression test in suicidal patients with unipolar depression. _Am J Psychiatry_ 140:877, 1983.

16. Shafii M, Carrigan S, et al: Psychological autopsy of completed suicide in children and adolescents. _Am J Psychiatry_ 142:1061-1064, 1985.

17. Eichelman B: Neurochemical and psychopharmacologic aspects of aggressive behavior, in Meltzer H (ed): _Psychopharmacology: The Third Generation of Progress_. New York, Raven Press, 1988.

18. Leicester J: Temper tantrums, epilepsy, and episodic dyscontrol. _Br J Psychiatry_ 141:262, 1982.

19. Jacobs D: Evaluation and management of the violent patient in emergency settings. _Psychiatr Clin North Am_ 6:259, June 1983.

20. Yudofsky SC, Silver JM, Schneider SE: Pharmacologic treatment of aggression. _Psychiatr Ann_ 17:397-407, 1987.

21. Eichelman B: Toward a rational pharmacotherapy for aggressive and vidolent behavior. _Hosp Community Psychiatr_ 39:31-39, 1988.

22. Franzen MD, Lovell MR: Behavioral treatments of aggressive sequelae of brain injury. _Psychiatr Ann_ 17:389-396, 1987.

23. Beck JC: The potentially violent patient: Legal duties, clinical practice, and risk management. _Psychiatr Ann_ 17:695-699, 1987.

# Chapter 8

# Anxiety Disorders

Anxiety is ubiquitous; anxiety disorders are not. <u>Anxiety</u> is an unpleasant and unjustified sense of apprehension often accompanied by physiological symptoms, while <u>anxiety disorder</u> connotes significant distress and dysfunction due to the anxiety. An anxiety disorder may be characterized by only anxiety, or it may display another symptom such as a phobia or an obsession and present anxiety when the primary symptom is resisted. <u>Fear</u> is also universal and can produce the symptom picture of acute anxiety states, yet, in contrast to anxiety, the cause is obvious and understandable. A feature common to all of the anxiety disorders is the unpleasant and unnatural quality of the symptoms (anxiety, phobia, obsession) - they are <u>ego-alien</u> or <u>ego-dystonic</u>.

The biological understanding of anxiety is limited. Anxiety is mediated through a complex system that involves (at least) the limbic system (amygdala, hippocampus) and frontal cortex anatomically and norepinephrine (locus ceruleus), serotonin (dorsal raphe nucleus), and GABA neurochemically. We don't yet know how these parts work.

### CHRONIC, MILD ANXIETY

Tension, irritability, apprehension, and mild distractibility are common (particularly in medical and psychiatric patients), often related to environmental factors, and treated with supportive and reality-oriented therapy. Medications are of little value chronically while iatrogenic addiction is a serious problem. Environmentally induced, short-lived, mild anxiety (<u>ADJUSTMENT DISORDER WITH ANXIOUS MOOD</u>, DSM-III-R p 331, 309.24) usually resolves with the disappearance of the stress.

## CHRONIC, MODERATELY SEVERE ANXIETY

A diagnosis of <u>GENERALIZED ANXIETY DISORDER</u> (<u>Anxiety Neurosis</u>; DSM-III-R p 251, 300.02) is made with more severe, chronic symptoms (longer than 6 months), including autonomic responses (palpitations, diarrhea, cold clammy extremities, sweating, urinary frequency), insomnia, fatigue, sighing, trembling, hypervigilance, and/or marked apprehension. It tends to run in families;[1] secondary depression is common. Usually no obvious etiologic stress is found, but look anyway. Psychotherapy helps (40% of patients). Encourage self-reliance and maintenance of productive activity. Train the patient in relaxation techniques; eg, biofeedback, meditation, self-hypnosis. Use benzodiazepines sparingly (diazepam, 5 mg, PO, tid-qid, or 10 mg HS) and for short periods (weeks - several months). Some patients prefer beta-blockers (eg, propranolol 80-160 mg/day), which seem to be equally effective.[2] Over 50% of patients become asymptomatic with time (months, years), but the rest retain a significant degree of impairment. Help the patient understand the chronic nature of the illness and the likelihood of having to live with some symptoms.

## ACUTE ANXIETY - PANIC ATTACKS

A <u>PANIC DISORDER</u> (DSM-III-R p 235, 300.01) has dramatic, acute symptoms lasting minutes to hours, is self-limited, and occurs in patients with or without chronic anxiety. Symptoms are perceived by the patient as medical and are characteristic of strong autonomic discharge - heart pounding, chest pains, trembling, choking, abdominal pain, sweating, dizziness - as well as disorganization, confusion, dread, and often a sense of impending doom or terror. Attacks may come "out of the blue" or may be initiated by crowds or stressful situations. They may be repeated several times daily, weekly, or monthly, and often disappear for months at a time (but may become chronic). A typical panic attack can be produced in 50-75% of patients with panic disorder, but not in normals, by the intravenous infusion of sodium lactate or the breathing of $CO_2$.[3]

Like other anxiety conditions, it runs in families (15%[+] of 1° relatives; 30%[+] of monozygotic twins). (Genetic evidence suggests a single dominant gene with incomplete penetrance - perhaps on chromosome 16.[4]) It often is associated with major depression and/or alcoholism and it occurs equally in men and women, particularly those who have had a disturbed childhood and early difficulty separating from their parents (separation anxiety disorder). In its milder forms, panic disorder tends to grade into the

Generalized Anxiety Disorder clinically (although it appears to be a distinct disorder). Patients often receive the "million dollar workup" for angina, thyrotoxicosis, or abdominal complaints. Effective treatment exists.

1. Medication is essential for panic disorder. Several effective drugs are available, although response to any one is unpredictable. Since some patients may respond to the initial doses of the drug with dysphoria or an amphetamine-like reaction, give a small test dose, then build up to a therapeutic level slowly. Consider:

   A. tricyclic antidepressants (eg, imipramine or desipramine, 150-300 mg/day);[5] expect 2-3 wks for response.
   B. MAOIs (particularly phenelzine, 30-75+ mg/day[6]); effective with a broad spectrum of patients but may take 4-6 weeks for a response.
   C. clonazepam (1-5 mg/day, bid); sedative but looks promising.[7]
   D. serotonin reuptake inhibitors; eg, fluoxetine,[8] but also trazodone;[9] new and unproven.
   E. alprazolam (2-8 mg/day, tid-qid); patients respond rapidly, but depression, potential addiction, and need for frequent doses can be problems.[10]
   F. other medication occasionally effective includes benzodiazepines, beta-blockers (propranolol), clonidine, and anticonvulsants (carbamazepine - particularly in patients with an abnormal EEG[11]).

2. Supportive psychotherapy is of use acutely but does not correct the condition or prevent relapses.


## ANXIETY WITH SPECIFIC FEARS - PHOBIC DISORDERS

Phobias[11] are fears which are persistent and intense, are out of proportion to the stimulus, make little sense even to the sufferer, lead to avoidance of the feared object or situation, and when sufficiently distressful or disabling are termed a PHOBIC DISORDER. Common, mild, irrational fears (of the dark, heights, snakes) receive no diagnosis. Phobias may wax and wane over months or years, continue for decades, and may gradually resemble a depressive disorder. They tend to generalize during their developing stages - eg, fear of a store generalizes to the street in front of the store and then to the entire shopping area.

7%+ of the population may have a phobic disorder in some circumstances, yet in less than 1% is it significantly disabling. The majority begin suddenly in women from stable families and of ages 15-30. Anxiety with ruminations may dominate the day-to-day picture, or anxiety may occur only when the phobic object is encountered directly. Relief occurs with escape, thus reinforcing the avoidance pattern—a vicious cycle. Phobics are at risk to abuse alcohol and drugs as self-medication. Three subtypes have been identified:

AGORAPHOBIA (DSM-III-R p 240, 300.22):

Multiple phobias with chronic anxiety: specifically fears of open and/or closed spaces, crowded places, unfamiliar places, and being alone. Many other fears and hypochondriacal concerns may be present, as well as multiple other symptoms including fainting, obsessional thoughts, depersonalization (feel unreal, detached), and derealization (feel surroundings are unreal).

Most patients with agoraphobia also have panic attacks: PANIC DISORDER WITH AGORAPHOBIA (DSM-III-R p 235, 300.21). Typically, they develop their agoraphobia as an extension of a panic disorder - ie, unpredictable panic attacks cause them to avoid public places for fear of having an attack (anticipatory anxiety). Constitutes 50%[+] of the phobic patients - the most disabling type. Women:men = 2:1. Genetics are similar to panic disorder (20%[+] of 1° relatives are similarly affected).

SOCIAL PHOBIA (DSM-III-R p 241, 300.23):

Fear of public speaking, using public lavatories, blushing, eating in public. Some patients exhibit marked general anxiety, others very little. Patient controls by avoidance - can be socially crippling. Don't mistake for the social withdrawal of depression, schizophrenia, or paranoid states; if symptoms have been present lifelong, consider AVOIDANT PERSONALITY DISORDER.

SIMPLE PHOBIAS (DSM-III-R p 243, 300.29):

Monophobias - of animals, thunderstorms, needles, etc. Usually begin in childhood, are more frequent among women, and have few associated symptoms or syndromes.


TREATMENT: Twofold.

1.  Behavior therapy - essential treatment for simple and social phobias,[13] and also agoraphobia with and without panic attacks. Key to treatment is **exposure** to the feared object. Systematic desensitization (by reciprocal inhibition) utilizes a graded hierarchy of frighten-

ing stimuli allowing the patient to "work up" to facing the phobic object. In _flooding_ the patient faces the feared object or situation directly while with _implosion_ the exposure is to the idea of the object or a vivid account of the "terrible" consequences produced by the object. Such treatment may require (and be enhanced by) support and/or antianxiety medication.

2. Medication. Minor tranquilizers are used temporarily to help the patient confront the phobia. Beta-blockers (eg, propranolol) can be used occasionally to help control incapacitating autonomic symptoms (eg, before a speech). Antidepressants may help social phobias.[14]

   If the course is complicated by panic attacks, use appropriate medication. Once the panic attacks are controlled with meds, an agoraphobic usually needs supportive exposure to the feared situations (without experiencing panic) before the phobia is resolved.

## DIFFERENTIAL DIAGNOSIS OF ANXIETY STATES

The various anxiety disorders are mimicked by other psychiatric conditions as well as by a number of medical illnesses. Always rule out an anxious depression (depressive symptoms appear first and usually predominate - be suspicious of anxiety that first appears after age 30). Alcohol and drug abuse (chronic hypnotic-sedative withdrawal, amphetamine use, caffeinism) are common primary problems in patients presenting with uncomplicated anxiety. Numerous unexplained physical complaints, with or without frequent operations, suggest Somatization Disorder. Anxiety is often prominent in schizophrenia and in borderline and histrionic personality disorders, while an acute schizophrenic episode may present as a panic attack (with disordered thinking). Hyperventilation Syndrome (HVS) may be a separate syndrome- a vicious cycle developed in susceptible persons: anxiety causes hyperventilation causes respiratory alkalosis causes vasoconstriction causes symptoms (light-headedness, paresthesias, carpopedal spasms) causes anxiety - treat with rebreathing, education.[15]

Medical conditions (most commonly cardiac disorders) may also mimic anxiety states, although often they produce no sense of apprehension or foreboding. If suggestive physical symptoms accompany anxiety, remember:

1. Abnormal EKG's and heart sounds help identify cardiac symptoms (chest pain, palpitations) due to _angina_ pectoris, prolapse of the mitral valve, and cardiac

arrhythmias (eg, PAT). <u>Mitral valve prolapse syndrome</u> (MVPS - midsystolic click, late systolic murmur, and echocardiographic findings) occurs with increased frequency (15-40+%) in patients with panic disorder;[16,17] however, anxiety and panic disorders may <u>not</u> be increased in patients with MVPS.[18] Thus, the relation between the two is not clear.

2. The apprehension and dyspnea associated with bronchial <u>asthma</u> or <u>COLD</u> ("pink puffers") usually has accompanying wheezing or characteristic spirometric and radiographic features.

3. Acute Intermittent <u>Porphyria</u> - anxiety with abdominal focus; look for fever, leukocytosis, pain in extremities, prior drug exposure, elevated urine porphobilinogen; Watson-Schwartz Test is positive.

4. Characteristic findings usually occur with <u>duodenal ulcer</u> (bleeding, relief of pain with food, persistent crater by X-ray, suggestive gastric analysis) and <u>ulcerative colitis</u> (bloody diarrhea, fever, weight loss, sigmoidoscopic findings) but without them, differentiation is sometimes difficult. <u>Internal hemorrhage</u> may be accompanied by pain and restlessness - the picture develops quickly.

5. The vertiginous, anxious patient with <u>Meniere's Disease</u> also has deafness, tinnitus, and nystagmus during the attack.

If there are no localizing features to the acute attack or if the anxiety is chronic, consider:

6. <u>Hypoglycemia</u> - at times indistinguishable from chronic or acute anxiety; obtain blood glucose at the time of the episode; 5 hr GTT.

7. <u>Hyperthyroidism</u> - anxiety symptoms occur with rapid onset type; skin warm and moist rather than cold and clammy; look for exophthalmos; get $T_3$, $T_4$; check for goiter; consider TRH stimulation test.

8. <u>Pheochromocytoma</u> - anxiety attacks with hypertension; visual blurring, headache, perspiration, palpitations; get 24 hr urinary VMA or free catecholamines.

Other medical conditions can mimic the anxiety syndromes: intracranial tumors, menstrual irregularities, hypothyroidism, hyper- and hypoparathyroidism, postconcussion syndrome, psychomotor epilepsy, Cushing's Disease. Appropriate tests help differentiate.

## ANXIETY WITH OBSESSIONS AND COMPULSIONS

<u>OBSESSIVE COMPULSIVE DISORDER</u> (DSM-III-R p 245, 300.30)
(<u>Obsessive Compulsive Neurosis</u>)

<u>Obsessions</u> are repetitive ideas, images, and impulses which intrude upon a patient who feels powerless to stop them. They are usually unpleasant, always unwanted, and may be frightening or violent (eg, the impulse to leap before a car; the thought of a friend being harmed). The patient can ruminate endlessly ("Did I lock the door?") and may develop rituals or <u>compulsions</u> (counting, touching) to ward off unwanted happenings or to satisfy an obsession (eg, an obsession with dirt leading to handwashing rituals). Compulsions are thus obsessions made manifest and occur in 75%[+] of obsessives. Their performance relieves the anxiety of the obsession temporarily. The thinking is often magical ("My son won't have an accident if I stamp each foot 30 times.") and the patient is generally aware of this.

OCD afflicts 1.5% of the population, presents varying degrees of severity, and is chronic, with some spontaneous cures.[19] There is increased concordance for obsessions in monozygotes and often a family history for obsessional disorder. First symptoms usually occur by the early 20's, may begin suddenly or slowly, and often have an episodic course. Often the clinical picture is dominated by the rituals, requiring them to be treated directly.

The cause of OCD is unknown, but CNS serotonin neurons are implicated in most severe cases.[20] Moreover, CNS damage (eg, head trauma), the frontotemporal lobes (eg, a few patients with TLE), and the cingulum clearly play roles in selected cases.

DIFFERENTIAL: Obsessive-compulsive problems are common in serious psychiatric illnesses. 20% of serious depressions have obsessive symptoms - major symptoms and family history help separate - treatment may be identical. Schizophrenics have bizarre obsessions and are usually comfortable with them. (Be cautious: OCD can reach psychotic proportions, so don't overdiagnose schizophrenia.[21]) Organic Mental Disorders may present early with obsessions and compulsions.

TREATMENT:

Treatment is moderately successful. Medication is useful and should be tried: ie, serotonin reuptake blocking antidepressants. (NOTE: the most useful drugs do not yet (1987) have FDA approval.) Consider <u>clomipramine</u> (Anafranil) (150-300 mg/day), fluvoxamine[22] or fluoxetine, or other drugs with serotonergic properties (eg, trazodone). Behavior therapy also helps. For ritualizers, use a combination of <u>exposure</u> to the feared situation and <u>response prevention</u> (blocking the compulsive behaviors). For patients with just obsessions, use <u>imaginal exposure</u> (mentally experiencing what "could happen") and <u>thought stopping</u> (the therapist, and then later the patient, interrupts obsessional thought with the shouted word "Stop!").

From the combination of meds and psychotherapy, expect moderate to significant improvement. For the rare, extremely chronic and disabled patient, consider psychosurgery: nerve fibers are interrupted in the cingulum (cingulotomy).[23]

## REFERENCES

1. Noyes R, Clarkson C, Crowe R, et al: A family study of generalized anxiety disorder. <u>Am J Psychiatry</u> 144:1019-1024, 1987.
2. Meibach RC, Dunner D, Wilson LG, et al: Comparative efficacy of propranolol, chlordiazepoxide, and placebo in the treatment of anxiety. <u>J Clin Psychiatry</u> 48:355-358, 1987.
3. Fyer MR, Uy J, Martinez J, et al: $CO_2$ challenge of patients with panic disorder. <u>Am J Psychiatry</u> 144:1080-1082, 1987.
4. Crowe RR, Noyes R, Wilson AF, et al: A linkage study of panic disorder. <u>Arch Gen Psychiatry</u> 44:933-937, 1987.
5. Aronson TA: A naturalistic study of imipramine in panic disorder and agoraphobia. <u>Am J Psychiatry</u> 144:1014-1019, 1987.
6. Buigues J, Vallejo J: Therapeutic response to phenelzine in patients with panic disorder and agoraphobia with panic attacks. <u>J Clin Psychiatry</u> 48:55-59, 1987.
7. Lydiard RB, Laraia MT, Ballenger JC, Howell EF: Emergence of depressive symptoms in patients receiving alprazolam for panic disorder. <u>Am J Psychiatry</u> 144:664-665, 1987.
8. Tesar GE, Rosenbaum JF, Pollack MH, et al: Clonazepam vs alprazolam in the treatment of panic disorder. <u>J Clin Psychiatry</u> 48 (10, Suppl):16-19, 1987.
9. Gorman JM, Liebowitz MR, Fyer AJ, et al: An open trial of fluoxetine in the treatment of panic attacks. <u>J Clin Psychopharmacol</u> 7:329-332, 1987.
10. Mavissakalian M, Perel J, Bowler K, Dealy R: Trazodone in the treatment of panic disorder and agoraphobia with panic attacks. <u>Am J Psychiatry</u> 144:785-787, 1987.
11. Edlund MJ, Swann AC, Clothier J: Patients with panic attacks and abnormal EEG results. <u>Am J Psychiatry</u> 144:508-509, 1987.

12. Marks IM: *Fears, Phobias, and Rituals: Panic, Anxieties, and Their Disorders*. New York, Oxford University Press, 1987.

13. Heimberg RG, Barlow DH: Psychosocial treatments for social phobias. *Psychosomatics* 29:27-37, 1988.

14. Lydiard RB, Laraia MT, Howell EF, et al: Alprazolam in the treatment of social phobia. *J Clin Psychiatry* 49:17-19, 1988.

15. Hoes MJAJM, Colla P, Van Doorn P, et al: Hyperventilation and panic attacks. *J Clin Psychiatry* 48:435-437, 1987.

16. Liberthson R, Sheehan DV, King ME, Weyman AE: The prevalence of mitral valve prolapse in patients with panic disorders. *Am J Psychiatry* 143:511-515, 1986.

17. Matuzas W, Al-Sadir J, Uhlenhuth EH, Glass RM: Mitral valve prolapse and thyroid abnormalities in patients with panic attacks. *Am J Psychiatry* 144:493-496, 1987.

18. Mazza DL, Martin D, Spacavento L, et al: Prevalence of anxiety disorders in patients with mitral valve prolapse *Am J Psychiatry* 143:349-352, 1986.

19. Jenike MA, Baer L, Minichiello WE: *Obsessive-Compulsive Disorders*. Littleton, MA., PSG Pub Co, 1986.

20. Zohar J, Insel TR, Zohar-Kadouch RC, et al: Serotonergic responsivity in obsessive-compulsive disorder. *Arch Gen Psychiatry* 45:167-172, 1988.

21. Insel TR, Akiskal HS: Obsessive-compulsive disorder with psychotic features: A phenomenologic analysis. *Am J Psychiatry* 143:1527-1533, 1986.

22. Perse TL, Greist JH, Jefferson JW, et al: Fluvoxamine treatment of obsessive-compulsive disorder. *Am J Psychiatry* 144:1543-1548, 1987.

23. Tippin J, Henn FA: Modified leukotomy in the treatment of intractable obsessional neurosis. *Am J Psychiatry* 139:1601-1603, 1982.

# Chapter 9

# Dissociative Disorders

These are uncommon conditions of uncertain etiology that reflect a psychologically altered state of consciousness.

## AMNESIA

Organic processes (usually involving the temporal lobes) account for the majority of cases of significant memory loss in adults.[1] These processes include intoxication or withdrawal from drugs or alcohol, various dementias, acute or chronic metabolic conditions (eg, hypoglycemia, hepatic encephalopathy), brain trauma (ie, postconcussive amnesia), brain tumors (particularly in the temporal lobes), cerebrovascular accidents, epilepsy (particularly temporal lobe epilepsy), and various degenerative or infectious CNS diseases. Transient Global Amnesia (TGA) is a sudden, self-limited, massive loss of memory in middle-aged or elderly patients due to a temporary (presumably vascular) cause. Always look for an organic cause for amnesia first.

Loss of memory from psychological causes is PSYCHOGENIC AMNESIA (DSM-III-R p 273, 300.12). Usually there is sudden anterograde loss of emotion-laden information following a severe physical or psychosocial stress. It occurs most frequently in women in their teens or 20's, or in men during the stress of war. The patient often appears confused and puzzled during the attack, but recovery is typically rapid, spontaneous, and complete.

If, usually following an acute stress, the patient suffers a severe memory loss, leaves home, and acts like a different person, he has PSYCHOGENIC FUGUE (DSM-III-R p 272, 300.13).[2] Although he presents himself well to strangers, on questioning he is usually unaware of his previous (real) identity and seems somewhat perplexed. However, occasional patients function for long periods of time in complex roles, undetected. The return of old memories and the old identity usually occurs abruptly within hours or days, but may not happen for months (or longer).    Fugue is more common in alcohol abusers.

The differential diagnosis of both conditions includes:

1. Various organic conditions (see above).
2. Psychiatric conditions - Amnesia may often accompany severe depressive or anxiety states.    Somnambulism may superficially resemble some fugues but has marked clouding of consciousness.
3. Malingering and secondary gain in patients with antisocial personality disorder.

Evaluate these patients with a careful history and physical exam, liver enzymes, blood alcohol level, and drug screen.    Further evaluation may include a CAT scan and a sleep deprived EEG with NP leads.    Are old skills preserved during the attack (uncommon in organic conditions)?    Is there obvious secondary gain?    Is there a personal or family history for mental illness or epilepsy? The amytal interview is occasionally diagnostic - organic patients usually become more confused while patients with psychological amnesia may have a return of memory (see p 14).

MULTIPLE PERSONALITY DISORDER (DSM-III-R p 269, 300.14)

Patients with this dramatic disorder[3,4] (eg, The Three Faces of Eve) feel that they have at least two (and sometimes many) personalities within themselves.    One of the personalities is usually dominant, yet any one of them may dominate from time to time.    The patient's behavior is consistent with whatever personality is in "control" at that moment.    Each personality may or may not be aware of the presence of the others.

This poorly understood psychiatric condition begins in childhood (usually in response to abuse[5]), is more common among females (3-9:1), tends to be chronic, and may be a form of self-hypnosis.    (Some cases have been felt to be hypnotic states inadvertently produced by the treating physician.)    Once considered rare, it may be relatively common, particularly in milder forms or in patients felt to have the more flamboyant personality disorders, somatization disorder, and schizophrenia.[6,7]

DEPERSONALIZATION DISORDER (DSM-III-R p 275, 300.60)

These patients experience periods during which they have a strong and unpleasant sense of their own unreality (depersonalization), often coupled with a sense that the environment is also unreal (derealization).    The patient may feel mechanical and separated from his own thoughts, emotions, and self-identity. Although many people transiently experience this phenomenon in a mild form, the experience for those receiving a clinical diagnosis is much more intense and recurrent. An episode occurs suddenly (often during relaxation following stress), usually in persons in their teens or 20's, may last for minutes, hours, or days, and then gradually disappears. It may return many times over the years.

Treatment has been of little value. Rule out the symptom of depersonalization that may accompany psychiatric disorders (eg, schizophrenia, depression, anxiety disorders, and histrionic personality disorder) and organic conditions (eg, OBS, temporal lobe epilepsy, drug and alcohol use, brain tumor).

### REFERENCES

1. Khan AU: Clinical Disorders of Memory. New York, Plenum Medical Book Co., 1986.
2. Akhtar S, Brenner I: Differential diagnosis of fugue-like states. J Clin Psychiatry 40:381, 1979.
3. Putnam FW, Guroff JJ, et al: The clinical phenomenology of multiple personality disorder: Review of 100 recent cases. J Clin Psychiatry 47:285-293, 1986.
4. Kluft RP: An update on multiple personality disorder. Hosp Community Psychiatry 38:363-373, 1987.
5. Coons PM, Milstein V: Psychosexual disturbances in multiple personality. J Clin Psychiatry 47:106-110, 1986.
6. Bliss EL: Multiple personalities: A report of 14 cases with implications for schizophrenia and hysteria. Arch Gen Psychiatry 37:1388, 1980.
7. Bliss EL, Larson EM, Nakashima SR: Auditory hallucinations and schizophrenia. J Nerv Ment Dis 171:30, 1983.

# Chapter 10

# Grief and The Dying Patient

Everyone endures personal losses; many suffer chronic illnesses. Everyone dies. Physicians attend at all of these events and need to recognize normal and abnormal human responses to loss (grief reaction and unresolved grief), illness, and death.

## GRIEF REACTION

### NORMAL GRIEF:

#### Symptoms:

UNCOMPLICATED BEREAVEMENT (DSM-III-R p 361, V62.82) (grief, mourning) is a normal response to a significant loss (of spouse,[1] parent, child - but also of health, limb, career, savings, status, etc).[2,3] Expect to see it with major losses - be alert for future problems if the patient doesn't grieve (although 30% of widows mourn briefly and very little). If a loss is obviously approaching, mourning may begin before the loss actually occurs (anticipatory grief). Symptoms associated with divorce may also be coded as MARITAL PROBLEM (DSM-III-R p 360, V61.10).

Recognize grief by restlessness, distractibility, disorganization, preoccupation, "numbness," feelings of sadness, apathy, crying, anxious pining, a need to talk about the dead, and intense mental pain during the days, weeks, and months after a loss. Somatic distress is common and includes generalized weakness, a tightness in the throat, choking, shortness of breath, palpitations, headaches, and GI complaints. Do not be surprised if the patient displays marked but short-lived irritability, hostility, or anger towards you, others, or the dead (you didn't "do enough"; they don't "care enough"; he died; etc). This often alternates with listlessness, social withdrawal, depression, and feelings of guilt (about that which was left undone or could have been done differently). Patients become preoccupied with their loss. They constantly think about the dead and review past experiences, visit the grave, and may even briefly deny the death.

25-35% of patients have symptoms suggesting a major depression: anorexia, feelings of worthlessness, impaired memory, suicidal thoughts, and hopelessness. 10% have delusional thoughts and hallucinations. Be careful not to "over-read" temporary bizarre behavior in the bereaved. Some patients develop psychophysiologic disorders, hypochondriasis, major anxiety symptoms, or phobias. A few begin to drink too much, some deteriorate physically, and major psychiatric illnesses (eg, acute schizophrenia) may be precipitated in those predisposed (eg, positive family history). Moreover, bereavement has been associated with increased ACTH and cortisol, decreased immune function and natural killer cell activity,[4] and an increased rate of heart disease and malignancy.[5] Death from suicide and illness is increased during the first year after the loss.[6]

UNRESOLVED GRIEF:

Loss not dealt with through a normal mourning process may produce chronic symptoms.

- Prolonged Grief: Grief develops into a chronic depression in 15%.[7] Lowered self-esteem and guilt tend to be prominent.[8]
- Delayed Grief: The patient who doesn't grieve at the time of a loss is at risk for later depression, social withdrawal, anxiety disorders, panic attacks, overt or covert self-destructive behavior, alcoholism, and psychophysiologic syndromes. Chronic anger and hostility, marked emotional inhibition, or distorted interpersonal relationships also may be displayed. Unresolved grief may be an unsuspected cause of psychiatric disability in many people - always inquire about a past history of significant losses.
- Distorted Grief: Exaggerated (bizarre, hysterical, euphoric, or psychosis-like) reactions occur in a few patients which have the effect of postponing the normal grieving process. Alternately, the patient may present with physical complaints (eg, pain or "chronic illness behavior") and may be mistaken for having a primary medical problem.

Persons at risk for developing an abnormal grief reaction include those who:

1. Received little support or understanding from others

following their loss (eg, abortion, suicide, death of an illicit lover).

2. Are social isolates - either "psychological loners" or those without family or friends nearby. Multiple strong supports help truncate the mourning process.

3. Are inhibited, compulsive, or uncomfortable with any form of emotion.

4. Have experienced <u>multiple</u> recent losses or a sudden, severe, unexpected loss.

5. Have unresolved past losses.

6. Had ambivalent feelings about the deceased when alive and have reacted to the death with guilt.

<u>TREATMENT</u>:

Encouraging satisfactory mourning is an important activity for the physician.

- Encourage mourning. Say it is <u>OK</u>. Say it is <u>important and necessary</u>. Explain that the anguish he undoubtedly will experience during this process is essential and curative. However, do <u>not</u> force the patient - let him set the pace.

- Help the patient identify and experience his emotions- sadness, hopelessness, despair, anxiety, fear, anger. Assure him that these are normal, expected, and under- standable. Do not be embarrassed by these emotions yourself.

- Help the patient review his loss. Be an active listener. Ask for a description of the deceased - ask for particu- lars, details, shared intimacies, etc. Become a support.

- See the patient frequently. Be interested. Be available, particularly over time. Recognize and tolerate relap- ses. Be alert to the presence of anniversaries.

- Do <u>not</u> use medication to attenuate normal grief - help the patient work through the grief instead. Sleeping medi- cation may be useful. If anxiety or restlessness is excessive, consider a temporary use of minor tranquili- zers (eg, diazepam 5 mg PO tid) <u>as therapy is begun</u>. Treat a major depression or psychosis with medication.

- Work with the family. Help develop a sympathetic support system. Mourners are social outcasts - help decrease the "social isolation of the bereaved." Self-help groups can be very valuable (eg, groups of parents who have lost a child, etc).[9]

- Keep the mourner "involved in life" - slowly at first, but insist on increasing independence.

## POST-TRAUMATIC STRESS DISORDER (PTSD)

If a patient suffers a severe loss or stress (eg, rape, serious car accident, harm to a child or spouse, natural disaster, combat, prison camp, etc), he may develop the clinical syndrome of <u>POST-TRAUMATIC STRESS DISORDER</u> (DSM-III-R p 247, 309.89). A mixture of the following symptoms are present initially:

Marked anxiety
Personality change with irritability and poor concentration
An exaggerated startle response
Insomnia and nightmares
Intrusive thoughts of the event
Reliving the feelings experienced at the time
Avoidance of anything associated with the trauma
Emotional blunting which can impair interpersonal relationships and day-to-day functioning

Later, depression, emotional numbing, and preoccupation with the trauma may predominate. The more severe the stress, the more likely PTSD is (1) to develop and (2) to be long-lasting. It may resolve after months or, untreated, last for decades.[10,11] Occasional patients present primarily with physical symptoms[12] or chronic pain.[13]

Patients with PTSD are more likely to have a personality disorder, a previous history of depression or substance abuse, or a family history of psychopathology,[14] but presumably PTSD can occur in anyone who has experienced sufficient stress. Psychophysiologic arousal at the time of the stress seems to be necessary to develop PTSD, while conditioned arousal keeps it going.[15,16]

PTSD patients are notoriously noncompliant: 70-80%[+] drop out of treatment,[17] presumably because they can't tolerate reliving the event in therapy. Medication is useful in many cases: benzodiazepines briefly for anxiety but primarily tricyclic antidepressants (imipramine 150-300 mg/day) and MAOIs (phenelzine 45-75 mg/day). Carbamazepine has been found useful in controlling flashbacks, nightmares, and intrusive recollections[18] (400-600 mg/day; 5-10 $\mu$g/mL). Psychotherapy should accompany medication: primarily education, support, cognitive-behavioral therapy, and hypnosis. The patient should be engaged in treatment <u>as soon after the incident as possible</u>. (For example, the rape victim needs special and sensitive care - often in the ER - after the assault, for psychiatric as well as legal reasons.[19] Many of her interpersonal relationships may have been altered by that episode. Work with the family - the married victim often needs to establish a new equilibrium with her husband.)

## THE DYING PATIENT

Few patients stress physicians as much as those who are dying. This need not be. Even if little can be done to change a fatal outcome, careful handling by the physician and crucial others can help turn a patient's death (whether expected or untimely) into a time of genuine relief, satisfaction, and (even) growth. When time is so limited, new realities and priorities emerge which must be dealt with if life is to be concluded satisfactorily.

NORMAL RESPONSES IN THE DYING:

The news that one is dying produces a special kind of grief reaction. A typical series of "stages" or psychological reactions to the threat of imminent death are seen frequently.[20]

1st Stage - Shock and denial: Denial is the initial reaction of many patients to being told that they are dying-particularly severe in those "caught by surprise." They may refuse to believe the diagnosis, actively begin doctor-shopping, or be dazed and appear oblivious to the significance of the diagnosis. This may be fleeting, but some patients may never pass beyond this stage.

2nd Stage - Anger: A frustrated, hopeless, angry, bitter "Why me?" response often accompanies the realization of impending death. The anger is directed at the physicians (or family, God, fate, etc) for the "unfairness" of this turn of events.

3rd Stage - Bargaining: The patient attempts to bargain with physicians or God for more time - promising good behavior, good intentions, etc, in exchange for "a chance to see my boy be graduated from college," etc.

4th Stage - Depression: The patient despairs and begins to grieve. Be alert to suicide, particularly in the irritable, demanding, agitated depression.[21]

5th Stage - Acceptance: The patient is quiet and resigned. He has little outside interests but seeks the presence of loved ones or a few close friends.

These stages are not necessarily stepwise and invariable. Just as often the person will shift back and forth between stages (eg, from denial to anger and then back to denial), exhibit varying degrees of denial throughout, but gradually become more detached. The younger the adult, the more likely the stages are to be turbulent and the problems severe.

Specific psychiatric problems occur often and should be identified and treated:

1. Depression is common but not "normal," and thus, if a depression is not relieved by support and time, a Major Depression may have developed. Consider treatment with antidepressants.
2. Organic brain syndromes (usually waxing and waning) develop frequently and can be frightening to patients. Help them see the disorders as separate from themselves - as just another thing to be experienced.
3. Acute anxiety is common but usually temporary, particularly if treated with medication.
4. Communication failures between the patient and loved ones are very common and troublesome - often taking the form of a "tyranny of silence" or a lack of understanding on either one's part of the distress of the other. These need to be dealt with directly.

## TREATMENT:

### Telling the Patient:

- Choose a quiet and private spot, be relaxed, sit down with the patient, and briefly reveal the diagnosis. Use the patient's response as an indicator of how much to tell.
- Patients need to know and need a chance to ask questions but, most of all, they need someone (usually the physician, but also spouse, pastor, etc) available - someone to help them grieve.
- Be truthful (but allow them to deny if they insist on it) and realistically hopeful ("We will begin treatment. Sometimes remissions occur. Etc"). Don't encourage false hopes, but don't dwell on the fatal outcome.
- Strong negative reactions do occur. Sedation can be helpful temporarily.

### Treating the Patient:

- Be supportive, empathic, warm, a good listener, hopeful (eg, about goals to be achieved before death), and available. Get to know the patient as a person-attention to exclusively medical matters is "dehumanizing." Be tolerant of ups and downs. Recognize that the patient may become hostile towards you - be patient.
- Always take your lead from the patient. Some days some topics are too stressful. Other days they "have" to talk. Only force the issue if their denial, anxiety, or anger is seriously obstructing good care. Occasionally confrontation may be required.

- Make them comfortable. Treat pain aggressively - narcotics are OK. Attend fastidiously to basic physical needs. Make their room pleasant and cheerful. Hallucinogens (eg, LSD) have been used experimentally with success.
- Certain fears are common and need to be looked for and dealt with: eg, fear of pain, of physical dependency, of being isolated, of losing control (emotional and physical), of being helpless, of the unknown, of leaving loved ones to flounder (financially or emotionally).
- It is essential to help the patient "work through" the process of dying. Help him set new priorities and goals (eg, get his affairs in order). Help him resolve old problems and feel good about current relationships. Help him be responsible. Encourage him to consider not only how he will die but also how he will live the rest of his life.
- Do not insist that patients march through the "stages of dying" in a set order and on schedule.
- Allow the patient "terminal dependency" - it is OK finally to regress.

Treating the Family:

- Family members show many of the signs of grief. Like the patient, they also may be angry, hostile, or denying. They may need treatment - help them mourn.
- It is important to keep the family (ie, loved ones) involved. Help the patient die "with their blessing."
- It can be enormously beneficial (to the patient, to the family) if the patient can be supportive to the family members in their grieving.

Treating the Staff:

- Recognize that the physician, nurses, aides, etc. are all affected by death. Anxiety, intellectualization, avoidance, and grieving frequently occur among staff - don't let them impair care. Staff conferences to ventilate and explore these issues may help.

THE CHRONICALLY ILL PATIENT

Chronic illness is another form of stress which entails grieving. Like the dying patient, these patients may deny their illness, become angry and resentful, regress, or become depressed. Common to all these reactions is anxiety associated with a loss of health and attractiveness, a loss of self-esteem, and the threat of dependency or even death. Certain personality types are at risk - eg, the narcissistic or the very independent. Treatment principles useful with the grieving or dying patient apply here as well.

## REFERENCES

1. Zisook S, Shuchter SP: The first four years of widow-hood. Psychiatr Ann 16:288-294, 1986.
2. Parkes CM: Bereavement: Studies of Grief in Adult Life. New York, International Universities Press, 1972.
3. Zisook S: Biopsychosocial Aspects of Bereavement. Washington, DC, American Psychiatric Press, 1987.
4. Irwin M, Daniels M, Bloom ET, et al: Life events, depressive symptoms, and immune function. Am J Psychiatry 144:437-441, 1987.
5. Fredrick JF: The biochemistry of bereavement. Omega 13:295-303, 1982-1983.
6. Clayton PJ: Mortality and morbidity in the first year of widowhood. Arch Gen Psychiatry 30:747, 1974.
7. Belitsky R, Jacobs S: Bereavement, attachment theory, and mental disorders. Psychiatr Ann 16:276, 1986.
8. Barry MJ: Therapeutic experience with patients referred for "prolonged grief reaction" - some second thoughts. Mayo Clin Proc 56:744, 1981.
9. Marmar CR, Horowitz MJ, Weiss DS, et al: A controlled trial of brief psychotherapy and mutual-help group treatment of conjugal bereavement. Am J Psychiatry 145:203-209, 1988.
10. Goldstein G, Van Kammen W, Shelly C, et al: Survivors of imprisonment in the Pacific theater during World War II. Am J Psychiatry 144:1210-1213, 1987.
11. Kluznik JC, Speed N, et al: Forty-year follow-up of United States prisoners of war. Am J Psychiatry 143:1443-1446, 1986.
12. Schottenfeld RS, Cullen MR: Occupation-induced post-traumatic stress disorders. Am J Psychiatry 142:198-202, 1985.
13. Benedikt RA, Kolb LC: Preliminary findings on chronic pain and posttraumatic stress disorder. Am J Psychiatry 143:908-910, 1986.
14. Davidson J, Swartz M, Storck M, et al: A diagnostic and family study of posttraumatic stress disorder. Am J Psychiatry 142:90-93, 1985.
15. Kolb LC: A neuropsychological hypothesis explaining posttraumatic stress disorders. Am J Psychiatry 144:989-995, 1987.
16. Pitman RK, Orr SP, Forgue DF, et al: Psychophysiologic assessment of posttraumatic stress disorder imagery in Vietnam combat veterans. Arch Gen Psychiatry 44:970-975, 1987.
17. Burstein A: Treatment noncompliance in patients with posttraumatic stress disorder. Psychosomatics 27:37-40, 1986.

18. Lipper S, Davidson JRT, Grady RA, et al: Preliminary study of carbamazepine in post-traumatic stress disorder Psychosomatics 27:849-854, 1986.
19. Falk N: Clinical management of rape. Hosp Phys 6:34, 1977.
20. Kubler-Ross E: On Death and Dying. London, Tavistock, 1970.
21. Brown JH, Henteleff P, Barakat S, et al: Is it normal for terminally ill patients to desire death? Am J Psychiatry 143:208-211, 1986.

# Chapter 11

## Conditions which Mimic Physical Disease

It is essential to differentiate organic illness from psychogenic illness in patients complaining of physical symptoms. Patients with physical concerns in whom no medical illness can be found and/or who don't improve with treatment are common. These frustrating patients often exhaust one doctor after another and usually end up being labeled "hysterics" or "crocks." This occasionally angry response by the physician does a disservice to these patients since, although some may be consciously "faking it" (malingering), most patients have as yet undiagnosed organic conditions or have symptoms which are unconsciously and involuntarily produced.

There are several discrete involuntary psychiatric syndromes (somatoform disorders - see below) which mimic organic disease. These disorders have typical clinical presentations, family histories, recommended treatments, and likely prognoses.

Failure to identify an organic etiology for a physical symptom does not necessitate a diagnosis of a somatoform disorder or malingering - these are not diagnoses by exclusion but rather should be based on specific characteristics. Consider the following diagnoses in any patient with a poorly specified or uncertain medical condition.

1. <u>UNDETECTED PHYSICAL ILLNESS</u>:

The possibility of an underlying, unrecognized illness must continue to be considered throughout the course of diagnosis and treatment, however long. Follow-up studies find 15-30% of conversion reaction diagnosis to represent misdiagnosed organic disease. Physical illness may produce symptoms which mimic a somatoform disorder or may predispose susceptible patients to develop concurrent psychiatric conditions (it's not "either, or"). Some patients with subtle CNS disease are at risk for conversion symptoms, so always carefully evaluate neurologically. The physical conditions commonly found (on follow-up) among these "false positive hysterics" include:

- CNS disease: Particularly epilepsy, MS, and post-concussion syndrome, but also CNS infections (eg, encephalitis), dementia, brain tumor, and cerebro-vascular disease.
- Degenerative disorders: Of musculoskeletal and con-nective tissues; including SLE, polyarteritis nodosa, early rheumatoid arthritis, myasthenia gravis.
- Others: Syphilis, TB, hyper- and hypothyroidism, hyper-parathyroidism, porphyria, hypoglycemia, duodenal and gallbladder disease, pancreatic disease, etc.

Be suspicious of any somatoform disorder which develops late in life. Psychological testing is of little help in differentiation - don't be misled by a "neurotic" picture on the MMPI into prematurely abandoning the search for a physical cause.

## SOMATOFORM DISORDERS[1-3]

2. <u>CONVERSION DISORDER</u> (Hysterical Neurosis, Conversion Type) (DSM-III-R p 257, 300.11):

A patient whose predominant problem is an obvious loss of function of some part of the nervous system which no identified organic pathology completely explains (conversion symptom) may have a conversion disorder.[4,5] Conversion symptoms include:

Motor - paralysis, astasia-abasia, seizures, urinary retention, aphonia, globus hystericus ("lump in the throat" which prevents swallowing).
Sensory - paresthesia, anesthesia, anosmia, blindness, tunnel vision, deafness.
Other - unconsciousness, vomiting.

In addition, the particular symptom appears to serve one of two specific psychological purposes.

1. As <u>primary gain</u>, the symptom "buries" an unconscious mental conflict. An unacceptable, painful thought is repressed, and the emotional energy is converted to a physical symptom. Usually the specific symptom "chosen" represents the conflict symbolically (eg, the negligent mother of a burned child develops anesthesia over the corresponding part of her body).

2. As <u>secondary gain</u>, the symptom gets the patient something he wants (eg, paralysis permits dependency on wife
   or justifies workman's compensation) or allows him to
   avoid something he doesn't want (eg, seizures prevent a
   court appearance).

As obvious as these relationships may be to the observer,
the patient is unaware of them (unconscious), and the
patient does not grasp their significance, even if they are
explained (lacks insight).

DIAGNOSIS

     In the apparent absence of organic pathology, it is
necessary to identify features in addition to a presumed
conversion symptom before making the diagnosis. Realize
also that as many as 25% of patients with conversion
disorders have associated organic pathology (eg, epilepsy in
a patient with pseudoseizures), so also investigate symptoms
only partially explained by the physical abnormalities.
Features associated with conversion disorders include:

- The symptom occurs abruptly and frequently follows an
  acute stress.
- There is often a past history of the same or a different
  conversion symptom.
- The disorder usually is seen first during adolescence or
  in the patient's 20's and in a person predisposed by a
  dependent, histrionic, antisocial, or passive-aggressive
  personality disorder.
- The patients often have associated moderate anxiety and
  depression.
- The patients are frequently immature, shallow, and
  demanding, although they tend to cooperate with
  examinations. They tend to have lower intelligence,
  limited insight, and lower socioeconomic status.
- Indifference to the symptom may be found (<u>la belle
  indifference</u>).

     The individual neurologic symptoms may have some
characteristics which distinguish them from those of an
organic etiology. In general, they tend to be variable,
atypical, and inconsistent with anatomy.

<u>Conversion Seizures</u>[6-8]: Seizures are often atypical and
   bizarre (patient may laugh or cry throughout seizure).
   Only infrequently is there incontinence, cyanosis,
   physical self-harm, tongue-biting, or complete loss of
   consciousness during the seizure. Good muscle tone is
   preserved during the typically brief postictal stage

(arm dropped onto face may land lightly or miss the face altogether). The onset is usually dramatic, and seizures rarely occur when the patient is alone.  Sit patient quickly upright - seizures often stop.

**Conversion Unconsciousness**:  The loss of consciousness is usually light and incomplete with the patient showing some awareness of environmental events, particularly when he feels unobserved.  VS and reflexes are normal, and the patient usually responds to painful stimuli. The eyes are held tightly shut, and some movements may be purposive (eg, move to keep from falling from exam table).

**Conversion Paralysis**:  The paralysis is often variable- even during one exam.  Paralysis of one limb or part of a limb, or hemiparesis are most common but the specific involvement is often inconsistent with anatomy, and the related changes (eg, tone, etc) are atypical.  DTR changes are variable, and pathological reflexes (eg, Babinski) are not present.  The paralyzed limbs often show little resistance to passive movement but resist the pull of gravity.  If there is resistance to a forced movement, it tends to give way abruptly (vs gradually as in organic conditions).  There may be movement when startled by a painful stimulus.  Palpate the antagonists - they often contract to simulate agonist weakness. There are usually associated conversion sensory changes.

**Astasia-abasia**:  This exaggerated and bizarre conversion ataxia varies from moment to moment.  The patient falls toward walls and people, rarely falls to the floor, and rarely hurts himself in spite of a dramatic presenta- tion.

**Conversion Sensory Changes**:  These are often dramatic, sometimes vague, and usually inconsistent with anatomy (eg, "stocking and glove" anesthesia, loss of all senses on one side or below a certain level on a limb, loss of which stops exactly at midline.  Careful testing differentiates most cases.

**Conversion Blindness**:  Visual disturbances are usually blurring, double vision, or tunnel loss but may be total blindness.  Response to a bright light (check with EEG) and avoidance of threatening objects are often inconsistent with the degree of presumed visual loss.

When the diagnosis is in doubt, a single dose of IV sodium amobarbital (Amytal) often temporarily removes the conversion symptom, thus clarifying the diagnosis.  Slowly give a 10% solution intravenously (1 ml/min - maximum of 500 mg). When the patient's words begin to slur, stop administration and observe for disappearance of symptom.

DIFFERENTIAL DIAGNOSIS:

- Carefully rule out physical illness.
- Some patients with conversion symptoms require a primary diagnosis of major depression or schizophrenia.
- Two somatoform disorders (see below) have features in common with conversion disorders - somatization disorder and psychogenic pain disorder.
- Differentiation from malingering is difficult (see below).

TREATMENT[9]:

Some patients have a short course and are "spontaneous cures"; a few may be chronic (eg, some paralyzed patients actually develop contractures), but most improve over weeks or months. A physical process is later identified in a significant minority (25%).

It is uncertain what treatment is best. Long-term psychoanalysis appears to effect real change in a few but is not for the majority of patients. Use minor tranquilizers if anxiety predominates. Behavior modification has had mixed success.

Crucial to any therapy is the formation of a supportive therapeutic alliance, but these patients are generally resistant to treatment. Direct confrontation about the "hysterical" nature of the symptom rarely works- the patient usually withdraws. Help the patient ventilate. Help the patient explore areas of stress in her life but relate that to symptoms only after an alliance has been formed. Gradually identify the symbolic nature of the symptoms, if present.

Work with the family. Help restructure the patient's environment to remove the secondary gain, if possible. Educate other involved medical personnel about the disorder - help them avoid countertherapeutic hostility.

3. SOMATIZATION DISORDER (Hysteria, Briquet's Syndrome) (DSM-II-R p 261, 300.81):

This syndrome has been delineated in the last few years and may or may not be coequal to the traditional diagnosis of hysteria. The patients have numerous vague and dramatic physical symptoms (usually presented in a dramatic way) which typically involve several organ systems.

- Conversion symptoms of all types
- Vague and ill-defined pains
- Menstrual problems; inhibited organism
- GI, GU, and cardiopulmonary difficulties
- Poorly characterized altered states of consciousness

The symptoms wax and wane but usually are presented forcefully by the patient, who insists on examination and treatment. These patients often receive multiple operations[10] and are at risk for iatrogenically induced drug addiction.

Analytically oriented researchers argue that symptoms are produced when forbidden impulses are repressed and the emotional energy associated with those drives is converted (conversion) into a physical symptom. Although definitive information remains incomplete, features currently associated with Briquet's Syndrome include:

- A chronic condition beginning in adolescence or during the 20's.
- Primarily in women;[11] 1% of all women.
- Anxiety, irritability, and depression common;[12,13] frequent suicide attempts (but few successful).
- Patients usually of lower intelligence and lower socioeconomic groups.[14]
- Frequent interpersonal and marital problems.
- Patients often have a previous or concurrent history of antisocial behavior and a poor school history.
- Patients may have histrionic personality disorder or antisocial personality disorder.
- First-degree female relatives have a 20% incidence of somatization disorder. First-degree male relatives have increased prevalence of alcoholism and antisocial personality disorder.

Somatization disorder is difficult to distinguish from malingering, and occasionally there are elements of both present. It is essential to rule out inconstant and confusing medical syndromes (eg, SLE, acute intermittent porphyria, temporal lobe epilepsy, MS, hyperparathyroidism), although most can be differentiated from the full Briquet's Syndrome (reliable diagnostic screening tests are available). Follow-up studies find few cases of undiagnosed organic illness (unlike conversion disorder). Rule out somatization in schizophrenia and depression.

TREATMENT:

Treatment success is limited. Focus usually should be

placed on management rather than cure. Develop a therapeutic alliance by being sympathetic and interested in the patient and her health but don't make that your exclusive focus. Gradually encourage an examination of the patient's general life problems and coping styles. Help the patient develop mature social, occupational, and intimate interpersonal skills. Treat depression and anxiety with medication, if indicated, but recognize the risk for addiction.

4. <u>SOMATOFORM PAIN DISORDER</u> (DSM-III-R p 264, 307.80):

These patients (often women) experience pain for which no cause can be found. It appears suddenly, usually following a stress, and may disappear in days or last years.[15] This condition is very similar to conversion disorder, and the patients may differ only by experiencing pain rather than neurological deficit as the predominant symptom. Treatments are also similar.

5. <u>HYPOCHONDRIASIS</u> (Hypochondriacal Neurosis) (DSM-III-R p 259, 300.70):

Although many people may mentally expand a minor symptom into a major physical illness (particularly during times of stress), they rarely become preoccupied with it and can easily be dissuaded when examination and laboratory tests are normal.[16] The hypochondriac, on the other hand, is convinced he is ill, angrily rejects evidence to the contrary, insists on further tests and treatments, and feverishly doctor shops. The patient appears pleased only if assured he is sick, and he eagerly seeks additional medical attention.[17] This common chronic condition begins in adolescence or middle age, is common among the elderly, and is resistant to therapy. The patient rarely sees a psychiatrist but rather drifts from internist to surgeon to neurologist, etc.

The patient is hyperalert to symptoms and presents them in great detail during the history. He usually has some specific idea of "what the trouble is" and merely may want the physician to concur. Physicians frequently become angry and rejecting towards the patient, which leads to further "shopping around." In severe cases, the patient becomes an invalid.

Many of these patients display anxiety or depression. Hypochondriacal features occur frequently in serious psychiatric conditions like schizophrenia, major depression, dysthymic disorder, and organic brain syndromes. Rule out other somatoform disorders, chronic factitious disorder, and malingering.

Treatment is unpromising.[18,19] Symptoms may disappear if an associated depression or psychosis is successfully treated. Don't expect a "cure" but rather work with the patient to help _control_ his symptoms.[20] "Assure" the patient that the problem is persistent but not debilitating or fatal. See the patient frequently for short periods of time. Assure him that you will be available if needed but schedule regular appointments (to be kept whether or not he is feeling ill). Consider giving a mild medication (eg, antihistamine, vitamin) which can be a focus of attention during appointments and will be evidence that he is taken seriously. This form of palliation can restore the patient to functional health more readily than any definitive medical treatment.

## SIMULATION OF PHYSICAL SYMPTOMS

Two categories of patients _voluntarily_ mimic physical symptoms:

### 6. MALINGERING (DSM-III-R p 360, V65.20):

These people knowingly fake symptoms for some obvious gain. They may be trying to get drugs, avoid the law, get a bed for the night, etc. In spite of their physical comlaints, they tend to be evasive and uncooperative during evaluation and therapy, and they avoid medical procedures. When exposed, they may angrily give up their symptoms and sign out AMA. Antisocial personality disorder and drug abuse are common associated conditions.

### 7. FACTITIOUS DISORDER WITH PHYSICAL SYMPTOMS (Munchausen Syndrome) (DSM-III-R p 316, 301.51):

These patients also knowingly fake symptoms but do so for unconscious psychological reasons that become evident after a thorough psychiatric evaluation. They usually prefer the sick role and move from hospital to hospital in what is a chronic life pattern.[21] They are usually loners with an early childhood background of trauma and deprivation. They are unable to establish close interpersonal relationships and generally have severe personality disorders. Unlike many malingerers, they follow through with medical procedures and are at risk for drug addiction and for the complications of multiple operations.

Both groups of patients can be difficult to distinguish from the somatoform disorders and from organic illness, yet careful and _repeated_ examinations will usually uncover their deceptions. The most common presentations include:

- Abdominal pain:   May have an abdomen "like a railroad yard."
- Heart:  Complains of pain.  May induce arrhythmias with digitalis or produce tachycardia with amphetamines or thyroid.
- Bleeding:  Patient may take anticoagulants or add blood from a scratch to lab samples.
- Neurological:   Weakness,  seizures,  unconsciousness-difficult to differentiate from conversion symptoms.
- Fever:  Produced by manipulating the thermometer (eg, hot coffee in the mouth).
- Skin:  Look for lesions in a linear pattern in areas the patient can reach.

Although they both produce symptoms consciously, they should be dealt with differently.  The malingerer should be handled formally (and often legally).  The patient with a factitious disorder should be treated sympathetically and every effort made to convince him to enter psychotherapy (difficult).   Unlike the malingerer, these patients are unable to control their self-destructive behavior, and that should be tactfully pointed out to them.

## REFERENCES

1.  Ford CV: <u>The Somatizing Disorders</u>. New York, Elsevier Biomedical, 1983.
2.  Ford CV: The somatizing disorders. <u>Psychosomatics</u> 27: 327-337,1986.
3.  Sigvardsson S, von Knorring A, Bohman M, Cloninger R: An adoptions study of somatoform disorders. <u>Arch Gen Psychiatry</u> 41:853-859, 1984.
4.  Ford CV, Folks DG: Conversion disorders: An overview. <u>Psychosomatics</u> 26:371-383, 1985.
5.  Weintraub MI: <u>Hysterical Conversion Reactions</u>. New York, SP Med & Scient Bks, 1983.
6.  Riley TL,Roy A: <u>Pseudoseizures</u>. Baltimore, Williams & Wilkins, 1982.
7.  Guberman A: Psychogenic pseudoseizures in non-epileptic patients. <u>Can J Psychiatry</u> 27:401, 1982.
8.  Lesser RP: Psychogenic seizures. <u>Psychosomatics</u> 27:823-829, 1986.
9.  Swartz MS, McCracken J: Emergency room management of conversion disorders. <u>Hosp Community Psychiatry</u> 37:828-832, 1986.
10. Smith Jr, GR, Monson RA, Ray DC: Psychiatric Consultation in somatization disorder. <u>NEJM</u> 314:1407-1413, 1986.

11. Cloninger CR, Martin RL, Guze SB, Clayton PJ: A prospective follow-up and family study of somatization in men and women. Am J Psychiatry 143:873-878, 1986.
12. Liskow B, Othmer E, Penick EC, et al: Is Briquet's Syndrome a heterogeneous disorder? Am J Psychiatry 143:626-9, 1986.
13. Zoccolillo M, Cloninger CR: Somatization disorder: Psychologic symptoms, social disability, and diagnosis. Compr Psychiatry 27:65-73, 1986.
14. Swartz M, Blazer D, George L, Landerman R: Somatization disorder in a community population. Am J Psychiatry 143:1403-1408, 1986.
15. Drossman DA: Patients with psychogenic abdominal pain: six years observation in the medical setting. Am J Psychiatry 139:1549, 1982.
16. Barsky AJ, Wyshak G, Klerman GL: Hypochondriasis. Arch Gen Psychiatry 43:493-500, 1986.
17. Barsky AJ, Klerman GL,: Overview: hypochondriasis, bodily complaints, and somatic styles. Am J Psychiatry 140:273, 1983.
18. Adler G: The physician and the hypochondriacal patient. NEJM 304:1394, 1981.
19. Kellner R: Prognosis of treated hypochondriasis. Acta Psychiatr Scand 67:69, 1983.
20. Kellner R: Psychotherapeutic strategies in hypochondriasis: a clinical study. Am J Psychotherapy 36:146, 1982.
21. Henderson LM, Bell BA, Miller JD: A neurosurgical munchausen tale. J Neurol Neurosurg Psychiatry 46:437, 1983.

# Chapter 12

# Psychosomatic Disorders

A psychosomatic disorder is a physical disease <u>partially</u> caused or exacerbated by psychological factors (<u>PSYCHOLOG-ICAL FACTORS AFFECTING PHYSICAL CONDITIONS</u>, DSM-III-R p 333, 316.00). This classification applies only to those condi-tions in which psychological influence is of <u>major</u> signifi-cance - but be aware that <u>any</u> physical disease may be modi-fied by psychological stress. The term "psychosomatic" does <u>not</u> refer to:

1. A physical symptom or clinical presentation caused by psychological factors for which there is no organic basis (eg, conversion disorder, psychogenic pain disor-der, somatization disorder).
2. A patient with numerous physical complaints but without organic pathology (eg, somatization disorder, hypochon-driasis, malingering).
3. Physical complaints related to habit disorders - eg, dyspnea due to excessive smoking.

<u>MECHANISMS OF DISEASE PRODUCTION</u>:

There are many specific diseases which are influenced greatly by the "psyche" (see below) but, although much studied, the mechanisms by which the brain produces such organic pathology are unclear.

<u>Psychological mechanisms</u>:

"<u>Stress</u>," either internal or external, is required but is much more likely to cause disease if:

1. The stress is severe (eg, death of a loved one, divorce or separation, major illness or injury, financial crisis, incarceration). Holmes and Rahe[1] developed a ranked scale of stressful life events (rated by life change units - LCU) and found a close correlation between an event's stress (in LCU's) and the patient's

likelihood of developing a physical illness.
2. The stress is chronic.
3. The patient perceives the stress as stressful.
4. The patient has an increased level of general instability
   eg, difficult job, troubled marriage, urban dweller,
   socially disrupted environment, etc.

It was once thought (F. Dunbar) that _specific_ superficial personality traits produced specific organic diseases (eg, that there is a "coronary personality," an "ulcer personality," etc.). It was also held (F. Alexander) that _specific_ deep and unconscious, unresolved neurotic conflicts caused specific physical disorders. Currently, the specificity that is generally accepted associates the "Type A" personality (ie, sense of time urgency, impatience, aggressiveness, upward striving, competitiveness, tendency to anger when frustrated) with coronary artery disease.[2]

More generally accepted are _nonspecific_ hypotheses which link a wide variety of stresses to the development of disease in an individual placed at risk by one or more of the following:

1. A genetic susceptibility.
2. A degree of chronic debilitation, a current illness, or
   "an organ vulnerability."
3. A tendency to react to stress with anger, resentment,
   frustration, anxiety, or depression.
4. A "psychological susceptibility" (eg, patient is pessimistic and "expects the worst" vs being optimistic
   and actively working to overcome stress).
5. An "alexithymic" personality - eg, a person who is in
   poor contact with his emotions and has an impoverished fantasy life.[3]

Physiological mechanisms:

These mechanisms are poorly understood, and only the broad outline can be sketched.[4] Stress is perceived cognitively (by the cerebral cortex) but, once recognized, is mediated primarily by the limbic system which, under chronic stress, chronically stimulates the hypothalamus and the vegetative centers in the brain stem. This stimulation produces a direct effect on the various organs by:

1. Activation of the autonomic nervous system (sympathetic and adrenal medulla; parasympathetic).
2. Involvement of the neuroendocrine system - ie, _releasing hormones_ from the hypothalamus travel through the pituitary portal system to the anterior pituitary where they cause the release of the trophic hormones

(eg, ACTH, TSH, GH, FSH) which either act directly or release other hormones from the endocrine glands (eg, cortisol, thyroxin, epinephrine, NE, sex hormones).[5] These produce a variety of changes in structures throughout the body. Hans Selye (1976)[6] emphasized the central role of cortisol as a primary mediator of the body's stress response (general adaptation syndrome - GAS) - if cortisol is released too chronically, various organs are damaged, producing psychosomatic diseases.

The details have yet to be worked out - there remain more questions than answers. The recently identified hormones, endorphins, may play a major role in stress response regulation. Central to all of these physiological systems is the concept of homeostasis - psychosomatic diseases occur when the body's "natural balance" is upset, particularly if it is chronically upset.

Although psychosomatic medicine has been concerned primarily with those diseases felt to be "psychosomatic," recently the concept has been broadened to include (or overlap with) the new field of Behavioral Medicine. The essence of behavioral medicine is the application of behavior modification techniques derived from learning theory to various medical problems - eg, chronic pain, hypertension and other psychosomatic diseases, habit disorders, etc. Techniques used include behavioral self-management methods, biofeedback, hypnosis, and various relaxation procedures.

SPECIFIC PSYCHOSOMATIC DISORDERS:

Although (1) stress can increase the susceptibility to any disease and (2) most diseases are currently viewed as multifactorially determined, those that most clearly have a major psychosomatic contribution include the following disorders.

CARDIOVASCULAR:

Coronary artery disease: More common in "Type A" personalities. These patients have increased serum cholesterol, low-density lipoproteins, and triglycerides; also increased urinary 17-ketosteroids, 17-hydroxycorticosteroids, and NE. Sudden death by MI is increased in patients experiencing a severe recent loss (1st 6 months).

Hypertension: Chronic psychosocial stress probably plays a role in its development in genetically predisposed patients. Mechanism is uncertain but may not be related to the brief hypertension that occurs during periods of acute stress. May occur more frequently in Type A people and in compulsive people who "store resentment" and who handle angry feelings poorly. Treat first with antihypertensives. Relaxation therapy (eg, progressive relaxation, meditation, hypnosis) is an effective adjunct to drugs - biofeedback may also help.

<u>Arrhythmias</u>: Palpitation, sinus tachycardia, and worsening of pre-existing arrhythmias may all be produced by stress - probably via a sympathetic-parasympathetic imbalance.

<u>Hypotension</u> (fainting): Produced by fear - probably due to peripheral vasodilation and a decreased ventricular filling.

<u>Congestive heart failure</u>: Frequently develops following periods of stress. Anxiety tends to exacerbate the condition.

<u>Raynaud's Disease</u>: Can often be treated effectively with progressive relaxation or biofeedback.

<u>Migraine</u>: Attacks are often precipitated by stress. Treatment should include medication <u>and</u> biofeedback. Consider relaxation and psychotherapy also.

RESPIRATORY:

<u>Bronchial asthma</u>: Occurs in people with a genetic predisposition - made worse by acute and chronic stress. These patients are at risk for developing neurotic emotional reactions secondary to the respiratory disorder. There is good evidence that a wide variety of problem-solving and stress-reducing techniques (eg, psychotherapy, family therapy, systematic desensitization, hypnosis, etc) are effective at preventing attacks in many asthmatics and should be used in conjunction with medication.

<u>Hay fever</u>: Patients have an increased sensitivity to their allergens when stressed but may also develop characteristic symptoms when no allergens can be identified.

<u>Tuberculosis</u>: Chronic stress often precedes development of the disease.

<u>Hyperventilation syndrome</u>: A common ER presentation (see chapter 8). Differentiate from panic disorder.

GASTROINTESTINAL:

<u>Peptic ulcer</u>[7]: Stress contributes to ulcer development, probably through its influence on the hypothalamic-pituitary-adrenal axis. The chronically frustrated and angry patient with increased gastric HCL (hypersecretor) is at risk. Help the patient develop more stress-free life patterns. Relaxation therapy may be of value.

<u>Ulcerative colitis</u>: Stressful emotional factors often

precede disease development and can induce a relapse but the mechanism is unclear.   Nonconfrontive, supportive psychotherapy is indicated to help the patient adapt better to stress and to his illness and to help him deal with the frequently associated anxiety and depression, but psychiatric care alone will not prevent relapses. Other intestinal conditions which are markedly influenced by psychosocial stress include <u>regional enteritis</u> (Crohn's Disease) and <u>irritable bowel syndrome</u>.[8]

<u>Obesity</u>:    Genetic and psychological factors interact.[9] Improper conditioning around food habits, an over-valuation of food, and a negative body image (eg, "fatso") are central.   "Binge eaters" are particularly susceptible to stress.   Supportive psychotherapy may be of some value but behavior modification is most useful. Long-term success is limited - initial weight loss is frequent but relapses are very common.   A change in life-style appears essential.

<u>ANOREXIA NERVOSA</u> (DSM-III-R p 65, 307.10)[10]:  This disor-der of profound weight loss without loss of appetite usually develops in adolescence  (F:M = 10:1), continues through the early 20's, and may end in death by starva-tion (5-10%).   It is increasingly common in upper middle class females.

These patients have a disturbed body image (feel fat in spite of dramatic visual evidence to the contrary) and are preoccupied with losing weight.   They diet, exercise, and dangerously abuse diuretics and laxatives, even while family members and professionals attempt to stop them.   Many anorexics (50% at some time during their course) also binge eat.

A  related  condition,  <u>BULIMIA</u>  (DSM-III-R p 67, 307.51), is a chronic disorder characterized primarily by episodic eating binges in adolescent or early adult females (F:M = 10-20:1) <u>of normal weight</u> who follow the gorging by self-induced vomiting or by inducing diarrhea with laxatives.   These individuals are weight conscious and markedly depressed by their uncontrolled eating. Self-deprecation and suicidal ruminations are common. Endocrinological, family history, and treatment findings are similar to those of anorexia, and many patients slip back and forth between the two conditions over time.

Anorexics  often  have  hormone  imbalances  (eg, amenorrhea), numerous signs of starvation (eg, edema, bradycardia, and hypothermia), and associated features like ritual behavior (eg, hand-washing).   The etiology is uncertain.   The families frequently have disturbed interpersonal patterns and an increased incidence of eating and affective disorders.  Be certain to rule out a primary affective or schizophrenic disorder.

Treatment[11] should involve hospitalization for severe cases, individual <u>and</u> family therapy,[12] and behavior modification. Some patients (particularly bulimics) improve with group therapy[13] and/or antidepressants,[14,15] while a few require antipsychotics. In its early stages this condition is frequently overlooked yet treatment can be lifesaving. Develop a high index of suspicion in thin, young females.

MUSCULOSKELETAL:
<u>Rheumatoid arthritis</u>[16]: Symptoms frequently worsen following emotional stress. Stress may be acting as an immunosuppressant. Depression is common in these patients. Psychotherapy is of little value in altering the course of the disease.
<u>Tension headaches</u>: Caused by chronic muscular tension. Treat with mild analgesics and EMG feedback from the frontalis muscles or with relaxation techniques (often coupled with vigorous activity).
<u>Spasmodic torticollis</u>: Exacerbated by stress. EMG biofeedback may be useful.
<u>Low back pain</u>: Treat multimodally.

ENDOCRINE:

Conditions which are exacerbated by stress include <u>hyperthyroidism</u> and <u>diabetes mellitus</u>.[17] Acute and chronic stress may precipitate a thyroid crisis in genetically predisposed patients. Ketosis may be produced and maintained by stress in diabetics. Patients with either condition should receive psychotherapy if they have adopted self-destructive life habits and if they experience frequent relapses.

GENITOURINARY:

Most gynecological disorders reflect primarily an endocrine imbalance, but many of these conditions also can be influenced significantly by psychosocial stress. Psychosomatic influences are most evident for: menstrual disorders (premenstrual tension, amenorrhea, oligomenorrhea), dyspareunia, frigidity pseudocyesis, premature ejaculation, and impotence. Spontaneous abortion can be produced by major stress.

CHRONIC PAIN:

Chronic pain patients are common. The sources of their pain may or may not be identifiable. They often have been thoroughly evaluated medically, have experienced several unsuccessful surgical or medical procedures, and may or may not be currently iatrogenically addicted to analgesics (be wary of requests for Demerol, Percodan, Codeine, Darvon, Talwin, Valium, etc). Nothing has helped, and the patients show evidence of depression, hopelessness, chronic anxiety, insomnia, chronic anger, interpersonal withdrawal, and/or somatic preoccupation.[18] Their lives may be totally dominated by the pain.

Be certain that you are not dealing with conditions which mimic or complicate chronic pain (see chapter 11):

1. Unrecognized, treatable organic pathology.
2. Primary depression, anxiety disorder, or psychosis.
3. Unrecognized, early OBS.
4. Drug addiction.
5. Conversion disorder.
6. Somatization disorder.
7. Somatoform pain disorder.
8. Hypochondriasis.
9. Histrionic personality disorder.
10. Malingering.
11. Compensation factors.

Always treat the chronic pain patient globally. Do not become overly concerned about whether the pain is "real" or "psychological" - it invariably will have elements of both, and treatments will be similar. Use whatever medical and surgical means are of value but do not stop there. Always explore and apply the multiplicity of psychological treatments that are available.[19]

- First, detoxify the patient, if necessary.
- Take the patient and his pain seriously. Be interested, sympathetic, and hopeful. Be a continuing presence - see the patient regularly and do not abandon him.
- Help the patient identify and accept reasonable expectations. Encourage him to continue functioning - avoid hospitalization.
- Recognize that chronic administration of analgesics has limited usefulness and great risks yet can be done therapeutically. Attempt to use no drugs or nonaddicting drugs (eg, antidepressants, major tranquilizers, antihistamines). Codeine is the preferable narcotic.
- Have the patient keep a pain diary. Work with the patient over time to help him determine what variables improve or worsen the pain.
- Consider the variety of psychological techniques available - eg, hypnosis, biofeedback, relaxation therapy, etc. Encourage the patient to discover that he is "in control of his own pain." Use these methods within the context

of a good therapeutic alliance. Consider family and group therapy. Help others in the patient's environment become more appropriately responsive to his pain.
- Consider some physical procedures - eg, nerve block dorsal column stimulators, acupuncture, rhizotomy, etc. Avoid surgery if possible.
- Recognize that not all patients will improve markedly.

OTHER:

Skin: A wide variety of psychosocial stressors can exacerbate certain skin conditions, including psoriasis, chronic urticaria, pruritus, neurodermatitis (eczema), and trichotillomania. Research suggests that warts (a contagious disease) responds to hypnosis.[20]

Malignant disease: Psychological stressors appear to influence the development (but perhaps not the course[21]) of a malignancy. This may be related to the effect of stress on the immune system. Much work remains to be done, yet there is some suggestion that psychological treatments (eg, hypnosis) may play a future role in cancer treatment.

Hematological: Stress may aid clotting among hemophiliacs. Changes in levels of various blood elements may occur in normals under acute stress.

Accident proneness: Some people are chronically at risk for accidental trauma due to psychological characteristics (eg, impulsive, anxious, hostile).

Seizures: Emotional stress can trigger seizures (both neurogenic and conversion). Psychotherapy and stress management is effective in helping to control seizure disorders, particularly in patients with partial seizures.

## REFERENCES

1. Holmes TH, Rahe RH: The social readjustment rating scale. J Psychosom Res 11:213, 1967.
2. Friedman M, Rosenman RH: Type A behavior pattern: Its association with coronary heart disease. Am Clin Res 3: 300, 1971.
3. Lesser IM: Alexithymia. NEJM 312:690-692, 1985.
4. Kandel ER: From metapsychology to molecular biology: Explorations into the nature of anxiety. Am J Psychiatry 140:1277-1293, 1983.
5. Axelrod J, Reisine TD: Stress hormones: Their interaction and regulation. Science 224:452-459, 1984.
6. Selye H: The Stress of Life, 2nd ed. New York, McGraw-Hill Book Co, 1976.
7. Christodoulou GN, Alevizos BH, Konstantakakis E: Peptic ulcer in adults. Psychother Psychosom 39:55-64, 1983.

8.  Latimer PR: Irritable bowel syndrome. Psychosomatics 24:205, 1983.
9.  Stunkard AJ: The current status of treatment for obesity in adults. Psychiatr Ann 13:862, 1983.
10. Herzog DB, Copeland PM: Eating disorders. NEJM 313:295-303, 1985.
11. Hsu LKG: The treatment of anorexia nervosa. Am J Psychiatry 143:573-581, 1986.
12. Russell GFM, Szmukler GI, Dare C, Eisler I: An evaluation of family therapy in anorexia nervosa and bulimia nervosa. Arch Gen Psychiatry 44:1047-1056, 1987.
13. MacKenzie KR, Livesley WJ, Coleman M, et al: Short-term group psychotherapy for bulimia nervosa. Psychiatr Ann 16:699-708, 1986.
14. Pope HG, Hudson JI: Antidepressant drug therapy for bulimia. J Clin Psychiatry 47:339-345, 1986.
15. Herzog DB: Antidepressant use in eating disorders. Psychosomatics 27 (No 11, Suppl):17-23, 1986.
16. Vollhardt BR, Ackerman SH, Grayzel AI, Barland P: Psychologically distinguishable groups of rheumatoid arthritis patients. Psychosom Med 44:353-362, 1982.
17. Kemmer FW, Bisping R, Steingruber HJ, et al: Psychological stress and metabolic control in patients with type 1 diabetes mellitus. NEJM 314:1078-1084, 1986.
18. Katon W, Egan K, Miller D: Chronic Pain: Lifetime psychiatric diagnoses and family history. Am J Psychiatry 142:1156-1160, 1985.
19. Latimer PR: External contingency management for chronic pain: Critical review of the evidence. Am J Psychiatry 139:1308, 1982.
20. Surman OS, Gottlieb SK, Hackett TP, Silverberg, EL: Hypnosis in the treatment of warts. Arch Gen Psychiatry 28:439, 1973.
21. Cassileth BR, Lusk EJ, Miller DS, et al: Psychosocial correlates of survival in advanced malignant disease? NEJM 312:1551-1555, 1985.

# Chapter 13

# Psychiatric Symptoms of Nonpsychiatric Medication

Many medical patients develop psychiatric symptoms due to treatment with medical drugs[1-3] - (1) as a common side effect, (2) as an idiosyncratic response, (3) from administration of toxic amounts, or (4) as the result of an untoward combination of drugs.[4,5] Unrecognized, the responsible medications might be continued. Likely offenders include:

ANTICONVULSANTS:

Diphenylhydantoin, phenacemide: Irritability, emotional lability, confusion, and occasionally hallucinations and psychotic thinking - at times with normal blood levels. Symptoms occur more frequently in patients who also demonstrate tremor and ataxia.

Phenobarbital: Normal blood levels occasionally may produce irritability and/or confusion in the elderly while excessive dosage will produce oversedation. Symptoms of withdrawal may occur if phenobarbital is stopped abruptly.

ANTI-INFLAMMATORY AGENTS:

Phenylbutazone (Butazolidin): Anxiety, nervousness, emotional lability.

Indomethacin (Indocin): Dizziness, disorientation, and confusion; also occasionally depression, hallucinations, and psychosis.

Salicylates: In high doses, can produce elation and euphoria grading into depression and confusion.

HORMONES:

Exogenous thyroid: Excess can result in symptoms varying from restlessness and anxiety to a psychosis mimicking mania or acute schizophrenia. Inadequately treated patients may display symptoms of hypothyroidism; eg, fatigue, depression, psychosis (myxedema madness).

Adrenal corticosteroids (eg, cortisone,[6] dexamethasone, prednisone): In addition to physical complications, excessive or chronic use can produce widely varying affective syndromes (eg, euphoria and hypomania, fatigue and depression) and/or degrees of a toxic psychosis.[7] Steroid withdrawal can produce complaints of weakness and fatigue - suspect pseudotumor cerebri if coupled with headache, vomiting, and confusion.

Estrogens: Restlessness, a sense of well-being, euphoria.

Progesterones: May produce fatigue, irritability, tearfulness, and depression when given either alone or in combination as oral contraceptives (2-30% of patients).

Androgens: Restlessness, agitation, aggressiveness, euphoria.

## ANTICHOLINERGICS:

An anticholinergic psychosis (see chapter 23) can be caused by a variety of medical drugs; they also can produce milder peripheral (dry mouth, hypotension) and central (lability, distractibility, restlessness) side effects.

Antihistamines: eg, Benedryl, Phenergan, Teldrin, Ornade, Dramamine.

Antispasmodics: eg, Banthine.

Ophthalmic drops: eg, atropine, homatropine, cyclopentolate.

Antiparkinsonian drugs: eg, Cogentin, Artane, Tremin, Kemadrin, Akineton.

Others: Compoz, Excedrin PM, Sleep-Eze, Sominex and others containing scopolamine.

Treat psychosis with physostigmine 1-2 mg, IM or slowly IV; repeat in 20 minutes if needed.

## ANTIHYPERTENSIVES[8,9]:

Rauwolfia alkaloids (reserpine): Can cause nightmares, confusion, and profound depression in susceptible patients taking normal doses.

Diuretics (thiazides, furosemide, ethacrynic acid): Fatigue and mild depression.

Methyldopa (Aldomet): Persistent lassitude; verbal memory impairment; depression with obtundation and confusion (on normal dosage).

Guanethidine (Ismelin): mild depression.

Clonidine: sedation, depression; antagonized by tricyclic antidepressants; hypomania on withdrawal sometimes.[10]

Propranolol (and other beta-blockers): <u>depression</u>,[11] confusion, hyperactivity, paranoia.

## CARDIAC DRUGS:

Digitalis and the cardiac glycosides:  Fatigue, apathy, depression, and/or toxic delirium - particularly in the elderly.

Propranolol (Inderal):  Fatigue, insomnia, nightmares, verbal memory impairment, and depression; rarely confusion and a toxic psychosis.

Antiarrhythmics (quinidine, procainamide, lidocaine): mild confusion; mild-to-major delirium; occasionally depression.

## SYMPATHOMIMETICS:

Both catecholamine and noncatecholamine stimulants may produce restlessness, anxiety, fear and panic, weakness, dizziness, irritability, and insomnia in recommended dosages.

## BROMIDE:

Acute intoxication is rare - bromide is too irritating to allow ingestion of large doses.  Symptoms of chronic intoxication (weeks, months) (bromism) range from mild disorientation to full toxic psychosis.  Look for "classic" acneiform rash of face and hair roots (30% of patients) in persons using some over-the-counter sedatives (eg, Bromo-Seltzer).

## L-DOPA:

The depression and apathy of Parkinson's disease may be relieved, but anxiety and agitation are produced frequently.  15% of patients develop more serious psychiatric problems including an acute organic brain syndrome with confusion or frank delirium, hypomania, acute psychosis, or major depression.  Often hard to differentiate from the progression of the disease.

## HYPOGLYCEMICS (insulin, tolbutamide, phenformin):

Symptoms of hypoglycemia - restlessness, anxiety, disorientation.

## ANTIBIOTICS and related drugs:

Tetracyclines:  Can produce emotional lability, depression, and confusion - from vitamin deficiencies

secondary to alteration of colonic bacteria.
Nalidixic acid and nitrofurantoin:   Lethargy; rarely confusion.
Isoniazid   (INH):      Euphoria,   transient   memory   loss,
agitation, psychotic reaction, paranoia, catatonic-like
syndrome.
Cycloserine:   Lethargy and confusion, agitation, severe
depression, psychosis, paranoid reactions.

ANTINEOPLASTICS:

Acute organic brain syndromes and depression can be
produced by a variety of these agents - either by a direct
CNS effect or due to involvement of other systems (eg,
anemia).

## REFERENCES

1.   David K: Psychological effects of non-psychiatric drugs,
     in Barchas J: Psychopharmacology: From Theory to Prac-
     tice. New York, Oxford University Press, 1977.
2.   Shader RI: Psychiatric Complication of Medical Drugs.
     New York, Raven Press, 1972.
3.   Drugs That Cause Psychiatric Symptoms. The Medical Let-
     ter 28:81-86, August 29, 1986.
4.   Bernstein JG: Drug interactions. In Hackett TP, Cassem
     NH: Handbook of General Hospital Psychiatry. St Louis,
     CV Mosby Co, 1987.
5.   Glassman R, Salzman C: Interactions between psychotropic
     and other drugs: An update. Hosp Community Psychiatry
     38:236-242, 1987.
6.   Carpenter WT, Gruen PH: Cortisol's effects on human
     mental functioning. J Clin Psychopharmacol 2:91-101,
     1982.
7.   Hall RC, Popkin MK, Stickney SK, Gardner ER: Presenta-
     tion of the steroid psychoses. J Nerv Ment Dis 167:229,
     1979.
8.   Solomon S, Hotchkiss E, Saravay SM, et al: Impairment of
     memory function by antihypertensive medication. Arch Gen
     Psychiatry 40:1109, 1983.
9.   Benson D, Peterson LG, Bartay J: Neuropsychiatric mani-
     festations of antihypertensive medications. Psychiatr
     Med 1:205-214, 1983.
10.  Tollefson GD: Hyperadrenergic hypomania consequent to
     the abrupt cessation of clonidine. J Clin Psychopharm
     1:93-95, 1981.
11.  Avorn J, Everitt DE, Weiss S: Increased antidepressant
     use in patients prescribed beta-blockers. JAMA 255:
     357-360, 1986.

# Chapter 14

# Psychiatric Presentations
of Medical Disease

Physical and psychiatric illnesses are closely
interwoven.[1-5] Both medical and psychiatric physicians
should appreciate this interrelationship.[6,7]

- 60% of patients needing mental health care are being
  treated by medical physicians.
- 50-80% of the patients treated in medical clinics have a
  diagnosable psychiatric illness, and 10-20% of medical
  patients suffer primarily from an emotional disorder.
- 50% of patients in psychiatric clinic populations have
  undiagnosed medical conditions.
- 10% of self-referred psychiatric patients have symptoms
  which are due solely to a medical illness.

Always evaluate psychiatric patients medically. Be
particularly alert to patients presenting with depression,
confusion, memory loss, anxiety, personality changes,
psychosis of rapid onset, visual hallucinations, and
illusions. Always be suspicious of symptoms of sudden onset
in a patient, particularly one over 35 years old, who previously has been problem-free. Recognize that patients (or
their physicians) often can identify a "precipitating event"
for even the most organic of psychiatric conditions - don't
be fooled.

Always consider psychiatric possibilities for physical
symptoms in medical patients. Take a good history including
past emotional problems. Why is the patient coming for help
now?

PSYCHIATRIC SYMPTOMS:

There are only a few typical psychiatric presentations
and many different medical illnesses which can cause them.
Some of the most common associations are listed below,
although almost any physical condition can contribute to
symptom production.

| Presentation | Disease |
|---|---|
| Anxiety[8] | hyperthyroidism<br>hypoglycemia<br>pneumonia<br>acute intermittent porphyria<br>pheochromocytoma<br>mitral valve prolapse<br>angina pectoris<br>cardiac arrhythmias<br>hyper- and hypoparathyroidism<br>hypothyroidism<br>Cushing's Disease<br>menstrual irregularities |
| Depression | hypothyroidism<br>debilitating disease<br>pneumonia, other infections<br>Cushing's Disease[9,10]<br>Addison's Disease<br>pancreatic carcinoma<br>intracranial tumors<br>Pernicious Anemia<br>hyper- and hypoparathyroidism |
| Confusion, memory loss | Numerous medical conditions<br>(see chapters 5 and 6) |
| Mixed psychotic-<br>hysterical symptoms[11] | MS<br>Wilson's Disease[12]<br>SLE<br>intracranial tumors<br>hyperthyroidism<br>psychomotor epilepsy<br>general paresis<br>Huntington's Chorea<br>metachromatic leukodystrophy<br>porphyria |

## MEDICAL DISEASES:

No medical illness produces pathognomonic psychiatric symptoms, yet each has a typical range of presentations. Some of the most characteristic are listed below, but more comprehensive sources are available. In many of these diseases, the patient develops psychiatric pathology before any medical signs or symptoms are noticed.

Endocrine:

Hyperthyroidism[13] - anxiety, restlessness, emotional lability, weight loss, sweating, fine tremor, atypical depression with confusion in older patients.

Hypothyroidism - depression, fatigue, apathy, occasionally anxiety and psychosis ("myxedema madness"), dry skin, EEG slowing, cold intolerance.

Hyperparathyroidism[14] - anxiety and irritability; depression, apathy, and fatigue; confusion and delirium; abdominal and bone pain, kidney stones, duodenal ulcer. Symptoms progress to psychosis and coma as the serum calcium levels rise.

Hypoparathyroidism - similar to hyper- but with anxiety and emotional lability more common; seizures, tetany.

Hypoadrenalism (Addison's Disease) - fatigue, apathy, depression, weakness, occasional confusion.

Pheochromocytoma - anxiety, restlessness, apprehension and panic, flushing, headaches; all during attacks.

Hypoglycemia - symptoms vary with blood sugar; episodic anxiety, tremor, sweating, personality changes, bizarre behavior.

Diabetes Mellitus - depression, apathy, confusion, intellectual dullness.

Premenstrual Syndrome (PMS)[15-17] - as many as 25% of women develop significant physical/psychological discomfort during the 4-5 days prior to menses, ending shortly after flow begins. Common symptoms include irritability, tension, tearfulness, moderate depression, a sense of bloating, swelling of the extremities, and headaches, but may include more severe symptoms such as profound depression, aggressiveness, and even psychosis. The etiology is unknown but may be related to hormonal imbalance: possibly prolactin, estrogen, or prostaglandins. Women with a preliminary affective disorder may be at risk for problems.[18] No treatment is certain, but progestogenic oral contraceptives, bromocriptine, Li, and/or psychotherapy may help.

Infections:

Depression, anxiety, OBS, and acute psychosis all can occur due to a variety of infectious processes, depending upon the patient's sensitivity, his age and physical condition, the site of the infection, and the agent. Particularly common are symptoms with pneumonia (particularly delirium with bacterial and depression with viral), infectious mononucleosis (anxiety and psychosis may be the first symptoms of mono; depression is commonly late), viral hepatitis (the posthepatitic syndrome - weakness, irritability, lethargy, depression), syphilis (general paresis), and TB.

Other:

Acute Intermittent Porphyria[19] - 15% of cases present first with psychiatric symptoms: anxiety, irritability, emotional outbursts, depression, acute psychosis; abdominal pain, peripheral neuropathies and bulbar palsies, vomiting and constipation.

Hepatolenticular degeneration (Wilson's Disease) - May present with a labile mood, explosive outbursts, and psychotic behavior in a young man before the development of cirrhosis, portal hypertension, rigidity, Kayser-Fleischer rings, and dementia.

Pellagra - dementia, diarrhea, and dermatitis; also depression, personality changes, and a confusional psychosis.

Systematic lupus erythematosus (SLE) - Patient may present with confusion, an affective state, and psychotic behavior before physical signs appear.

Pernicious Anemia - depression and fatigue but also an organic psychosis. Look at blood for characteristic megaloblastic anemia.

Pancreatic carcinoma - severe depression in 40%[+] of patients. Also depression with CA of lung and brain.[20]

Prolapse of the mitral valve - associated with generalized anxiety disorder, panic disorder, and agoraphobia with panic attacks, but the significance of the association is not known.

COPD - anxiety, depression, and mild-moderate organicity are common.[21]

## REFERENCES

1. Hall RCW: Psychiatric Presentations of Medical Illness. New York, SP Med & Scientific Books, 1983.
2. Jefferson JW, Marshall JR: Neuropsychiatric Features of Medical Disorders. New York, Plenum Med Book Co, 1981.
3. Korami EK: Physical Illness in the Psychiatric Patient. Springfield, IL, Charles C Thomas, 1982.
4. Levenson AJ, Hall RCW: Neuropsychiatric Manifestations of Physical Disease in the Elderly. New York, Raven Press, 1981.
5. Lishman WA: Organic Psychiatry. Oxford, Blackwell Pub, 1978.
6. Dvdoredsky AE, Cooley HW: Comparative severity of illness in patients with combined medical and psychiatric diagnoses. Psychosomatics 27:625-630, 1986.

7. Hayes JR, Butler NE, Martin CR: Misunderstood somato-psychic concomitants of medical disorders. Psychosomatics 27:128-133, 1986.
8. Raj A, Sheehan DV: Medical evaluation of panic attacks. J Clin Psychiatry 48:309-313, 1987.
9. Cohen SI: Cushings syndrome: A psychiatric study of 29 patients. Br J Psychiatry 136:120, 1980.
10. Kelly WF, Checkley SA, Bender DA, Mashiter K: Cushing's syndrome and depression - a prospective study of 26 patients. Brit J Psychiatry 140:1194, 1983.
11. Cummings JL: Organic psychosis. Psychosomatics 29:16-26, 1988.
12. Bornstein RA, McLean DR, Ho K: Neuropsychological and electrophysiological examination of a patient with Wilson's disease. Int J Neuroscience 26:239-247, 1985.
13. Hall RCW: Psychiatric effects of thyroid hormone disturbance. Psychosomatics 24:7, 1983.
14. Borer MS, Bhanot VK: Hyperparathyroidism: Neuropsychiatric manifestations. Psychosomatics 26:597-601, 1985.
15. DeJong R, Rubinow DR, Roy-Byrne P, et al: Premenstrual mood disorder and psychiatric illness. Am J Psychiatry 142:1359-1361, 1985.
16. Keye WR: Medical treatment of premenstrual syndrome. Can J Psychiatry 30:483-488, 1985.
17. Rubinow DR, Roy-Byrne P: Premenstrual syndromes. Am J Psychiatry 141:163-172, 1984.
18. Price WA, DiMarzio L: Premenstrual tension syndrome in rapid-cycling bipolar affective disorder. J Clin Psychiatry 47:415-417, 1986.
19. Tishler PV, Woodward B, O'Connor J, et al: High prevalence of intermittent acute porphyria in a psychiatric patient population. Am J Psychiatry 142:1430-1436, 1985.
20. Silberfarb, PM, Greer S: Psychological concomitants of cancer. Am J Psychother 36:470, 1982.
21. Grant I, Prigatano GP, Heaton RK, et al: Progressive neuropsychologic impairment and hypoxemia. Arch Gen Psychiatry 44:999-1006, 1987.

# Chapter 15

# Psychiatric Presentations of Neurological Disease

Many of the psychiatric symptoms caused by various neurological diseases (eg, CNS tumor, trauma, seizure,[1] infection) can be correlated directly to the CNS site involved.

Frontal lobes:

   Prefrontal damage - the frontal lobe syndrome occurs with unilateral or bilateral damage (personality changes, irritability, euphoria, apathy, pseudodepression, impulsivity, social inappropriateness). Do not mistake for depression or mania. Intelligence is usually unimpaired in unilateral damage. Symptoms are milder if only one side is involved.

   If the premotor area is involved (on left), there may also be apraxia of the left hand and Broca's (expressive) aphasia. Don't confuse with psychosis.

Temporal lobes:

   Stimulation or lesions may produce visual and olfactory hallucinations, non-complex auditory hallucinations, and aggressive psychotic behavior.
   Dominant lobe lesion may produce agnosia for sounds, intonations, and music.
   Bilateral lesions may produce the amnestic disorder of Korsakoff and the Kluver-Bucy Syndrome (placidity and hypersexuality).

Parietal lobes:

   Dominant lobe lesions may produce language difficulties (eg, inability to express or understand spoken words, perform simple tasks, read, and/or write), tactile agnosia, apraxia, and intellectual deterioration.
   Nondominant lobe lesions may produce anosognosia.

Occipital lobes:

Some lesions produce crude, flashing visual illusions and hallucinations.

Limbic system:

Effects are diverse but usually involve primitive and emotional behavior - eg, emotional lability, fear, rage, impulsivity, depression, memory loss. Also amnestic syndrome when mammillary bodies involved (Korsakoff's Syndrome).

NEUROLOGICAL DISEASES:

Neurological disorders can produce a variety of psychiatric symptoms - consult a comprehensive source for detailed descriptions of specific conditions. Some major diseases are presented below.

Parkinson's Disease - frequently accompanied by apathy and depression.[2]

Huntington's chorea - may present first with psychiatric symptoms[3] (eg, emotional lability, impulsiveness, depression, hallucinations, delusions). Don't mistake for schizophrenia, major depression, or mania. Look for family history, movement disorder, and dementia.

Multiple sclerosis (MS) - early psychiatric symptoms are common, particularly emotional lability, euphoria, transient psychotic episodes, depression, and an "hysterical" presentation.

Intracranial tumors - 50% of patients develop psychiatric symptoms, and occasionally they may be the presenting symptoms.[4] Pattern is site-related, although there is usually a degree of generalized OBS. Early personality changes are often subtle - "He's not the same person any more." Aphasias due to tumor (or any other cause) may mimic psychotic language disorders - there are qualitative differences between these two types of speech.

Head trauma[5,6] - a postconcussion syndrome: includes irritability, emotional lability, and personality changes. Depression and mania may occur.[7]

CNS infection - typically presents with OBS (usually irritability and restlessness initially). General paresis (CNS syphilis)[8,9] usually presents as a gradually developing dementia but can produce a variety of confusing symptoms - eg, may mimic schizophrenia, mania, depression, somatization disorder.

Stroke - <u>poststroke depression</u>[10] is common (50%+ of pts) but the type of mood disorder tends to vary with the anatomical location of the damage: major depression (L-frontal); dysthymia (L- & R-posterior); and unnatural cheerfulness, anxiety, and anhedonia (R-frontal).    Major depression lasts for 9-12 months and responds to antidepressants or ECT.[11]

AIDS - Some combination of apathy and depression, anxiety and agitation, and denial occur in the majority of AIDS patients[12] and requires traditional therapies.    50%+ develop neurological complications that typically begin as slowed mentation and grade into delirium; the majority of these patients then progress to dementia.[13]

<u>GILLES DE LA TOURETTE SYNDROME</u> (DSM-III-R p 79,   307.23) - This neuropsychiatric syndrome of uncertain etiology usually develops in latency or early adolescence with the onset of one or more poorly controlled symptoms, including head or extremity tics, eyeblinks, and the spasmodic production of coughs or grunts which occasionally can include verbal obscenities (coprolalia).    It is often severe and lifelong, occurs (along with other tic phenomena) with increased incidence in families, may[14] (or may not[15]) have a major genetic component, and is associated (genetically?) with obsessive-compulsive disorder.[16]    All symptoms are worsened by stress and may be improved by psychotherapy, but primary treatment is pharmacological: haloperidol[17] (the mainstay;     80-90% of patients improve;   2-12 mg/day), but consider clonidine[18,19] (0.1-0.5 mg/day), pimozide[20] (2-12 mg/day), clonazepam,[21] or fluphenazine.[22]    Stimulant medication can precipitate or worsen Tourette symptoms but can also help,[23] so use cautiously, if at all.

REFERENCES

1.   McKenna PJ, Kane JM, Parrish K: Psychotic syndromes in epilepsy. <u>Am J Psychiatry</u> 142:895-904, 1985.

2.   Mayeux R, Stern Y, Williams JBW: Clinical and biochemical features of depression in Parkinson's disease. <u>Am J Psychiatry</u> 143:756-759, 1986.

3.   Caine ED, Shoulson I: Psychiatric syndromes in Huntington's disease. <u>Am J Psychiatry</u> 140:728-733, 1983.

4.   Binder RL: Neurologically silent brain tumors in psychiatric hospital admissions. <u>J Clin Psychiatry</u> 44:94-97,

1983.
5.  Garoutte B, Aird RB: Behavioral effects of head injury. Psychiatr Ann 14:507-514, 1984.
6.  Goethe KE, Levin HS: Behavioral manifestations during the early and long-term stages of recovery after closed head injury. Psychiatr Ann 14:540-546, 1984.
7.  Robinson RG, Boston JD, Starkstein SE, Price TR: Comparison of mania and depression after brain injury: Causal factors. Am J Psychiatry 145:172-178, 1988.
8.  Rundell JR, Wise MG: Neurosyphilis: A psychiatric perspective. Psychosomatics 26:287-295, 1985.
9.  Simon RP: Neurosyphilis. Arch Neurol 42:606-613, 1985.
10. Robinson RG: Depression and stroke. Psychiatr Ann 17: 731-740,
11. Murray GB, Shea V, Conn DK: Electroconvulsive therapy for poststroke depression. J Clin Psychiatry 47:258-260, 1986.
12. Faulstich ME: Psychiatric aspects of AIDS. Am J Psychiatry 144:551-556, 1987.
13. Price RW, Brew B, Sidtis J, et al: The brain in AIDS: Central nervous system infection and AIDS dementia complex. Science 239:586-592, 1988.
14. Pauls DL, Leckman JF: The inheritance of Gilles de la Tourette's syndrome and associated behaviors. NEJM 315: 993-997, 1986.
15. Zausmer DM, Dewey ME: Tics and heredity. Br J Psychiatry 150:628-634, 1987.
16. Pauls DL, Towbin KE, Leckman JF, et al: Gilles de la Tourette's syndrome and obsessive-compulsive disorder. Arch Gen Psychiatry 43:1180-1182, 1986.
17. Weiden P, Bruun R: Worsening of Tourette's disorder due to neuroleptic-induced akathisia. Am J Psychiatry 144: 504-505, 1987.
18. Leckman JF, Detlor J, Harcherik DF, et al: Short- and long-term treatment of Tourette's syndrome with clonidine. Neurology 35:343-351, 1985.
19. Leckman JF, Ort S, Caruso KA, et al: Rebound phenomena in Tourette's syndrome after abrupt withdrawal of clonidine. Arch Gen Psychiatry 43:1168-1176, 1986.
20. Shapiro AK, Shapiro E: Controlled study of pimozide vs placebo in Tourette's syndrome. J Am Acad Child Psychiatry 23:161-173, 1984.
21. Merikangas JR, Merikangas KR, Koop U, Hanin I: Blood choline and response to clonazepam and haloperidol in Tourette's syndrome. Acta Psychiatr Scand 72:395-399, 1985.
22. Goetz CG, Tanner CM, Klawans HL: Fluphenazine and multifocal tic disorders. Arch Neurol 41:271-272, 1984.
23. Erenberg G, Cruse RP, Rothner AD: Gilles de la Tourette syndrome: Effects of stimulant drugs. Neurology 35:1346-1348, 1985.

# Chapter 16

# Psychiatry of Alcohol

Alcohol is the major substance of abuse. 68% of Americans drink, 12% are heavy drinkers (men 2:1), 10 million have alcohol abuse problems, and 50% of homicides and auto deaths are alcohol-related. Certain populations are at risk: eg, urban blacks, some Indian tribes, bartenders.

## CLASSIFICATION

Normal (recreational) drinking grades into pathological use. ALCOHOL ABUSE (DSM-III-R p 173, 305.00) is diagnosed if there is at least one month of impaired social and occupational functioning due to alcohol use. Individual patterns can vary from continuous consumption to periodic binges, but all demonstrate the inability to abstain from drinking or to stop drinking once started. Such drinking usually results in depression and anxiety. Beginning often as evening and weekend drinking, the pattern usually becomes established by the late 20's in males (later in females) with gradual deterioration in some during their 30's and 40's. Spontaneous remissions can occur. Blackouts (anterograde amnesia for events that occurred during acute intoxication but while conscious and quite functional) often follow more severe drinking.

If the patient also demonstrates tolerance (increased amounts needed to achieve effect) or withdrawal, he has ALCOHOL DEPENDENCE (ALCOHOLISM) (DSM-III-R p 173, 303.90). Broader definitions of alcoholism are used by some; eg, "patients with significant impairment due to persistent and excessive alcohol use, possibly involving physiological, psychological, or social dysfunction" (AMA Manual of Alcoholism).

The etiology of alcoholism is unknown although evidence for genetic, biological characteristics grows. Adoption studies indicate a genetic factor in some families: increased frequency of alcohol abuse and sociopathy among male, and possible increased somatization among female relatives of alcoholics. Recent research[1] identifies two groups of alcoholics:

Type 1 - alcohol-seeking from adolescence and early adult-hood; impulsive; distractible; risk-taking; antisocial characteristics with recklessness and aggression; strong family history; primarily males; very treatment resistent; 25% of all alcoholics.

Type 2 - adult onset; steady, gradually escalating consumption; guilty, worried, rigid, perfectionistic, dependent, introverted; modest family history; both males and females; some recover completely; 75% of alcoholics.

Moreover, certain biological features seem to be inherited by $1^o$ relatives (particularly males) of alcoholics: eg, a resistance to intoxication, a subnormal cortisol rise after drinking,[2] and a subnormal epinephrine release following stress.[3]

Cultural groups are differently affected (eg, low among Jews and Orientals). All social strata are affected - fewer than 5% are "skid row" types. There is no "typical alcoholic personality." Patients with chronic anxiety, mood disorders (particularly females), schizophrenia, dementia, and antisocial personality disorder are at risk to "self-medicate" with alcohol. Always rule out these primary psychiatric disorders.


## RECOGNIZING THE ALCOHOLIC

The majority of alcohol abusers go unrecognized by physicians until their social and occupational life and their physical health have been significantly harmed. Early recognition is important. These patients frequently conceal alcohol use - keep a high index of suspicion. Be suspicious if the predominant complaints include:

1. Chronic anxiety and tension
2. Insomnia
3. Chronic depression
4. Headaches, blackouts
5. Nausea and vomiting, vague GI problems
6. Tachycardia, palpitations
7. Frequent falls or minor injuries

Ask about absenteeism, job loss, financial difficulties, family trouble. Ask, "Do you drink?" Be encouraging and nonjudgmental. Get drinking specifics (number of beers/

day, oz/glass, drink alone?, etc). Interview relatives and friends, if possible.

Use a brief screening questionnaire. Two are quick and reliable: the MAST[4] (Michigan Alcoholism Screening Test - 24 "yes or no" questions; can be administered by an office worker) and the CAGE[5] (consists of 4 questions; two or more positive answers are suggestive of alcoholism)

1. "Have you ever felt you should cut down on your drinking?"
2. "Have people annoyed you by criticizing your drinking?"
3. "Have you ever felt bad or guilty about your drinking?"
4. "Have you ever had a drink first thing in the morning to steady your nerves or get rid of a hang-over (Eye-Opener)?"

Chronic drinking frequently elevates serum gammaglutamyltransferase (GGT) and RBC MCV. These measures, coupled with evidence of more acute alcoholic insult (protein, Alk Phos, LDH, SGOT, SGPT, etc) constitute a fairly reliable laboratory screen for alcoholism. (Recent work suggests that inhibition of platelet MAO by ethanol and stimulation of platelet adenylate cyclase by other chemicals may be a specific test for alcoholism.[6] Time will tell.)

CLINICAL PRESENTATIONS

When presenting acutely, always determine the patient's recent drinking history:
1. Is he currently intoxicated?
2. Time since last drink?

Intoxication Syndromes

ALCOHOL INTOXICATION (DSM-III-R p 127, 303.00): Alcohol is a CNS depressant which initially disinhibits, then depresses. Early intoxication includes liveliness, a sense of well-being, and a smell of alcohol on the breath (blood alcohol levels up to 100 mg/100 ml); grading into irritability, emotional lability, and incoordination (100-150 mg%), which grades into apathy, slurred speech, and ataxia (150-250 mg%) which can become alcoholic coma (above 250-400 mg%; an emergency - get blood alcohol level and check for presence of other drugs; treat with intubation, CPR, etc, if necessary). Blood alcohol levels vary with drinking experience and thus are only approximate.
Acute intoxication can mimic schizophrenia, mania, depression, hysteria, etc, so delay detailed interview and

final diagnosis until patient is sober. Evaluate <u>carefully</u>
for medical problems (see below) - differential includes
hypoglycemia, CNS infection, and toxic psychosis of other
etiology. Intoxicated patients may be uncooperative, as-
saultive, and dangerous - be civil, nonthreatening, accepting, respectful, patient, but prepared with force. Attempt
nonpharmacological management (quiet room, support, coffee),
but sedation may be necessary: eg, diazepam 5-20 mg or IM
(erratically absorbed), but be cautious of oversedation.
Decide if the patient just needs to "sleep it off," is at
risk for withdrawal, or is becoming comatose. Should he go
home with family, be observed overnight, be hospitalized, or
go to jail? Be familiar with community resources.

<u>ALCOHOL IDIOSYNCRATIC INTOXICATION (Pathological Intoxica-</u>
<u>tion</u>) (DSM -III-R p 128,  291.40)  is an unusual and contro-
versial condition of marked aggressiveness and emotional
lability, occasionally of psychotic proportions, which follows ingestion of small quantities of alcohol in an otherwise normal person. Etiology is unknown. Some patients
retain this pattern for life. Episodes appear suddenly and
may last for hours or a day or more, often with amnesia for
the episode afterward. Sedate (benzodiazepines, Haldol) and
control until sober. Rule out temporal lobe epilepsy.
<u>Alcoholic paranoia</u> has a similar presentation but with
strong paranoid delusions. It usually occurs in chronic
alcoholics who are actively drinking.


## Alcohol Withdrawal Syndromes

These may occur in heavy drinkers or alcoholics who
stop drinking or who just reduce their consumption. Don't
overlook them in the "closet" alcoholic - eg, the business-
man or housewife who temporarily abstains while in the
hospital for other reasons. If the patient is withdrawing,
delay final diagnostic conclusions.

<u>UNCOMPLICATED ALCOHOL WITHDRAWAL</u> (DSM-III-R p 129, 291.80)
- <u>tremulousness</u>, hyperreflexia, weakness, nausea, and
vomiting, "dry heaves," anxiety, insomnia and bad dreams,
mild  illusions  and  hallucinations,  hypervigilance,
paresthesias, numbness, tinnitus, and/or blurred vision
beginning with the first 12-18 hours of reduced drinking,
leading to a vicious cycle. There is no EEG slowing-
instead, the waves are normal or fast.    Debilitated,
medically ill patients are at risk. <u>Alcoholic convulsions</u>
(generalized, self-limited, single or in small groups) occur
in some, usually in the first two days of withdrawal, but
sometimes later.  If the seizure is focal - suspect CNS
pathology (eg, subdural).

ALCOHOL WITHDRAWAL DELIRIUM (Delirium Tremens - DTs) (DSM-III-R p 131, 291.00) is a life-threatening delirium with disorientation, agitation, memory disturbances, hallucinations (usually visual, but also tactile, auditory, vestibular, etc), delusions, powerful autonomic discharge (hypertension, tachycardia, sweating), tremor, ataxia, and fever beginning 2-8 days after reduced drinking.    Tremulousness and seizures can precede, and often are mistaken for, the much less common DTs.    Malnourishment and medical illness increases the risk of delirium.    Mortality rate is 10-15% for the complete syndrome (often from secondary infection or acute heart failure).    Less than 5% of alcoholics ever experience DTs.

ALCOHOLIC HALLUCINOSIS (DSM-III-R p 131, 291.30) displays striking auditory hallucinations (voices, sounds) and mixed other withdrawal symptoms (mild tremor, anger, apprehension) but the patient typically has a clear sensorium and is oriented.    It usually occurs in the first three days after cessation of drinking in patients who have had years of heavy drinking.    Patients may be dangerous or self-destructive while hallucinating.    Usually self-limited (within one week), occasional cases last for months or become chronic (chronic alcoholic hallucinosis).    Differential includes alcoholic paranoia and toxic psychosis (amphetamine, cocaine).    Differentiation from paranoid schizophrenia is difficult in chronic cases (look for other signs of schizophrenia).


## COMPLICATIONS OF CHRONIC ALCOHOLISM

Chronic alcoholics have numerous complicating diseases.

Medical:    gastritis, gastric ulcer, diarrhea, anemia, hypertension, pancreatitis, cirrhosis (in less than 10% of alcoholics - alcohol plus poor diet), persistent impotence, insomnia.

Neurological:
1. Peripheral neuropathy (vitamin B deficiencies)
2. Alcoholic cerebellar degeneration
3. Central pontine myelinolysis
4. Marchiafava-Bignami Disease
5. Cerebral atrophy
6. Alcoholic myopathy and cardiomyopathy
7. Wernicke's encephalopathy[7] (vertical and horizontal nystagmus, sixth nerve palsies, ataxia, and confusion) - due to thiamine deficiency (give 50 mg IV and 50 mg IM, then 50 mg IM daily until patient is eating).    An

emergency - if treated early, it usually quickly clears.

Psychiatric:
1. ALCOHOL AMNESTIC DISORDER (Korsakoff's Disease) (DSM-III-R p 133, 291.10) is a profound recent short-term memory loss (retrograde and anterograde) with confabulation, which follows untreated Wernicke's encephalopathy or develops insidiously. Typically, events are remembered for several minutes (ie, immediate memory is OK) and then are forgotten. Due to thiamine deficiency - lesions in the mammillary bodies and thalamus. Treat as in Wernicke's Disease. Impairment is often lifelong, yet 75% improve with time.
2. DEMENTIA ASSOCIATED WITH ALCOHOLISM (DSM-III-R p 133, 291.20) refers to a dementia (ie, all intellectual functions affected), ranging from mild to severe, following many years of alcohol abuse and with no other obvious etiology. Few alcoholics are affected and the predisposition is unknown.
3. Suicide.
4. Drug Abuse.

Other:
1. Fetal Alcohol Syndrome describes small, hyperactive, retarded children with variable anatomical abnormalities including ptosis, epicanthal folds, hypoplastic maxilla, cleft lip and palate, microcephaly, and hypospadias. Although not definite, it is thought to be due to a teratogenic effect on the fetus caused by alcohol consumed by the mother while pregnant. It is one of the most common causes of retardation.

TREATMENT OF WITHDRAWAL

Treatment varies with the severity of the symptoms. When in doubt, hospitalize temporarily; however, many patients manifesting mild withdrawal symptoms can be treated in a supportive environment, with good nutrition, and without medication.[8,9]

1. Be clear and unambiguous. Identify yourself. Explain procedures. Place patient in a lighted room. Include family and familiar people. Use restraints if needed. Keep under constant observation.

2. Carefully evaluate (PE, chest X-ray, chemistry, electrolytes including calcium and magnesium, CBC, CT,

occult blood in stool, occasionally an LP). Incidence
of complicating disorders is high - eg, pneumonia, TB,
UTIs, hypoglycemia, diabetic ketoacidosis, anemia,
shock, gastritis with hematemesis, acute hemorrhagic
pancreatitis, cirrhosis and hepatic failure, meningitis.
Be particularly careful to exclude (1) a subdural
hematoma due to a fall and (2) withdrawal from other
substances. Treat these conditions if present.

3. Use medication - to assure sleep, prevent exhaustion,
reduce agitation. Sedate until calm (but avoid
oversedation) then taper over 4-8 days (ie, decrease by
approximately 20% of total first day's dose each day).
The delirium often resolves within one day.
Benzodiazepines currently are preferred, but chloral
hydrate, paraldehyde, and barbiturates are also useful.
Phenothiazines lower seizure threshold, but may be
useful with chronic psychotics and alcoholic
hallucinosis.

> Tremulousness: eg, chlordiazepoxide 25-50 mg PO (or
> diazepam, 10-20 mg), q4-6 hr until comfortable.
> Lorazepam (6-12 mg/day) may be a better choice in
> patients with liver disease or confusion.[10]
> Delirium: eg, chlordiazepoxide 50-100 mg, PO or IM
> every hr until calm (able to stay in bed), then q4
> hrs. IM doses are often poorly absorbed - can lead
> to early undersedation, then cumulative overseda-
> tion. If patient is severe, give IV slowly.

Clonidine,[11] a sympathetic inhibitor, may relieve sweating, tremor, and tachycardia, but doesn't prevent DTs.
Beta-blockers (eg, atenolol, 50-100 mg/day) used with
benzodiazepines may shorten the course.[12]

4. If withdrawal seizures persist, consider 5-10 mg of diazepam slowly by IV or 100-150 mg of phenobarbital IM.
If a primary seizure disorder exists, begin diphenylhydantoin.

5. Give thiamine 100 mg IM, then 50 mg PO tid x 4 days. Also
provide a high carbohydrate diet and multivitamins daily
(and for weeks/months).

6. Correct fluid and electrolyte imbalances - particularly
hypokalemia (replace carefully over 24 hrs or longer
via IV) and hypomagnesemia (may exacerbate seizures -
give magnesium sulfate 2-4 ml of 50% solution IM q6 hrs
x 2 days).

7. Record pulse, BP, and temp every half-hour initially. Treat shock with fluids, whole blood, and vasopressors.

8. Check for and treat: hypoglycemia, prolonged PT (give vitamin K 10 mg IM), fever (aspirin, sponge baths - rule out superimposed infection).

9. Anxiety, irritability, depression, and insomnia may persist for weeks after the acute episode - a vulnerable period for the alcoholic. Even serious depression may spontaneously resolve after several weeks of sobriety[13] - don't over (or under) treat. Antianxiety agents may be of use for 1-2 weeks.

## TREATMENT OF ALCOHOLISM

Successful treatment of alcoholism is difficult but not hopeless.[14] However, there is no definitive treatment.[15]

1. Identify its presence. Get your facts straight (family drinking history, recent intake).
2. Develop a personal rapport with the patient - be warm and supportive but firm. Be open and matter-of-fact about the drinking but insist on abstinence. Encourage patient to maintain employment and social involvement.
3. Treat all medical complications of drinking.
4. Treat any complicating primary psychiatric illness (eg, schizophrenia, affective disorder, anxiety disorder). If the patient is likely to drink, recognize that tricyclics potentiate the CNS depressant effect of alcohol and that alcohol can promote lithium toxicity.
5. Enlist family members in treatment. Evaluate family's contribution to the problem. Consider family therapy; marital therapy.[16]
6. Lithium may help a few patients stay sober[17] (unpredictable); there are more promising drugs on the way.[18]
7. Consider disulfiram (Antabuse) use in cooperative but backsliding patients. It inhibits aldehyde dehydrogenase leading to toxic acetaldehyde buildup 15-30 minutes after alcohol consumption, which leads to anxiety and apprehension, sweating, nausea and vomiting, tachycardia, headache, and hypotension. Give 500 mg PO qd x 1 wk, then maintain on 250 mg daily (range 125-500 mg). Carefully inform patient of the possible reactions. Effects last up to two weeks after last dose; however, not every patient shows an Antabuse reaction. Occasional adverse effects include sedation, a metallic taste, mild GI disturbances, mild ataxia, and a peripheral neuropathy. Question its use in thoroughly irresponsible patients - hepatotoxicity and toxic psy-

choses can occur and severe reactions (to a large alcohol challenge) can lead to shock and coma. Contraindicated in patients with unstable medical conditions or histories of psychosis, OBS, MI, or heart failure. Biggest problem with disulfiram - patients stop taking it so they can drink.[19,20]

8. Group therapy appears to be the most effective technique. In most cases, work with or refer patient to a specialized multidisciplinary treatment team. Make referral personally, with the patient present. AA (Alcoholics Anonymous) can help - encourage patient's consideration. Also useful: Alanon (spouses of alcoholics). Hospitalize in an alcohol unit (milieu therapy) if even temporary sobriety cannot be achieved. Keep trying.

9. Be patient. Keep trying.

## REFERENCES

1. Cloninger CR: Neurogenetic adaptive mechanisms in alcoholism. Science 236:410-416, 1987.
2. Schuckit MA, Gold E, Risch C: Plasma cortisol levels following ethanol in sons of alcoholics and controls. Arch Gen Psychiatry 44:942-945, 1987.
3. Swartz CM, Drews V, Cadoret R: Decreased epinephrine in familial alcoholism. Arch Gen Psychiatry 44:938-941, 1987.
4. Powers JS, Spickard A: Michigan Alcoholism Screening Test to diagnose early alcoholism in a general practice. South Med J 77:852, 1984.
5. Ewing JA: Detecting alcoholism: The CAGE questionnaire. JAMA 252:1905, 1984.
6. Tabakoff B, Hoffman PL, Lee JM, et al: Differences in platelet enzyme activity between alcoholics and non-alcoholics. NEJM 318:134-139, 1988.
7. Reuler JB, Girard DE, Cooney TG: Wernicke's encephalopathy. NEJM 312:1035-40, 1985.
8. Whitfield C et al: Detoxification of 1,024 alcoholic patients without psychoactive drugs. JAMA 239:1049-1053, 1978.
9. Sellers E, Naranjo C: New strategies for the treatment of alcohol withdrawal. Psychopharm Bull 22:88-92, 1986.
10. Miller WC, McCurdy L: A double-blind comparison of the efficiency and safety of lorazepam and diazepam in the treatment of the acute alcohol withdrawal syndrome. Clin Ther 6:364, 1984.
11. Wilkins AJ, Jenkins WJ, Steiner JA: Efficacy of clonidine in treatment of alcohol withdrawal state. Psychopharmacology 81:78-80, 1983.
12. Kraus ML, et al: Randomized clinical trial of atenolol withdrawal. NEJM 313:905,1985.

13. Dackis CA, Gold MS, Pottash ALC, Sweeney DR: Evaluating depression in alcoholics. _Psychiatr Res_ 17:105-109, 1986.
14. Helzer JE, Robins LN, Taylor JR, et al: The extent of long-term moderate drinking among alcoholics discharged from medical and psychiatric treatment facilities. _NEJM_ 312:1678-1682, 1985.
15. Holden C: Is alcoholism treatment effective? _Science_ 236:20-22, 1987.
16. Kaufman E: The family of the alcoholic patient. _Psychosomatics_ 27:347-360, 1986.
17. Judd LL, Huey LY: Lithium antagonizes ethanol intoxication in alcoholics. _Am J Psychiatry_ 141:1517-1521, 1984.
18. Suzdak PD, Gilowa JR, Crawley JN, Schwartz RD, et al: A selective imidazobenzodiazepine antagonist of ethanol in the rat. _Science_ 234:1243-1247, 1986.
19. Fuller RK, Branchey L, Brightwell DR, Derman RM, et al: Disulfiram treatment of alcoholism. _JAMA_ 256:1449-1455, 1986.
20. Wilson A, Blanchard R, Davidson W, McRae L, Maini K: Disulfiram implantation: a dose response trial. _J Clin Psychiatry_ 45:242-247, 1984.

# Chapter 17

# Psychiatry of Drug Abuse

Drug abusers are common, often unrecognized, and poorly understood. There is great variability in the degree of drug use from patient to patient. <u>Abuse</u> occurs if the patient (1) has been using drugs for more than one month, (2) has difficulty controlling his use, and (3) has impaired social and/or occupational functioning because of that use. Drug <u>dependence</u> requires the presence of either tolerance or withdrawal. Patients may be classified by the type of drug abused (see below) or by the pattern and reason for abuse. Some recognized patterns of use (abuse) include:

- Recreational use - Patient takes drugs for "fun" and is not physically or psychologically dependent upon them. He may also take them "just to be part of the group" or because it is a counter-cultural requirement.
- Iatrogenic addiction - Patient addicted "by mistake." Patient (and physician) may or may not recognize the addiction. Many of these patients are convinced that they must have the drug to function (eg, to sleep, to interact with others) and may go to great lengths to talk their physicians into prescribing medication.
- The chronic drug addict - These patients usually abuse "street" drugs. Many have underlying depressions. Many have antisocial personalities. Some take drugs in an effort to self-medicate a chronic psychiatric disorder (eg, major depression, schizophrenia).[1]

Abusers are not "all alike," but they do have many common features, including the frequent presence of marked depression and anxiety, increased dependency needs (often hidden), low self-esteem, a familial association (genetic?) with antisocial personality disorder and alcoholism,[2] a disrupted family life, and a chronic course resistant to treatment. Also, evaluate for psychiatric illness.

Treatment of chronic drug abusers is difficult - frequently an inpatient setting is required. Whether inpatients or outpatients, drug abusers should be treated firmly but with support and understanding. Set clear limits and stick to them. Insist on dealing with the patient only when he is not intoxicated. Be reasonably confrontative. You will be tested and manipulated by many patients - don't respond with retribution. Follow many of the principles used in dealing with the alcoholic patient (see chapter 16).

The most common drugs of abuse, their clinical presentations, and treatment follow. Abusers of multiple drugs are common.

## OPIOIDS

<u>DRUGS INVOLVED</u>:

    opium
    morphine
    diacetylmorphine (Heroin, horse, smack)
    methadone
    codeine
    oxycodone (eg, Percodan, in mixture)
    hydromorphone (Dilaudid)
    levorphanol (Levo-Dromoran)
    pentazocine (Talwin)
    meperidine (Demerol)
    propoxyphene (Darvon)

Some of these compounds are naturally occurring (opium and its constituents morphine and codeine) while the others are semi-synthetic or wholly synthetic. Some of these drugs have legitimate uses (eg, morphine, meperidine) while others are solely substances of abuse (eg, heroin). Most are obtained illegally "on the street" and are used primarily by a young, lower socioeconomic population while others are abused more widely (eg, Demerol, Dilaudid, and Percodan are common drugs of abuse among professionals). Common routes of administration are IV (heroin, morphine, methadone- "mainlining"), SC (heroin, meperidine - "skin popping"), nasally (heroin, cocaine - "snorting"), orally (methadone, Percodan), and smoked (opium). It is frequently very difficult to determine the daily dose used because (1) the abuser often overestimates the dose and (2) the amount of active drug in a "bag" bought on the street is uncertain. Frequently a bag of heroin is 95% adulterants (eg, quinine, mannitol, lactose).

Abuse (<u>OPIOID ABUSE</u>, DSM-III-R p 182, 305.50) and dependency (<u>OPIOID DEPENDENCE</u>, DSM-III-R p 182, 304.00) are common in some populations, and the search for drugs or money for drugs accounts for the majority of the crime in some communities. Some people (less than 50%) are able to abuse opioids without becoming dependent (ie, without tolerance and/or withdrawal), and they often are used recreationally without addiction. Those persons who become dependent represent a high risk group.

- 1% of all heroin addicts in the USA die each year. Most common cause is an inadvertently fatal OD - eg, an addict using "bags" of 5% heroin accidently buys a supply containing 15% heroin. Also common is death during violent crime.
- 25%[+] of addicts have a personality disorder - usually antisocial type. They also have a high incidence of depression and anxiety.[3] Suicide rate is elevated.
- Heroin addicts are at markedly increased risk (due to dirty needles, poor nutrition, etc) for developing certain medical illnesses.

   AIDS, but also
   Hepatitis, serum and infectious
   Subacute bacterial endocarditis
   Tetanus
   Pneumonia; pulmonary edema, embolus, abscess; TB
   Cellulitis, thrombophlebitis, septicemia
   UTIs, glomerulonephritis, nephrosis
   Osteomyelitis
   Transverse myelitis
   Polyneuropathy (Guillain-Barre type)
   VD
   Nasal septum perforation (due to "snorting")
   Needle "tracts" on the arms (and legs)

Always carefully evaluate hospitalized addicts medically. Recognize that the analgesic properties of the opioids may obscure acute medical problems. The majority of addicts "grow out of" their habit over the years (or die), thus there are relatively few older abusers.

Treatment of the opioid addict usually means treatment of the acute episodes (eg, intoxication and withdrawal - see below). "Cure" of the addiction does occur in some well-motivated patients, yet most addicts continue their abuse over at least several years. The two major forms of long-term treatment (both with equivocal results) are:
1. Methadone Maintenance - Patients are maintained as outpatients on daily doses of methadone of 40-120 mg. This level controls the craving for (and eliminates the euphoria from) heroin. The patient can then develop some skills, hold a job, go to school, etc: psychotherapy can help some,[4] but treatment demands careful limit

setting.[5] Moderately motivated patients <u>may</u> succeed by this route. LAAM, a chemical congener of methadone, has recently found use as a long-acting replacement for methadone (patient takes it 3x/wk). Unfortunately, many of these patients continue to abuse other drugs while taking methadone (cocaine & "crack" are common).

2. Residential, drug-free, self-help programs - Patients (usually highly motivated) stay 1-2 years (or more) in a close "therapeutic community" which insists on the drug-free state and on personal responsibility. Confrontation and behavior modification are frequently used. Poor "candidates" usually drop out.

The two major features of illicit opioid use which bring patients to medical attention are intoxication (and overdosage) and withdrawal.

OPIOID INTOXICATION (DSM-III-R p 151, 305.50) develops rapidly after an IV dose (1-5 min). The time course varies with the drug used.

| Drug | Duration of action (hr) |
|------|------------------------|
| heroin | 4 - 6 |
| methadone | 12 - 24 |
| meperidine | 2 - 4 |

The abstinence syndrome begins after this period of time in the dependent patient. It is because of these kinetics that many heroin addicts "shoot up" 3-4 x/day, or more.

Symptoms are similar for most of the narcotics.

Psychological symptoms - a "rush" immediately follows IV administration (described as a "whole body orgasm" with the focus in the abdomen). This is accompanied by euphoria and a sense of well-being or dysphoria (usually anxiety and fear), a drowsiness and "nodding off," apathy, psychomotor retardation, and difficulty concentrating.

Physical symptoms - miosis (<u>pupillary constriction</u>), slurred speech, respiratory depression, hypotension, hypothermia, bradycardia, constipation, and nausea and vomiting. Skin ulcers are common with meperidine injection. Seizures may occur in the patient tolerant to meperidine.

An overdose (either accidental or intentional) is a medical emergency - these patients may die of respiratory depression and pulmonary edema. Look for needle tracts and pinpoint pupils in the unconscious patient but recognize that if the patient already has experienced significant CNS anoxia, the pupils may be dilated. Seizures occasionally occur (particularly with meperidine).

Treat the OD with intensive medical care (ICU) and the narcotic antagonist naloxone (Narcan). Give 0.4 mg IV and repeat x 5 at 3 min intervals. Expect a rapid response (ie, clearing in 1-2 min), and if this doesn't occur after four doses, suspect another etiology for the coma. If the patient improves, continue monitoring - patient may need additional doses of naloxone since it has a much shorter half-life than either heroin or methadone. Excessive naloxone may throw a dependent patient directly from coma into withdrawal - don't be confused. Multiple drugs may have been taken - be alert to the possibility of a more slowly developing coma from a second agent.

OPIOID WITHDRAWAL (DSM-III-R 162, 392.00): In spite of its reputation as a dramatic and traumatic withdrawal syndrome, opioid withdrawal is uncomfortable but usually not life-threatening in healthy young adults and is not nearly as dangerous or difficult to manage as the withdrawal from sedative-hypnotic drugs.

Symptoms are similar for each of the narcotics, but the time course varies (dependent partly on the "size of the habit").

| Drug | Time after last dose that symptoms begin | Sx peak | Sx disappear |
|------|------------------------------------------|---------|--------------|
| heroin | 4 - 8 hr | 1 - 3 days | 7 - 10 days |
| methadone | 12 - 48 hr | 4 - 6 days | 10 - 21 days |
| meperidine | 2 - 4 hr | 8 - 12 hr | 4 - 5 days |

  Psychological symptoms - Early there is often intense drug craving followed by severe anxiety, restlessness, irritability, insomnia, and decreased appetite. In this state, the hospitalized patient is frequently extremely demanding and manipulative.
  Physical symptoms - Yawning, diaphoresis, tearing, rhinorrhea, pupillary dilation, piloerection (hard to "fake" so look for it), muscle twitching, and hot flashes. Later there is nausea and vomiting, fever, hypertension, tachycardia, tachypnea, diarrhea, and abdominal cramps. Seizures occur with meperidine withdrawal.

Babies born to addicted mothers, including those on methadone maintenance, often experience an abstinence syndrome, including a high-pitched cry, irritability, tremor, fever, decreased food intake, vomiting, yawning, and hyperbilirubinemia.

Withdraw these patients gradually by using oral methadone to lessen the symptom severity. After a complete
history and physical (including urine screen for opioids and
other drugs), wait for signs of withdrawal and then give
methadone 10 mg PO. Establish the stabilization dose over
the first 1-2 days by adding 5-10 mg of methadone on a qid
schedule as the patient continues to show signs of
abstinence (recognize that some patients will vigorously
demand more drugs even while they are sedated by their
current dose). Once stabilized, give the methadone on a qd
or bid schedule and reduce the total daily amount by 5
mg/day (or 10-20% of the stabilization dose). Most withdrawals from heroin addiction take 7-10 days - methadone
addiction withdrawals should be done more slowly (eg, 2-3
weeks). Alternate methods of opiate withdrawal using
clonidine (Catapres)[6] or LAAM[7] have recently been developed
which show evidence of being safer and more effective than
methadone withdrawal. Withdraw patients from Talwin using
decreasing doses of Talwin.

If a patient is withdrawing from both opioids and
sedative-hypnotics (not uncommon), concentrate on a safe
sedative-hypnotic withdrawal by maintaining the patient on
10-30 mg of methadone until the first withdrawal has been
completed.

## SEDATIVE-HYPNOTICS

DRUGS INVOLVED:

| Drug | Dependency-producing Dose (mg/day) |
|------|:-----:|
| meprobamate (Equanil, Miltown) | 1600 |
| methaqualone (Quaalude, Sopor) | 600 |
| glutethimide (Doriden) | 250 |
| ethchlorvynol (Placidyl) | 1000 |
| chloral hydrate (Noctec) | 600 |
| secobarbital (Seconal) | 600 |
| pentobarbital (Nembutal) | 600 |
| amobarbital (Amytal) | 300 |
| chlordiazepoxide (Librium) | 300 |
| diazepam (Valium) | 60 |
| | |
| oxazepam (Serax) | |
| flurazepam (Dalmane) | |
| methyprylon (Noludar) | |
| phenobarbital (Luminal) | |

The minimum dependency-producing dose listed above should be considered only approximate - there are individual differences as well as a required period of continuous administration (usually at least 1-3 months) before withdrawal symptoms occur. Oral use is the rule. Street synonyms for some of the sedative-hypnotics include downers, reds, blues, blue velvet, yellows, yellow jackets, sopers, ludes.

## CLINICAL SYNDROMES:

The same variety of syndromes occurs with sedative-hypnotic use as occurs with alcohol. There is cross-tolerance between alcohol and the sedative-hypnotics as well as among the various drugs themselves. The clinical picture varies little from drug to drug although withdrawal phenomena are more severe with the shorter acting drugs and more prolonged with those that have a longer half-life.

SEDATIVE, HYPNOTIC INTOXICATION (DSM-III-R p 158, 305.40): Symptoms of intoxication are dose related. Mild intoxication includes a sense of well-being, talkativeness, irritability, and emotional disinhibition. Increased doses produce apathy, confusion, stupor, and coma. Physical signs of intoxication include slurred speech, ataxic gait, incoordination, reduced DTRs, lateral nystagmus, and constricted pupils. Look for fast activity on the EEG. Fatalities are frequent with sedative-hypnotic ODs, usually due to respiratory depression (uncommon with the benzodiazepines).

Always evaluate sedative-hypnotic abusing patients who present with intoxication for an overt or covert OD. If they are becoming increasingly lethargic, treat as a medical emergency with hospitalization and intensive medical care. Obtain blood and/or urine levels.

SEDATIVE, HYPNOTIC ABUSE (DSM-III-R p 184, 305.40): This condition results from the pathological use of one or more of this class of drugs for more than one month. These patients frequently can't abstain from use, once started - a psychological addiction. Abuse of sedative-hypnotics is common and, unlike other substances of abuse, there are two distinct populations and patterns of abuse.

1. Males and females in their teens or 20's who obtain these drugs illegally and use them (as well as many other kinds) for "fun" and to get "high" or to block things out and "get away from the hassle."
2. Middle-aged females who are frequently chronically anxious or depressed and who obtain legal prescriptions from (one or more) physicians for complaints of anxiety and insomnia, gradually increase the dosage themselves

in an effort to cope, and often become physiologically addicted. Although these patients are common, they are disproportionately frequently seen by physicians because they ultimately have to "doctor shop" to obtain drugs. Recognize them. Recognize also that these patients frequently vigorously deny their illness - both to their physicians <u>and</u>, sometimes, to themselves.

Without exception, if the patient takes enough drug long enough, he will develop tolerance to it and/or signs of physiological withdrawal when it is stopped; ie, <u>SEDATIVE, HYPNOTIC DEPENDENCE</u> (DSM-III-R p 184, 304.10). Some evidence suggests that there is a familial pattern to the abuse of these substances (eg, family members also abuse sedative-hypnotics and alcohol).

<u>SEDATIVE, HYPNOTIC WITHDRAWAL</u> (DSM-III-R p 159, 292.00): This is the most dangerous of the drug withdrawal syndromes and can occur both in the dependent person who abstains and also in the person who merely reduces his dose. Its severity depends upon the particular drug abused, the duration of use, and daily dose used (degree of tolerance). Keep a high index of suspicion. Recognize it (1) by a history of significant drug use (<u>often</u> denied by the patient), (2) by characteristic abstinence symptoms (see below), and (3) by a Tolerance Test.

<u>Withdrawal Symptoms</u>:

   Psychological: A subjective sense of severe anxiety, restlessness, apprehension, irritability, insomnia, and anorexia which has developed gradually over the past 24 hours (1-3 days with the longer acting sedative-hypnotics) and is worsening hour by hour. Delirium may occur (<u>SEDATIVE, HYPNOTIC WITHDRAWAL DELIRIUM</u>, DSM-III-R p 160, 292.00) with visual hallucinations and formication (sense of insects crawling on the skin).
   Physical: Tremulousness (coarse tremor - primarily the upper extremities), weakness, nausea and vomiting, orthostatic hypotension, tachycardia, hyperreflexia, diaphoresis. After several days this may progress to delirium, hyperpyrexia, and coma. Seizures may occur (typically after 2-5 days) - usually generalized and single or a short series, but occasionally status epilepticus.

<u>Tolerance Test</u>:

   There are several methods of determining the degree of dependence (and thus the probable severity and length of withdrawal). One method is given below. It can be used

regardless of the particular sedative-hypnotic drug of abuse
(ie, they are all cross-tolerant).

1. Hospitalize the patient for the test if possible.
2. Administer test to a patient who is comfortable or only
   mildly anxious (not to a patient who is intoxicated or
   presently withdrawing - test would be invalid).
3. Give 200 mg of pentobarbital orally.
4. At one hour, evaluate the patient.  If he is:
   a. asleep but arousable - patient has no tolerance.
   b. grossly ataxic, coarse tremor and nystagmus - daily
      tolerance is 400-500 mg of pentobarbital.
   c. mildly ataxic, mild nystagmus - daily tolerance is
      600 mg.
   d. comfortable, slight lateral nystagmus - daily toler-
      ance is 800 mg.
   e. asymptomatic or has continuing signs of mild with-
      drawal - daily tolerance is 1000 mg, or more.  Wait
      3-4 hours, then give an oral dose of 300 mg of
      pentobarbital.  Failure to become symptomatic at
      this larger dose suggests a daily tolerance of
      greater than 1600 mg.

Treat withdrawal vigorously and carefully.  Usually
hospitalize unless the addiction is mild and the patient
reliable.  Evaluate for medical illness.  Withdrawal can be
accomplished safely using several different sedative-
hypnotics although the most commonly used are pentobarbital
and phenobarbital.

To withdraw with pentobarbital, give the estimated daily
tolerance dose (obtained either by reliable history of all
cross-tolerant drugs and alcohol used or by a tolerance
test) equally divided on a Q6 hr schedule for the first and
second days and then reduce 10% of the initial dose each
day.  Expect the patient to be somewhat uncomfortable but,
if signs of serious withdrawal (or intoxication) appear,
slow (or quicken) the decrease slightly.  If the patient is
showing serious withdrawal symptoms before treatment, give
enough pentobarbital over several hours to make him comfortable, then begin the withdrawal procedure.

SEDATIVE, HYPNOTIC AMNESTIC DISORDER (DSM-III-R p 161,
292.83):  This profound, short-term, anterograde and retrograde memory loss (Korsakoff's Syndrome) is usually
reversible.

## HALLUCINOGENS

DRUGS INVOLVED:

lysergic acid diethylamide (LSD-25, acid)
2,5-dimethoxy-4-methylamphetamine (DOM, STP)
dimethyltryptamine (DMT)
trimethoxyamphetamine (TMA)
psilocybin
mescaline (peyote, tops, cactus)

phencyclidine (PCP, angel dust, hog)
thiocyclidine (TCP)
ketamine (Ketalar)

cannabis (marijuana, hashish, pot, weed, grass, reefer)
delta-9-tetrahydrocannabinol (THC)

LSD, MESCALINE, AND OTHERS:

Patients take these drugs orally, develop symptoms in 10-45 minutes, and are back to normal in several hours (eg, LSD) to 1-2 days. The typical consequence of ingestion (HALLUCINOGEN HALLUCINOSIS, DSM-III-R p 144, 305.30) is:

Psychological symptoms - Marked perceptual distortions (changing object shapes, changing body image), illusions and hallucinations (mostly visual geometric designs, but also auditory and tactile), depersonalization, derealization, and synesthesias (stimuli in one modality produce sensations in another - eg, sounds become colors) - all occurring in a clear sensorium. The patient is usually aware that what he is experiencing is due to drugs (ie, has insight - unlike the patient with amphetamine psychosis). Occasionally the patient experiences strong depressive or anxious feelings (eg, panic - a "bad trip"), but more typically the mood is euphoric and the patient feels he is receiving profound, staggering insights.
Physical symptoms - Tachycardia, palpitations, diaphoresis, pupillary dilation (responsive to light), blurred vision, tremor, incoordination, hyperreflexia, hyperthermia, piloerection.

The psychological symptoms are particularly sensitive to the "set" or expectations of the patient prior to drug usage. Occasionally the patient will experience brief hallucinations weeks, months, or even years after the period of drug use (flashbacks). Flashback experiences may be continued for years, even in the absence of additional LSD usage, if marijuana is used regularly. Although primarily used as recreational drugs, a few patients disrupt their lives with drug use (HALLUCINOGEN ABUSE, DSM-III-R p 179, 305.30). There are no withdrawal symptoms, although slight tolerance does develop.

Two clinical syndromes which may (infrequently) follow the use of these drugs by one or more days are:

HALLUCINOGEN DELUSIONAL DISORDER (DSM-III-R p 146, 292.11) - Delusions that occur with drug use may persist for a variable length of time after the drug is out of the body.

HALLUCINOGEN MOOD DISORDER (DSM-III-R p 146, 292.84) - A persistence of a dysphoric mood (usually depression or anxiety) for days, weeks, or longer after taking the drug. The presentation may be identical to or gradually develop into a major mood disorder.

Treatment for "bad trips" usually consists of support ("talking down") - patient usually clears within hours. Benzodiazepines and phenothiazines may be used (eg, diazepam 10-15 mg; haloperidol 4-5 mg).

## PHENCYCLIDINE (PCP):

PCP is a common drug of abuse (PHENCYCLIDINE ABUSE, DSM-III-R p 183, 305.90; PCP DEPENDENCE, 304.50), particularly among youth. It is eaten, smoked, or taken IV. Symptoms begin in 2-60 minutes, depending on the route of administration.

Psychological symptoms - Low doses produce euphoria, grandiosity, a feeling of "numbness," and emotional lability. Higher doses cause symptoms which range from perceptual distortions, anxiety, excitation, confusion, and synesthesias to a paranoid psychosis, rigidity, and a catatonic-like state to convulsions, coma, and death. Violent (and self-destructive) behavior is common when intoxicated.

Physical symptoms - Tachycardia, hypertension, vertical and horizontal nystagmus, ataxia, dysarthria, myoclonus, decreased pain sensitivity, diaphoresis, seizures.

The patient usually clears in 3-6 hr. The symptom picture can be quite variable and can include a delirium usually lasting several days but which may last weeks or longer (PHENCYCLIDINE DELIRIUM, DSM-III-R p 155, 292.81), delusions (PCP DELUSIONAL DISORDER, 292.11), or a varying organic mood disorder (PCP MOOD DISORDER, 292.84). Long-term organic symptoms may occur (memory loss, word-finding difficulty). Diagnosis is based on the clinical picture, a history of PCP use, the presence of PCP in urine,[8] and (possibly) hair analysis.[9]   Chronic, unadmitted PCP use can easily be misdiagnosed as "atypical psychosis," so be wary.

Treatment is controversial.  OD's can be fatal. Hospitalize and use gastric suction, urine acidification, and symptomatic medical maintenance.  If agitation must be controlled, use haloperidol (perhaps combined with ascorbic acid[10]).  Decrease external stimulation.

CANNABIS:

The active ingredient of cannabis is delta-9-tetra-hydrocannabinol (THC).  The various forms (eg, marijuana, hashish) are all either smoked or eaten, and the differences in the effects they produce depend primarily on their concentrations of THC.  Cannabis is used widely and usually produces mild physical and psychological alterations (CANNA-BIS INTOXICATION, DSM-III-R p 139, 305.20) which occur shortly after intake and last 2-4 hr.

Psychological symptoms - The primary effect is a sense of well-being, mild euphoria, and relaxation.  Mild alter-ations and intensifications of perceptions occur (greater with the more concentrated forms), as does a sense of indifference and slowed time.  A few persons find the use of cannabis dysphoric and develop depres-sion, anxiety, panic, or even a delusional syndrome (usually paranoid, often with depersonalization) CANNA-BIS DELUSIONAL DISORDER (p 140, 292.11).  Impaired psychomotor performance and recent memory during and shortly following use is common (expected).[11]
Physical symptoms - Tachycardia, conjunctival injection, dry mouth, increased appetite.

Toxic psychoses have been reported with high dose use.  Some persons are socially and occupationally handicapped by chronic drug use (CANNABIS ABUSE, DSM-III-R p 176, 305.20).[12]   These patients are frequently apathetic and "amotivational," but this may be more a reflection of their personality structure than an effect of cannabis.  If there is also a significant degree of tolerance, the patient has CANNABIS DEPENDENCE (DSM-III-R p 176, 304.30).[13]

Treat "bad trips" with support.  Surreptitious use of marijuana can be detected by a urine screen for delta-9-THC-11-oic acid (THCA) up to several days after use.[14]

## STIMULANTS

DRUGS INVOLVED:

    amphetamine (Benzedrine)
    dextroamphetamine (Dexedrine)
    methamphetamine (Methedrine, "speed")
    phenmetrazine (Preludin)
    cocaine

    These are effective orally (except cocaine) and nasally
(cocaine), but produce a more rapid and intense effect by
smoking (cocaine - "crack") and IV (an orgasm-like "rush").
Street terms for amphetamines include speed, bennies,
uppers, diet pills, crystal, double crosses; for cocaine
include coke, snow, and crack (rock); and "speedball" for
amphetamine or cocaine with an opioid. Crack, the alkaloi-
dal, free-base form of cocaine HCl, is inexpensive, widely
available, and extremely addicting.

CLINICAL SYNDROMES:

    The effects of AMPHETAMINE INTOXICATION (DSM-III-R p
134, 305.70) and COCAINE INTOXICATION (DSM-III-R p 145,
305.60) occur within minutes (depending on route) and
consist of:

    Psychological symptoms - Hyperalertness, restlessness,
        psychomotor agitation, pacing, talkativeness and pres-
        sure of speech, sense of well-being, elation. Frequent-
        ly aggressiveness, violent behavior, and poor judgement
        occur as well.
    Physical symptoms - Tachycardia, hypertension, pupillary
        dilation, chills and diaphoresis, anorexia, nausea and
        vomiting, insomnia. Occasionally there are stereotyped
        repetitive movements (eg, endlessly taking something
        apart and then reassembling it).

With brief use, symptoms usually disappear within hours of
stopping the drug. All these symptoms may disappear as
tolerance develops.

    If drug use becomes a consuming pattern which lasts for
at least one month and which interferes with social and
occupational functioning, the patient has AMPHETAMINE ABUSE
(DSM-III-R p 175, 305.70) or COCAINE ABUSE (DSM-III-R p 177,
305.60). Abuse usually develops over months and may include
a pattern of "runs" of frequent, large-dose IV administration over days or weeks. After a run, the person frequently
sleeps for 12-18 hr, then may begin another run. High dose
use places the patient at risk for developing:

AMPHETAMINE DEPENDENCE (DSM-III-R p 175, 304.40) - ie, tolerance and/or withdrawal present.

AMPHETAMINE DELIRIUM (DSM-III-R p 136, 292.81) - A characteristic organic delirium (see chapter 5) develops shortly after taking the drug and disappears as the blood level drops. Violence is common during these episodes.

AMPHETAMINE DELUSIONAL DISORDER (DSM-III-R p 137, 292.11) - Patient becomes markedly paranoid and develops persecutory delusions within a setting of clear consciousness, often accompanied by hostility, anxiety, ideas of reference, and psychomotor agitation. This condition may last for one week or longer than one year. It easily can be mistaken for paranoid schizophrenia, which it closely resembles.

AMPHETAMINE WITHDRAWAL (DSM-III-R p 136, 292.00) - Cessation of drug in heavy user may be followed by mild-to-severe depression (watch for suicide), profound fatigue, irritability, anxiety, fearfulness, nightmares, and insomnia or hypersomnia. Severe symptoms seldom last more than one week but may be followed by chronic low-level depression and/or anxiety. Abnormal EEG patterns may last for weeks.

Cocaine produces similar syndromes. Serious medical complications occur with cocaine[15] (and particularly crack): MI ($2^o$ to coronary artery constriction) and anoxia $2^o$ to seizures can be fatal. Depression, paranoid psychosis, marked anxiety, malnutrition, and pneumonia also can occur. Crack, when smoked, typically produces a high within seconds, followed by a dysphoric crash several minutes later[16,17] - leading to rapidly repeated administrations and addiction. It is a very bad drug.

Make the diagnosis by the clinical picture and history of drug use. Most sympathomimetics and cocaine can be identified by a urine drug screen (cocaine is difficult-check with your lab).

TREATMENT:

Stop the drug. If the patient is mildly or moderately excited, try to "talk him down" and use benzodiazepines. The patient may be agitated and violent - take appropriate precautions (eg, restraints). Treat severe intoxication, delirium, and delusional symptoms with an antipsychotic (eg, haloperidol 5-10 mg PO or 5 mg IM). Acidify the urine with ascorbic acid or ammonium chloride (maintain pH at 4-5). Be alert to potential suicide and to medical complications (eg, MI, stroke, intracranial hemorrhage). Severe withdrawal depressions may respond to antidepressants.

Cure is difficult. Consider hospitalization if symptoms or habit are severe or if life is severely disrupted. Group therapy (in- or out-patient) should be tried at some point.

## INHALANTS[18-21]

The types of glues, solvents, and cleaners "sniffed" for their psychic effects are numerous and include gasoline, kerosene, plastic and rubber cements, airplane and household glues, paints, lacquers, enamels, paint thinners, solvents, aerosols, furniture polishes, fingernail polish removers, nitrous oxide, cleaning fluids, etc. Several active constituents are probably involved in most substances. This is a major abuse problem, particularly among late latency and early to middle adolescent children, and particularly among lower socioeconomic groups. This is often a group activity.

The effects from this variety of substance are usually quite similar - typically mild euphoria, confusion, disorientation, impulsivity, and ataxia - all of which may progress to a toxic psychosis, seizures, and coma. Repeated and chronic abuse is common, but withdrawal symptoms have not been noticed. Death has occurred from asphyxiation, aspiration, cardiac arrhythmias, and kidney, liver, and bone marrow damage. An acute brain syndrome (delirium) typically occurs but only in the unusual or very severe case does the patient appear to develop a degree of chronic CNS damage.

Physical restraint and medical support may be needed in the acute situation, but the patient usually clears over hours or days. Evaluate carefully for liver, kidney, and pulmonary damage. Encourage these children and their families to enter therapy.

## REFERENCES

1.  Khantzian EJ: The self-medication hypothesis of addictive disorders. Am J Psychiatry 142:1259-1264, 1985.
2.  Cadoret RJ, Troughton E, O'Gorman TW, Heywood E: An adoption study of genetic and environmental factors in drug abuse. Arch Gen Psychiatry 43:1131-1136, 1986.
3.  O'Brien CP, Woody GE, McLellan AT: Psychiatric disorders in opioid-dependent patients. J Clin Psychiatry 45:9-13, 1984.

4. Woody GE, McLellan AT, Luborsky L, O'Brien CP: Twelve-month follow-up of psychotherapy for opiate dependence. Am J Psychiatry 144:590-596, 1987.
5. McCarthy JJ, Borders OT: Limit setting on drug abuse in methadone maintenance patients. Am J Psychiatry 142:1419-1423, 1985.
6. Charney DS, Heninger GR, Kleber HD: The combined use of clonidine and naltrexone as a rapid, safe, and effective treatment of abrupt withdrawal from methadone. Am J Psychiatry 143:831-837, 1986.
7. Judson BA, Goldstein A, Inturrisi CE: Methadyl acetate (LAAM) in the treatment of heroin addicts. Arch Gen Psychiatry 40:834, 1983.
8. Ragan FA, Hite SA, Samuels MS, et al: Extended EMIT-DAU phencyclidine screen. J Clin Psychiat 47:194-195, 1986.
9. Sramek JJ, Baumgartner WA, Tallos JA, et al: Hair analysis for detection of phencyclidine in newly admitted psychiatric patients. Am J Psychiatry 142:950-953, 1985.
10. Giannini AJ, Loiselle RH, DiMarzio LR, Giannini MC: Augmentation of haloperidol by ascorbic acid in phencyclidine intoxication. Am J Psychiatry 144:1207-1209, 1987.
11. Yesavage JA, Leirer VO, Denari M, Hollister LE: Carry-over effects of marijuana intoxication on aircraft pilot performance. Am J Psychiatry 142:1325-1329, 1985.
12. Schnoll SH, Daghestani AN: Treatment of marijuana abuse. Psychiatr Ann 16:249-254, 1986.
13. Tennant FS: The clinical syndrome of marijuana dependence. Psychiatr Ann 16:225-234, 1986.
14. Verebey K, Gold MS, Mule SJ: Laboratory testing in the diagnosis of marijuana intoxication and withdrawal. Psychiatr Ann 16:235-241, 1986.
15. Cregler LL, Mark H: Medical complications of cocaine abuse. NEJM 315:1495-1500, 1986.
16. Gold MS, Verebey K: The psychopharmacology of cocaine. Psychiatr Ann 14:714-723, 1984.
17. Siegel RK: Cocaine smoking disorders. Psychiatr Ann 14:728-732, 1984.
18. Evans AC, Raistrick D: Phenomenology of intoxication with toluene-based adhesives and butane gas. Br J Psychiatry 150:769-773, 1987.
19. Evans AC, Raistrick D: Patterns of use and related harm with toluene-based adhesives and butane gas. Br J Psychiatry 150:773-776, 1987.
20. Dinwiddie SH, Zorumski CF, Rubin EH: Psychiatric correlates of chronic solvent abuse. J Clin Psychiatry 48:334-337, 1987.
21. Westermeyer J: The psychiatrist and solvent-inhalant abuse. Am J Psychiatry 144:903-907, 1987.

*Chapter 18*

# Personality Disorders

<u>Personality</u> is a consistent style of behavior uniquely recognizable in each individual. <u>Personality disorders</u> (Axis II of DSM-III-R) refers to personality characteristics of a form or magnitude that are maladaptive and which cause poor life functioning. These <u>long-term</u> traits feel "natural" (ego syntonic), even though a person may be bothered by the results of his behavior. There are elements of the personality disorders in all of us, and the difference between health and pathology may be one of degree. Moreover, many patients display their pathology clearly only when under stress.

Most personality disorders develop in childhood and become fixed by the early 20's, yet some occur following organic insults to the brain. Some may have a biologic, and even a genetic, component (eg, schizotypal and borderline personality disorders[1]). Psychological testing may facilitate diagnosis: WAIS, MMPI, Bender Gestalt, and Rorschach. Atypical and mixed types are common, and some may grade into or be confused with similar psychoses (eg, paranoid type: paranoid schizophrenia). These patients often resist treatment and change slowly, but occasionally respond to a variety of treatment modalities, including individual or group therapy, and short-term use of antianxiety agents or low doses of major tranquilizers. Some may require inpatient treatment during periods of decompensation. Adolescents (under 18), and even children, may receive a personality disorder diagnosis if the pattern is stable, clear, and incompatible with a childhood disorder.

ANTISOCIAL P.D. (DSM-III-R p 342, 301.70)

Antisocial behavior begins in childhood or early adolescence: aggressiveness, fighting, "hyperactivity," poor peer relationships, irresponsibility, lying, theft, truancy, poor school performance, runaway, inappropriate sexual activity, drug and alcohol use. As adults there is criminality, assaultiveness, self-defeating impulsivity, hedonism, promiscuity, unreliability, and crippling drug and alcohol abuse. They fail at work, change jobs frequently, go AWOL and receive dishonorable discharges from the service, are abusing parents and neglectful mates, can't maintain intimate interpersonal relationships, and spend time in jails and prisons. These patients are frequently, if temporarily, anxious and depressed (suicidal gestures) and are second only to patients with hysteria in the production of conversion symptoms. The behavior peaks in late adolescence and the early 20's with improvement in the 30's, although the patients rarely recover from the "lost years." Males are involved more severely, earlier, and more frequently (3% of population) - M:F = 5-10:1.

Their rearing is generally impaired by rejection, neglect, desertion, poverty, and inconsistent discipline - they are frequently illegitimate and unwanted. The parents are often criminals (30% of fathers), alcoholics (50% of fathers), and chronically unemployed. Male first degree relatives have an increased incidence of antisocial personality disorder, alcoholism, and drug abuse, and female relatives have associated Briquet's Syndrome. A genetic component is likely.[2-4]

No tests are diagnostic, although a 4-9 MMPI profile is common, and there is an increased incidence of nonspecific EEG abnormalities (increased slow-wave activity, etc). It is necessary to rule out primary drug and alcohol abuse (difficult, look for normal childhood behavior), schizophrenia (thought disorder present), OBS (disorientation, memory impairment), early mania, explosive disorder, and ADULT ANTISOCIAL BEHAVIOR (DSM-III-R p 359, V71.01). Several very specialized disorders of impulse control can also mimic this disorder: PATHOLOGICAL GAMBLING (DSM-III-R p 324, 312.31), KLEPTOMANIA (DSM-III-R p 322, 312.32), and PYROMANIA (DSM-III-R p 325, 312.33). The patients are resistant and manipulative - don't rely on the patient's report; check your data. They rarely seek help for personality change and treatment is difficult and often unsuccessful. Best results follow closely supervised inpatient care: utilize strong, frequent, and accurate confrontation of interpersonal behavior, particularly by peers.[5] Individual outpatient psychotherapy is of little value. The terms Antisocial P.D., sociopathy, and psychopathy generally are used synonymously.

HISTRIONIC P.D. (DSM-III-R p 348, 301.50)

Histrionic patients initially seem charming, likeable, lively, and seductive but gradually become seen as emotionally unstable, egocentric, immature, dependent, manipulative, excitement-seeking, and shallow. They demand attention, are exhibitionistic, and present a "caricature of femininity," yet have a limited ability to maintain stable, intimate interpersonal relationships with either sex. This common disorder occurs predominantly in women.[6] There is an association with depression, transient psychoses, substance abuse, and Conversion and (particularly) Somatization Disorders.[7] Suicidal gestures and attempts are common. Lesser impaired patients respond to psychotherapy.

## BORDERLINE P.D. (DSM-III-R p 346, 301.83)

These usually socially adapted patients have complex clinical presentations, including diverse combinations of anger, anxiety, intense and labile affect, brief disturbances in consciousness (eg, depersonalization, dissociation), chronic loneliness, boredom, a chronic sense of emptiness, volatile interpersonal relations, identity confusion, and impulsive behavior, including self-injury. Stress can precipitate a transient psychosis. Many other diagnoses are often suggested or can also be made; eg, depression, brief reactive psychosis, other personality disorders, cyclothymic disorder. This is a heterogeneous group, some of whom may be related genetically to affective disorders.[8] Psychological testing is useful. Be sure to rule out organic states such as mild delirium, psychomotor epilepsy, or use of LSD. Insight-oriented and supportive psychotherapies (and their combination) are often beneficial.[9,10] Low-dose antipsychotic agents (thioridazine 100-300 mg hs), antidepressants,[11] or lithium carbonate may help selected patients.[12,13]

## NARCISSISTIC P.D. (DSM-III-R p 349, 301.81)[14]

Although often symptom-free and well functioning, these patients are chronically dissatisfied due to a constant need for admiration and habitually unrealistic self-expectations. They are impulsive and anxious, have ideas of omnipotence and of being a "special person," become quickly dissatisfied with others, and maintain superficial, exploitative interpersonal relationships. Under stress and when their needs are not met, they may become depressed, develop somatic complaints, have brief psychotic episodes, or display extreme rage. Mixtures with other personality disorders are common. Long-term psychotherapy helps.

## PASSIVE-AGGRESSIVE P.D. (DSM-III-R p 356, 301.84)

These patients are irritating and infuriating. They are oppositional, resentful, and controlling and thus have few friends and significantly impaired social and occupational functioning. Their enormous hostility is expressed passively - by intentional inefficiency, negativism, stubbornness, procrastination, "forgetfulness," withdrawal, and somatic complaints. They are overdependent on other people and institutions, yet resist demands made on them, even if able to perform. This disorder is common, stable over time, and associated with episodes of anxiety and depression as well as alcoholism, drug dependency, and an "inability to cope." Long-term individual psychotherapy may be useful.

## PARANOID P.D. (DSM-III-R p 337, 301.00)

These aloof, emotionally cold people typically display unjustified suspiciousness, hypersensitivity to slights, jealousy, and a fear of intimacy. They tend to be grandiose, rigid, contentious, and litigious and are thus isolated and disliked. They accept criticism poorly, blaming others instead. This disorder may be associated with chronic CNS impairment, drug use (eg, amphetamines), and obsessive-compulsive states. Psychotic decompensation sometimes occurs, requiring major tranquilizers. They rarely seek treatment.

## SCHIZOID P.D. (DSM-III-R p 339, 301.20)

These are seclusive people who have little wish or capacity to form interpersonal relations, derive little pleasure from social contacts, and yet can perform well if left alone (eg, night watchman). They have a limited emotional range, daydream excessively, and are humorless and aloof. They do not appear to have an increased risk of developing schizophrenia as was previously thought. Treatment seems of little help.

## SCHIZOTYPAL P.D. (DSM-III-R p 340, 301.22)

In addition to having features of the schizoid, these people are "peculiar." They relate strange intrapsychic experiences, reason in odd ways, and are difficult to "get to know" yet none of these features reach psychotic proportions. Schizophrenia occurs with increased frequency in family members, suggesting that this condition is part of the "schizophrenic spectrum" of disorders.[15-17]

## OBSESSIVE COMPULSIVE P.D. (DSM-III-R p 354, 301.40)[18]

These patients, frequently successful men, are inhibited, stubborn, perfectionistic, judgmental, overly conscientious, rigid, and chronically anxious individuals who avoid intimacy and experience little pleasure from life. They are indecisive, yet demanding, and are often perceived as cold and reserved. They are at risk to develop obsessive compulsive disorder and depression. Psychotherapy can effect changes over time.

AVOIDANT P.D. (DSM-III-R p 351, 301.82)

This is a fairly common disorder: an exceedingly shy, lonely, hypersensitive individual with low self-esteem who would rather avoid personal contact than face any potential social disapproval, even though desperate for interpersonal involvement (as opposed to the schizoid person). These patients are troubled by anxiety and depression.

DEPENDENT P.D. (DSM-III-R p 353, 301.60)

These are excessively passive, unsure, isolated people who become abnormally dependent on one or more people. Initially acceptable, the behavior can become very controlling, appear hostile, and blend into a passive-aggressive style. It is more common in women and is likely to lead to anxiety and depression, particularly if the dependent relationship is threatened.

### ATTENTION DEFICIT DISORDER (Residual State)[19]
### (DSM-III-R p 50, 314.01)

ADDH is a disorder of children which can continue to produce problems well into adulthood and which has many features of a personality disorder.[20] These patients have been distractible, impulsive, quick-tempered, unable to tolerate stress, and restless since childhood. Their lability impairs interpersonal relations and job stability and results in frequent depressions. They are at risk for drug abuse and alcoholism. Differentiate from personality disorders, cyclothymic disorder (more recent onset), intermittent explosive disorder (normal between episodes), and primary depression. ADDH is most effectively treated with stimulants (eg, methylphenidate 10 mg PO tid) but use them very cautiously due to abuse potential.[21] (Propranolol may be an alternative.[22]) Combine with supportive psychotherapy.

REFERENCES

1.  Siever LJ, Coccaro ER, et al: Psychobiology of personality disorders: Pharmacologic implications. Psychopharm Bull 23:333-336, 1987.
2.  Mednick SA, Gabrielli WF, Hutchings B: Genetic influences in criminal convictions: Evidence from an adoption cohort. Science 224:891-894, 1984.
3.  Reitsma-Street M, Offord DR, Finch T: Pairs of same-sexed siblings discordant for antisocial behavior. Br J Psychiatry 146:415-423, 1985.
4.  Cadoret RJ, O'Gorman TW, Troughton E, Heywood E: Alco-

holism and antisocial personality. <u>Arch Gen Psychiatry</u> 42:161-167, 1985.
5. Gabbard GO, Coyne L: Predictors of response of antisocial patients to hospital treatment. <u>Hosp Community Psychiatry</u> 38:1181-1185, 1987.
6. Thompson DJ, Goldberg D: Hysterical personality disorder <u>Br J Psychiatry</u> 150:241-245, 1987.
7. Lilienfeld SO, Van Valkenburg C, Larntz K, Akiskal HS: The relationship of histrionic personality disorder to antisocial personality and somatization disorders. <u>Am J Psychiatry</u> 143:718-722, 1986.
8. Gunderson JG, Elliott GR: The interface between borderline personality disorder and affective disorder. <u>Am J Psychiatry</u> 142:277-288, 1985.
9. Waldinger RJ: Intensive psychodynamic therapy with borderline patients: An overview. <u>Am J Psychiatry</u> 144:267-274, 1987.
10. Tucker L, Bauer SF, Wagner S, et al: Long-term hospital treatment of borderline patients. <u>Am J Psychiatry</u> 144:1443-1448, 1987.
11. Cowdry RW, Gardner DL: Pharmacotherapy of borderline personality disorder. <u>Arch Gen Psychiatry</u> 45:111-119, 1988.
12. Soloff PH: A pharmacologic approach to the borderline patient. <u>Psychiatr Ann</u> 17:201-205, 1987.
13. Cowdry RW: Psychopharmacology of borderline personality disorder: A review. <u>J Clin Psychiatry</u> 48 (8, Suppl):15-22, 1987.
14. Goldstein WN: DSM-III and the narcissistic personality. <u>Am J Psychother</u> 39:4-16, 1985.
15. Jacobsberg LB, Hymowitz P, Barasch A, Frances AJ: Symptoms of schizotypal personality disorder. <u>Am J Psychiat</u> 143:1222-1227, 1986.
16. McGlashan TH: Schizotypal personality disorder. <u>Arch Gen Psychiatry</u> 43:329-334, 1986.
17. Hymowitz P, Frances A, Jacobsberg LB, et al: Neuroleptic treatment of schizotypal personality disorders. <u>Compr Psychiatry</u> 27:267-271, 1986.
18. Pollak J: Obsessive-compulsive personality. <u>J Pers Disorders</u> 1:248-262, 1987.
19. Weiss G, Hechtman LT: <u>Hyperactive Children Grown Up</u>. New York, The Guilford Press, 1986.
20. Gittelman R, Mannuzza S, Shenker R: Hyperactive boys almost grown up. <u>Arch Gen Psychiatry</u> 42:937-947, 1985.
21. Wender PH, Reimher FW, Wood D, Ward M: A controlled study of methylphenidate in the treatment of attention deficit disorder, residual type, in adults. <u>Am J Psychiatry</u> 142:547-552, 1985.
22. Mattes JA: Propranolol for adults with temper outbursts and residual attention deficit disorder. <u>J Clin Psychopharmacol</u> 6:299-302, 1986.

# Chapter 19

# Psychosexual Disorders

These disorders are often first brought to the attention of the general physician. The three distinct categories are:

- Psychosexual dysfunction - inhibition in sexual desire and/or psychophysiological performance.
- Paraphilia - sexual arousal to deviant stimuli.
- Gender identity disorders - patient feels like the opposite sex.

PSYCHOSEXUAL DYSFUNCTION

Clinically observable features of the normal human <u>sexual response cycle</u> consist of:

<u>Stage I</u>: <u>Excitement</u> (minutes to hours)
  Males - psychological arousal and penile erection.
  Females - psychological arousal, vaginal lubrication, nipple erection, and vasocongestion of the external genitalia.

<u>Stage II</u>: <u>Plateau</u> (seconds to 3 min)
  Males - several drops of fluid appear at head of penis (from Cowper's gland).
  Females - tightening of outer third of vagina, breast engorgement.

<u>Stage III</u>: <u>Orgasm</u> (5-15 sec)
  Males - ejaculation, involuntary muscular contraction (eg, pelvis); followed by a refractory period.
  Females - contractions of outer third of vagina, some involuntary pelvic thrusting; may be multiple.

<u>Stage IV</u>: <u>Resolution</u>
  Males - relaxation, detumescence, sense of well-being.
  Females - relaxation, detumescence, sense of well-being.

Patients (or their partners) may complain of decreased sexual desire and/or of one or more specific abnormalities of the response cycle. The dysfunctions may be situational, partial rather than complete, and primary or acquired. The phases usually occur in a stepwise fashion, but that is not mandatory - identify the stage involved. Often there are marital problems, unrealistic expectations, long-standing personal "hangups," chronic difficulty establishing and maintaining intimate interpersonal relations, etc. Identify these through history and psychiatric evaluation. <u>Always</u> evaluate carefully for organic causes (particularly with impotence and dyspareunia). Organic conditions tend to be chronic and independent of the situation.

Treatment should be global with an emphasis on intimacy and relationship - not just technique.[1] Identify and treat psychosocial causes with dynamic psychotherapy, marital therapy, hypnotherapy,[2] and group therapy. Sedatives may help temporarily if anxiety is prominent. Even purely physical causes often have significant associated secondary interpersonal problems that must be addressed once the medical condition has been corrected. A good prognosis is associated with acute, recent dysfunction in a psychologically healthy patient with good past sexual functioning and strong sexual interests. Some relationships between partners are sufficiently hostile and destructive that, unless other matters are resolved, prognosis is very poor for a correction of the psychosexual dysfunction.

The "new sex therapy" (Masters and Johnson) uses individual psychotherapy, couples therapy, education, behavior modification techniques, and often a male-female therapist pair (dual-sex therapy). Their numerous techniques have wide applicability with sexual dysfunctions and should be considered for use. Many of these methods center on decreasing a patient's (or couple's) anxiety about making love. Essential principles include:

- Good communication with full exploration of sexual feelings.
- Training in specific stimulation and coital techniques (through "pleasuring sessions").
- Emphasis on the couple as a pleasure-giving team.
- Prohibition of intercourse early in therapy (to reduce performance anxiety).
- Emphasis on multimodal sensory pleasure (touch, sight, sound) and sensory awareness exercises.
- Insistence that physiological responses be ignored (erection, etc. - "Don't worry about it; it will happen").

MALE ERECTILE DISORDER; FEMALE SEXUAL AROUSAL DISORDER (DSM-III-R p 294, 302.72):

Males (Impotence): The failure to reach or maintain a complete erection in at least 75% of attempts.[3]  Two forms exist:

Primary impotence - Patient has never maintained an erection.
Secondary impotence - Patient has lost the ability: may be person or situation specific (selective impotence).

Impotence is a common sexual complaint of men - predominantly the secondary form.  It is not a "natural consequence" of aging.  Some feel 90% of cases are psychogenic, but recent studies emphasize the frequency of an organic etiology.[4]  Organic causes include:

- Disorders of the hypothalamic-pituitary-gonadal axis: Low serum testosterone level due to primary testicular hypofunction, pituitary tumors, etc.
- Endocrine: Hyperthyroidism (may have elevated testosterone), hyperprolactinemia, diabetes mellitus, acromegaly, Addison's disease, myxedema.
- Medication: Tricyclic antidepressants, MAOIs, major tranquilizers (particularly thioridazine), cholinergic blockers, antihypertensive drugs (particularly adrenergic blockers and false sympathetic neurotransmitters), estrogens, ethyl alcohol (alcoholism), addictive drugs (particularly narcotics and amphetamines), anticholinergic drugs.
- Illness: Any illness may cause impotence temporarily but particularly chronic debilitating disease, chronic renal disease, peripheral vascular disease, and local physical and neurological disorders.

Psychogenic causes include depression, anxiety (over cardiac status, performance, etc), hostility and marital conflict, etc.

First identify any physical cause - do a complete medical evaluation (look for physical illness, absent beard and body hair, small testes, gynecomastia), get serum testosterone (then further hormonal studies if low).  Early morning sleeping erection or occasional successful intercourse does not rule out an organic etiology, nor does a normal pattern of nocturnal penile tumescence (NPT - erections during REM sleep) rule in a psychogenic etiology, although most (all?) psychogenic cases have normal NPT.[5]  Treat medical causes (often curative).  Follow with global therapy, if needed. Therapy includes allowing the female to play the dominant role and insisting on a gradual shift from foreplay to intercourse.  Perhaps 30-40% will not improve.

Females (Frigidity): An inadequate genital sexual response (failure to reach the excitement or plateau stages) although the woman may find sexual activity pleasurable.  It often reflects personality or marital problems, but other specific causes include poor physical health, alcoholism, fatigue, depression, fear of pregnancy, and a postpartum state. Treat the couple.

PREMATURE EJACULATION (DSM-III-R p 295, 302.75):

The ejaculation occurs before the patient wishes it to (usually before his partner reaches orgasm) (40% of all patients with sexual complaints; 30% of all males).  Cause is usually functional and secondary to anxiety (determine the source of the anxiety).  It is much more common in stressful marriages.  "Squeeze technique" effective - just prior to ejaculation, woman squeezes head of glans.  This is coupled with the man practicing imagery control.  The young and vigorous male may benefit from 1% Nupercaine ointment applied to the coronal ridge and frenulum.

INHIBITED MALE ORGASM (Retarded Ejaculation) (DSM-III-R p 295, 302.74):

The patient fails to ejaculate.  Differentiate from retrograde ejaculation ("ejaculation" into the bladder - due to organic factors, eg, anticholinergic drugs, prostatectomy).  Some patients can have an orgasm only under certain conditions (eg, with masturbation, with a stranger) - identify the circumstances in which orgasm can take place. Psychological causes include lack of interest (eg, primary sexual deviation), anxiety, compulsive personality, marriage stresses, and sexual "hangups."  Physical causes include medication (guanethidine, methyldopa, phenothiazines - particularly thioridazine, MAOIs), GU surgery, and lower spinal cord impairment (eg, parkinsonism, syringomyelia). First train the patient to ejaculate by himself, then treat the interpersonal relationship - individual psychotherapy is often needed.  The technique of the female self-inserting her partner's penis may be effective.

INHIBITED FEMALE ORGASM (Anorgasmia) (DSM-III-R p 294, 302.73):

The patient persistently fails to reach orgasm during intercourse.  There are primary (5% of cases) and secondary forms, although be aware that many women become orgasmic as they get older (peak at age 35).  There may be a hormonal basis in some, but most causes are psychological. This condition is very situation specific - some women never have orgasm in spite of ample excitement (10%); others have orgasm only with masturbation, still others require clitoral manipulation during intercourse, and a minority of women can have an orgasm with intercourse alone. Psychotherapy often involves first training the woman to have an orgasm by herself, then treating the couple.

DYSPAREUNIA (DSM-III-R p 295, 302.76):

Pain with intercourse. It often is related to a physical condition (50%): cervical or vaginal infection or anatomic abnormality, endometriosis, tumor, or other pelvic pathology. Anxiety about sexual activity (for a variety of reasons) can produce pelvic muscle tightening and pain but, remember, pain from organic causes can produce anxiety which exacerbates the pain. Also, dyspareunia can produce vaginismus, and vaginismus can produce dyspareunia.

VAGINISMUS (DSM-III-R p 295, 306.51):

The patient has an involuntary spasm during coitus of the muscles surrounding the outer third of the vagina which prevents penile entrance. It may be related to physical causes producing pain - dyspareunia. Psychological causes include past sexual trauma (eg, rape), a hostile marital relationship (perhaps from a vicious cycle), or sexual "hangups." Individual therapy and relaxation techniques are usually required. Hegar dilators (size increased over 3-5 days) may be useful.

HYPOACTIVE SEXUAL DESIRE DISORDER (DSM-III-R p 293, 302.71):

Common (20% of population, more F than M) and difficult to treat. It may present as inhibited excitement or inhibited orgasm - don't be misled. Causes usually are functional. It varies with time, the sexual partner, depression, anxiety, and the stresses of the relationship. It may reflect a fear of intimacy or pregnancy, a passive-aggressive personality style, strong religious orthodoxy, or homosexuality, among others. Individual or couple therapy is useful.

SEXUAL AVERSION DISORDER (DSM-III-R p 293, 302.79):

Similar to hypoactive sexual desire disorder but represents an active avoidance of sexual activity. Patient has often been sensitized by past (unpleasant) experiences.

PARAPHILIA (Sexual Deviation)

These patients become sexually excited only by unusual or bizarre stimuli (practices or fantasies). The particular type of arousing stimulus determines the diagnosis. Orgastic release usually occurs by masturbation during or following the event. Etiology is uncertain - possibly biological, learned, and/or dynamic-instinctual. Most types are rare (courts see them most frequently), although physicians will occasionally encounter them. Men predominate although women may display sadomasochism, voyeurism, exhibitionism,[6] and homosexuality.

These patients may not be troubled by their desires (ego syntonic) and thus are difficult to treat, although depression, anxiety, and guilt do occasionally occur. These conditions frequently coexist with personality disorders, alcohol and drug abuse, and other psychiatric disorders - treat them. The patients often have impaired interpersonal relationships, particularly heterosexual relations.

Psychotherapy is frequently unsuccessful. Specific behavior modification techniques to eliminate the deviation are most successful (eg, aversion - covert conditioning) although these must be paired with a more global retraining program.[7] Hypersexual states and some other sexual deviations may benefit from medroxyprogesterone acetate (Depo-Provera) or cyproterone acetate.[8]

PEDOPHILIA (DSM-III-R p 284, 302.20):

These patients repeatedly approach prepubertal children sexually (touch, explore, mutually masturbate; occasionally intercourse). They are usually timid, inadequate males who know the child involved (a neighbor, relative). Three general types are recognized: heterosexual pedophilia (prefers preadolescent girls), homosexual pedophilia (prefers early teenage boys - most resistant to therapy), and mixed pedophilia (younger children, either sex). Don't confuse with child molestation due to decreased impulse control (eg, OBS, intoxication, retardation, psychosis) or a one-time event (eg, due to loneliness or following a marital crisis). There may be biological,[9] familial[10] roots. Behavior modification is the treatment of choice.

EXHIBITIONISM (DSM-III-R p 282, 302.40):

Usually timid males who become sexually aroused by exposing their genitals to an unsuspecting female (adult or child). They are only rarely aggressive. They may masturbate during the exposure and needs a shock reaction from the female for satisfaction. Very resistant to treatment.

Less frequent paraphilias include:

<u>FETISHISM</u> (DSM-III-R p 282, 302.81): Sexual arousal to inanimate objects. May be combined with other sexual preferences.

<u>FROTTEURISM</u> (DSM-III-R p 283, 302.89): Arousal from touching or fondling a nonconsenting person, usually in a crowded place where escape is possible. Usually teenage or young adult males.

<u>TRANSVESTIC FETISHISM</u> (DSM-III-R p 288, 302.30): Aroused by female clothing and cross-dressing. Don't confuse with transsexualism (the wish to <u>become</u> a female) or effeminate homosexuality (cross-dressing to attract others - not to produce arousal itself).

<u>VOYEURISM</u> (DSM-III-R p 289, 302.82): Sexual arousal by watching unsuspecting people who are naked or sexually active. Masturbation usually takes place concurrently.

<u>SEXUAL MASOCHISM</u> (DSM-III-R p 286, 302.83): Arousal from being sexually bound, beaten, humiliated, etc.

<u>SEXUAL SADISM</u> (DSM-III-R p 287, 302.84): Sexual excitement following inflicting psychological or physical (sexual or nonsexual) harm on a consenting or nonconsenting partner. Some rapists deserve this diagnosis.

## GENDER IDENTITY DISORDER

<u>TRANSSEXUALISM</u> (DSM-III-R p 74, 302.50):

These adults have experienced at least two continuous years of discomfort about their anatomic sex and have a desire to change their sex. Males predominate, and their clinical characteristics are more variable. They may have experienced the discomfort since childhood or only recently. They may be homosexual, heterosexual, or have little sexual interest.[11] Many have an effeminate appearance and cross-dress. Females with this disorder are usually homosexual and masculine appearing.

Etiology is unclear - it may be predominantly biological and/or psychological, although the mother/child bond always appears disturbed (often too close). Check karyotype and sex hormone levels. These patients are very likely to have personality disorders, particularly of the borderline type. The course is chronic, and there is significant risk for depression, suicide, anxiety, and genital self-mutilation. Rule out effeminate homosexuality (patient does <u>not</u> want to be the other sex), schizophrenia, and hermaphroditism.

Treat with supportive psychotherapy and feminizing-masculinizing hormones. Sex change surgery (castration, penectomy, vaginoplasty, phalloplasty) is falling out of fashion: it is irreversible and the results appear no better (perhaps worse) than psychotherapy alone. There have been isolated reports of gender identity changes with intensive behavior modification.[12]

## HOMOSEXUALITY

Homosexuality (an arousal to and preference for sexual relations with adults of the same sex) is not currently considered to be a mental disorder, except if the patient is chronically distressed by it ("ego-dystonic homosexuality"; classed as SEXUAL DISORDER NOS, DSM-III-R p 296, 302.90). It may be a temporary phase during adolescence.

Homosexuality is common in the USA - 5-10% of males and perhaps 2-4% of females. In spite of numerous theoretical explanations,[13] the cause(s) is unknown. There may be congenital, prenatal, familial,[14] and/or biological[15] etiologies for some but environmental factors probably dominate in the choice of a sexual orientation.

Ego-dystonic homosexuals have internalized a negative attitude toward homosexual behavior and chronically and consistently want to change. They suffer from depression, anxiety, and shame. Most psychotherapy is of little value. However, specialized behavior modification techniques (concentrating on decreasing deviant arousal, stimulating heterosexual arousal, and teaching heterosocial skills) may help as many as 50%.

## REFERENCES

1.  Cole M: Sex therapy - A critical appraisal. Br J Psychiatry 147:337-351, 1985.
2.  Araoz DL: Uses of hypnosis in the treatment of psychogenic sexual dysfunctions. Psychiatr Ann 16:102-105, 1986.
3.  Bancroft J, Wu FC: Erectile impotence. Br Med J 290: 1566-1568, 1985.
4.  Spark RF, White RA, Connolly PB: Impotence is not always psychogenic. JAMA 243:750-755, 1980.
5.  Karacan I: Nocturnal penile tumescence as a biologic marker in assessing erectile dysfunction. Psychosomatics 23:349-360, 1982.

6.  Grob CS: Female exhibitionism. <u>J Nerv Ment Diseases</u> 173: 253–256, 1985.
7.  Barlow DH: The treatment of sexual deviation: Toward a comprehensive behavioral approach, in Calhoun K, Adams H, Mitchell K: <u>Innovative Treatment Methods in Psychopathology</u>. New York, John Wiley & Sons, 1974.
8.  Berlin FS, Meinecke CF: Treatment of sex offenders with antiandrogenic medication. <u>Am J Psychiat</u> 138:601, 1981.
9.  Gaffney GR, Berlin FS: Is there hypothalamic-pituitary-gonadal dysfunction in paedophilia? <u>Br J Psychiatry</u> 145:657–660, 1984.
10. Gaffney GR, Lurie SF, Berlin FS: Is there familial transmission of pedophilia? <u>J Nerv Ment Disease</u> 172:546–548, 1984.
11. Green R. Gender identity in childhood and later sexual orientation. <u>Am J Psychiatry</u> 142:339–341, 1985.
12. Barlow DH, Abel GG, Blanchard EB: Gender identity change in transsexuals. <u>Arch Gen Psychiatry</u> 36:1001, 1979.
13. Stoller RJ, Herdt GH: Theories of origins of male homosexuality. <u>Arch Gen Psychiatry</u> 42:399–404, 1985.
14. Pillard RC, Weinrich JD:L Evidence of familial nature of male homosexuality. <u>Arch Gen Psychiatry</u> 43:808–812, 1986.
15. Gladue BA, Green R, Hellman RE: Neuroendocrine response to estrogen and sexual orientation. <u>Science</u> 225:1496–1499, 1984.

# Chapter 20

# Sleep Disturbances

Sleep disorders are extremely common - 10-20% of the population have had trouble sleeping within the past year; 3-4% have had hypersomnia.

Current classification and understanding of sleep problems rests on recent advances in knowledge of normal sleep.[1] Much of this has been obtained through physiological (sleep, EEG, EMG, etc) measures of patients in sleep laboratories.

## NORMAL SLEEP

Normal sleep is cyclical (4-5 cycles/night) and active, not passive. Distinct stages (measured by EEG) occur, and a person passes stepwise through them. Patients enter stage 1, descend by steps over approximately 30 min to stage 4, plateau there for 30-40 min, and then ascend to lighter stages (1-2) in order to enter REM sleep 90-100 minutes after falling asleep. Then the cycle repeats. As the night progresses, the REM periods lengthen, stage 4 disappears, and the sleep is generally lighter. The length of time spent in any one stage varies in a characteristic fashion with age. The significance of each stage is not known.

Waking - alpha waves (8-12 cps)

NREM Sleep (Nonrapid eye movement) - low level of activity: lowered BP, heart rate, temperature, and respiratory rate. Good muscle tone and slow, drifting eye movements.

Stage 1 - lightest sleep, a transition stage; low voltage, desynchronized waves.
Stage 2 - sleep spindles (13-15 cps) and high spikes (K complexes).
Stage 3 - some delta waves (high voltage at 0.5-2.5 cps).
Stage 4 - deepest sleep, mostly in first half of night; mostly delta waves.

REM Sleep - active sleep characterized by rapid synchronous eye movement, twitching of facial and extremity muscles, penile erections, and variation in pulse, BP, and respiratory rate. Muscular paralysis (absent tone) is present. Depth is similar to stage 2. Dreaming can occur in several stages but is most common in REM sleep.

For clinical purposes, patients with sleep disorders can be divided into those presenting with complaints of insomnia or hypersomnia. In each category, there are several distinct syndromes which must be ruled out.

INSOMNIA

(PRIMARY INSOMNIA, DSM-III-R p 301, 307.42)

Sleep laboratory studies usually are not needed for diagnosis and treatment. Take a good history of the sleep problem, including the 24-hr sleep-wake cycle. Identify the pattern: trouble falling asleep, trouble staying asleep (frequent awakenings), early morning awakenings. Inquire about life stresses, drug and alcohol use, marital and family problems.[2,3] Consider the following:

- Is the insomnia simply normal sleep?
    a. Some "insomniacs" get ample sleep (pseudoinsomnia). The problems are psychological and lie elsewhere - use psychotherapy and reassurance about the adequacy of the sleep.
    b. Sleep time lessens with age - explain to concerned elderly. Help them avoid a complicating "worry over sleeplessness" cycle.
    c. Some patients are substance abusers seeking drugs.

- Is the insomnia transient (situational insomnia)?
    Patient usually has trouble falling asleep. Identify the stress. Help the patient correct and deal with it. Consider the time-limited (1-2 wk) use of sleeping medication (eg, flurazepam, 15-30 mg, PO, HS; triazolam, 0.25-0.5 mg, PO, HS).

- Is there a chronic, minor psychiatric illness?
    Insomnia is due most frequently to chronic depression and/or anxiety. Antisocial and obsessive-compulsive features are also common among these patients. They often self-medicate, producing more insomnia. Insomniacs often have trouble expressing aggressive feelings, internalize their problems, and/or have a fear of losing control. The resulting problem is usually sleep onset

in type with decreased stage 4 sleep. These patients
must be differentiated from those with <u>conditioned
insomnia</u>, in which the patient has inadvertently trained
himself to stay awake at bedtime.

- Is there a major psychiatric illness?  (<u>INSOMNIA RELATED
  TO ANOTHER MENTAL DISORDER</u>, DSM-III-R p 300, 307.42)
  a. <u>Acute psychosis</u>: Often produces major sleep disrup-
     tion - treat with antipsychotics.
  b. <u>Mania or hypomania</u>: Very short sleep time - use
     antipsychotics or lithium.
  c. <u>Major Depression</u>: Usually there is early morning
     awakening, but frequent awakenings during the night
     are also common.  REM sleep begins very quickly.
     Treat the depression (tricyclics decrease REM
     sleep).

- Is there a medical problem?  (<u>INSOMNIA RELATED TO A KNOWN
  ORGANIC FACTOR</u>, DSM-III-R p 300, 780.50)
  a. Chronic pain and related anxiety and depression - eg,
     back pain, headache, arthritis, asthma, nocturnal
     angina (increased pains during REM sleep), duodenal
     ulcer.
  b. Hyperthyroidism, epilepsy, general paresis.
  c. Is the patient simply worried about a medical
     problem?

- Is there substance use or abuse?  Very common so always
  inquire.
  a. Alcohol - The most common self-prescribed hypnotic.
     Chronic use produces fragmented sleep.
  b. Hypnotic medication - Often prescribed by physicians
     for insomnia.  Tolerance develops to each of them
     with, ironically, sleep disruption ("sleeping-pill
     insomnia").  Severe rebound insomnia usually occurs
     with withdrawal - least with the long acting benzo-
     diazepines (eg, flurazepam).  Treatment <u>must</u> begin
     with withdrawal of the medication - at the rate of
     one therapeutic dose/wk.
  c. Caffeine - patients often overlook.  Ask.
  d. Cigarettes (nicotine) can stimulate.
  e. Amphetamines, methylphenidate, hallucinogens, amino-
     phylline, ephedrine, and steroids all can interrupt
     sleep.

- Is there <u>sleep cycle disruption</u>?  (<u>SLEEP-WAKE SCHEDULE
  DISORDER</u>, DSM-III-R p 305, 307.45)  Sleepiness may
  become out of phase if there is "jet lag" or night shift
  work.  Usually self-limited.

- Is there <u>Nocturnal Myoclonus</u>? Restless sleep with frequent awakenings secondary to muscle contractions
(jerks) in the legs. Ask the bed partner. However,
recent evidence suggests that nocturnal myoclonus plays
little role in producing insomnia. There is no assured
treatment but consider a trial of a small dose of
clonazepam (0.5-2 mg) or nitrazepam[4] at bedtime.

- Is it caused by the <u>Restless Legs Syndrome</u>? Legs feel
"uncomfortable." Relieved by moving; clonazepam[5] may
help.

- Are there frequent <u>nightmares</u> (<u>DREAM ANXIETY DISORDER</u>,
DSM-III-R P 308, 307.47), <u>night terrors</u> (pavor nocturnus
- <u>SLEEP TERROR DISORDER</u>, DSM-III-R p 310, 307.46), or
<u>sleepwalking</u> (somnambulism - <u>SLEEPWALKING DISORDER</u>, DSM-
III-R p 311, 307.46)?[6]
a. Nightmares (REM sleep) can be chronic and disruptive
- psychotherapy <u>may</u> help.
b. Night terrors (stage 4 sleep) occur early in the
night in children, are terrifying to observers, but
are not remembered by the patient. They usually
disappear with adulthood. Some respond to low doses
of minor tranquilizers (eg, diazepam).
c. Somnambulism (stage 4 sleep) can persist into adult-
hood.[7] The patient's behavior appears strange to an
observer - there is marked clouding of consciousness. Protect the patient from his actions. Diazepam, 15 mg, HS, or imipramine 50 mg, HS may help.

GENERAL TREATMENT OF INSOMNIA[8,9]

1. Rule out, or treat, specific syndromes.
2. Maintain a regular bedtime. Keep room dark and quiet.
Develop a "sleeping ritual." Arise promptly in the
morning.
3. Regular exercise during the day helps. Avoid vigorous
mental activities late in the evening. Try a bedtime
snack but <u>don't</u> drink alcohol after supper.
4. Provide support and reassurance. Psychotherapy may be
essential.[10]
5. Try relaxation techniques: progressive relaxation, biofeedback, self-hypnosis, meditation, etc.
6. Use sedative-hypnotics for a limited time only (see
chapter 23). Most hypnotic medications (exception is
flurazepam) become ineffective within two weeks if used
nightly. Try initially for one week in an effort to
establish a successful sleep pattern (eg, flurazepam 15-
30 mg, PO, HS but be aware that flurazepam can produce a
gradual worsening of psychomotor performance). If used
longer than a week, introduce drug holidays and don't

exceed recommended dosage. L-tryptophan (a serotonin precursor in food) may relieve insomnia in a few patients.

## HYPERSOMNIA

(<u>PRIMARY HYPERSOMNIA</u>, DSM-III-R p 305, 780.54)

1. Hypersomnia is associated more commonly with purely psychological causes (<u>HYPERSOMNIA RELATED TO ANOTHER MENTAL DISORDER</u>, DSM-III-R p 303, 307.44): depression (particularly in younger patients), anxiety, and withdrawal. It is a means of escape from stress. These patients usually sleep excessively at night rather than during the day.

2. Does the patient have <u>NARCOLEPSY</u>?[11] Narcolepsy is a lifelong disorder which usually begins at puberty, is more common in males, probably has a genetic component, occurs with a frequency of about 1/2000, and is characterized by the <u>narcoleptic tetrad</u>:

   a. Daytime <u>sleep attacks</u> - The patient falls abruptly asleep (REM activity on EEG) during the day, in spite of efforts to stay awake. He usually sleeps for several minutes and wakes refreshed but may have from several to more than 100 episodes during a day. The attacks are likely to occur while he is active and engaged and can be embarrassing or dangerous (during a speech, driving a car).
   b. <u>Cataplexy</u> - A sudden loss of muscle tone which may result in a fall to the ground or just a feeling of weakness. It usually is precipitated by a strong emotion (eg, anger, laughter) and can last from seconds to many minutes. The patient is conscious throughout.
   c. <u>Hypnagogic hallucinations</u> - Dreamlike and often frightening auditory and/or visual hallucinations which occur as the patient falls asleep or as he awakens (hypnopompic).
   d. <u>Sleep paralysis</u> - A flaccid, generalized paralysis lasting for several seconds in a fully conscious patient, either while waking or falling asleep, and accompanied by a strong sense of fear. It resolves spontaneously or when the patient is touched or his name is called.

Some patients suffer only sleep attacks, many also have cataplexy (more than two-thirds), and less than 50% also display hallucinations or sleep paralysis. 10-20% of patients have the complete tetrad. Most patients with narcolepsy also have disturbed nighttime sleep with frequent awakenings and nightmares.

TREATMENT:
- Train the patient to avoid dangerous occupations and precipitating stimuli. Planned daytime naps can help.
- Sleep attacks - methylphenidate (Ritalin), 5-10 mg, PO, tid. Insist on occasional drug holidays. This treatment is unsatisfactory, but psychopharmacological advances are on the horizon.[12,13]
- Narcolepsy with cataplexy - add imipramine, 10-25 mg, PO, tid (suppresses REM sleep).
- Consider sedation for insomnia (ie, benzodiazepines).

3. Does the patient have SLEEP APNEA?[14] This serious abnormality of nighttime respiratory function can cause long-standing daytime sleepiness, particularly during quiet times (unlike narcolepsy), but is not a likely cause of insomnia. It occurs in three types: (1) a few patients briefly cease nighttime breathing efforts (Central Sleep Apnea), (2) the majority struggle to draw air through nose and mouth passageways which have markedly increased sleep-induced resistance (Obstructive Sleep Apnea), and (3) some suffer both phenomena (Mixed S.A.). There may be from 30 to several hundred episodes each night lasting from 10 seconds to more than 2 min. Males are affected 20:1.[15] The patients may experience a variety of symptoms, including frequent awakenings, impaired libido, loud snoring, sleepwalking, hypertension, headaches, depression, and intellectual and personality changes. Only a few cases will demonstrate anatomical abnormalities of upper airway structures. In serious chronic cases pulmonary hypertension, right heart failure, and/or cardiac arrhythmias may occur.

   No treatment has been clearly effective for Central Sleep Apnea. A permanent tracheostomy may be dramatically successful in Obstructive Sleep Apnea, but try weight loss and medication (theophylline, pemoline, thioridazine) first. Hypnotics can further compromise nighttime breathing - don't use them.

4. Rule out current use of sedative drugs or rebound in chronic amphetamine users.

5. Rule out medical conditions (HYPERSOMNIA RELATED TO A KNOWN ORGANIC FACTOR, DSM-III-R p 303, 780.50): eg, myxedema, hypercapnia, any brain tumor but particularly those involving the mesencephalon and walls of the 3rd ventricle, seizures, cerebrovascular disease, hypoglycemia. Severe hypersomnia with marked postawakening

confusion occurs with both the Pickwickian syndrome (obesity and respiratory insufficiency) and the Kleine-Levin syndrome (attacks of hyperphagia, hypersomnia, and hypersexuality).

## REFERENCES

1. Coleman RM, Roffwarg HP, Kennedy SJ, et al: Sleep-wake disorders based on a polysomnographic diagnosis. JAMA 247:997-1003, 1982.
2. Mendelson WB, James SP, Garnett D, et al: A psychophysiological study of insomnia. Psychiatry Res 19: 267-284, 1986.
3. Kales JD, Kales A, Bixler EO, et al: Biopsychobehavioral correlates of insomnia. Am J Psychiatry 141:1371-1376, 1984.
4. Moldofsky H, Tullis C, Quance G, Lue FA: Nitrazepam for periodic movements in sleep. Can J Neurol Sci 13: 52-54, 1986.
5. Boghen D, Lamothe L, Elie R, et al: The treatment of the restless legs syndrome with clonazepam. Can J Neurol Sci 13:245-247, 1986.
6. Vela-Bueno A, Soldatos CR, Julius DA: Parasomnias: Sleepwalking, night terrors, and nightmares. Psychiatr Ann 17:465-449, 1987.
7. Berlin RM, Qayyum U: Sleepwalking: Diagnosis and treatment through the life cycle. Psychosomatics 27:755-760, 1986.
8. Kales A, Kales JD: Evaluation and Treatment of Insomnia New York, Oxford University Press, 1984.
9. Mellinger GD, Balter MB, Uhlenhuth EH: Insomnia and its treatment. Arch Gen Psychiatry 42:225-232, 1985.
10. Berlin RM: Psychotherapeutic treatment of chronic insomnia. Am J Psychotherapy 39:68-74, 1985.
11. Manfredi RL, Cadieux RJ: Sleep disorders of organic origin: Narcolepsy and sleep apnea. Psychiatr Ann 17: 470-478, 1987.
12. Scharf MB, Brown D, Woods M, et al: The effects and effectiveness of gamma-hydroxybutyrate in patients with narcolepsy. J Clin Psychiatry 46:222-225, 1985.
13. Salin-Pascual R, Ruente J, Fernandez-Guardiola A: Effects of clonidine in narcolepsy. J Clin Psychiatry 46:528-531, 1985.
14. Kwentus J, Schulz SC, Fairman P, Isrow L: Sleep apnea: A review. Psychosomatics 26:713-724, 1985.
15. Ancoli-Israel S, Kripke DF, Mason W: Characteristics of obstructive and central sleep apnea in the elderly. Biol Psychiatry 22:741-750, 1987.

# Chapter 21

# Mental Retardation

There are 2-2.5,000,000 mentally retarded persons in the USA (1% of population) of whom 80-85% are only mildly retarded.   Retardation requires a decreased intellectual functioning (as measured by standard IQ tests), but its presentation is modified by social and occupational adaptation, age and maturation, and the environmental and cultural setting.[1]   Adults with intellectual impairment which developed before age 18 have <u>retardation</u>, and those developing it after age 18 have <u>dementia</u>.

## CLASSIFICATION

<u>MILD MENTAL RETARDATION</u> (DSM-III-R p 32, 317.00) - IQ 50-70. Usually recognized when they enter school - requires special education.   85% of the retarded (but its prevalence decreases markedly with adulthood).   The majority become self-supporting.

<u>MODERATE MENTAL RETARDATION</u> (DSM-III-R p 32, 318.00) - IQ 35-50.   10% of all retarded.   They are trainable, can learn simple work skills, and can be partly self-supporting in sheltered settings.

<u>SEVERE MENTAL RETARDATION</u> (DSM-III-R p 33, 318.10) - IQ 20-35.   4% of all retarded.   They are capable of simple speech but require institutional or other intensely supportive care.

<u>PROFOUND MENTAL RETARDATION</u> (DSM-III-R p 33, 318.20) - IQ below 20.   1% of all retarded. They are totally dependent upon others for survival.

A presumably retarded patient who is untestable is considered to have <u>UNSPECIFIED MENTAL RETARDATION</u> (DSM-III-R p 33, 319.00).

## CAUSES

Distinct causes (usually biological) are identified for only 25% of patients, and those occur predominantly in the moderately-to-profoundly retarded patients.[2,3] The rest appear to be due to environmental factors with an uncertain polygenic contribution in some cases. Moderate-to-profound retardation is distributed uniformly across social classes, while mild retardation occurs primarily in the lower classes.

Major biological causes include:

Chromosomal abnormalities - numerous types including Down's Syndrome (mongolism, trisomy 21),[4] Cri Du Chat Syndrome, Klinefelter's Syndrome (XXY), Turner's Syndrome (XO/XX).

Dominant genetic inheritance - Neurofibromatosis (Von Recklinghausen's Disease), Huntington's Chorea, Marfan's Syndrome, Sturge-Weber Syndrome, tuberous sclerosis.

Metabolic disorders - Phenylketonuria (PKU), Hartnup Disease, fructose intolerance, galactosemia, Wilson's Disease, a variety of lipid disorders, hypothyroidism, hypoglycemia.

Prenatal disorders - maternal rubella (particularly in the 1st trimester), syphilis, toxoplasmosis, or diabetes; maternal alcohol abuse (Fetal Alcohol Syndrome) and use of some drugs (eg, thalidomide); toxemia of pregnancy; erythroblastosis fetalis; maternal malnutrition.

Birth trauma - difficult delivery with physical trauma and/or anoxia, prematurity.

Brain trauma - tumors, infection (particularly encephalitis, neonatal meningitis), accidents, poisons (eg, lead, mercury), hydrocephalus, numerous types of cranial abnormalities.

Social causes include substandard education, environmental deprivation, childhood abuse and neglect, restricted activity.

Rule out Specific and Pervasive Developmental Disorders, dementia, and Residual Schizophrenia. Rule out BORDERLINE INTELLECTUAL FUNCTIONING (DSM-III-R p 359, V40.00). Look for associated psychiatric or neurological syndromes.

## TREATMENT AND PROGNOSIS

Most mildly retarded individuals demonstrate significantly improved functioning with education and a supportive environment. They are at risk for adjustment reaction, depression, psychotic reactions, and behavioral disturbances

2° to a negative self-image. Treat the patient with supportive, reality-oriented psychotherapy. Determine the patient's coping style and temperamental strengths and encourage them but don't demand too much. Simple behavior modification techniques may be very effective and should be part of any treatment program.

Consider psychopharmacology in patients with psychiatric syndromes.[5] Low doses of minor or major tranquilizers may help behavior problems (eg, aggressiveness) - don't over-use (It's easy to do).[6] Lithium or propranolol[7] may moderate self-abuse and aggression in some cases.

Severely retarded persons may require some form of institutionalization, yet training in sheltered settings should be considered.

If the patient lives with his family - treat the family. Parents and siblings frequently display anger, rejection, overprotection and overcontrol, denial, and/or guilt - all of which should be recognized and dealt with by the physician. Provide genetic counseling. Coordinate with outside agencies and specialists, when available.

The majority of mildly retarded adults, when no longer in school, are indistinguishable from the general population, and no longer receive the diagnosis of mental retardation (ie, they develop skills, adapt, and "grow out of it"). Prognosis is good for a productive, self-sufficient life.

## REFERENCES

1. Bowlby J: Maternal Care and Mental Health. Geneva, World Health Organization, 1951.
2. Carter CH: Medical Aspects of Mental Retardation, ed 2. Springfield, IL, Charles C Thomas Pub, 1978.
3. Eaton LF, Menolascino FJ: Psychiatric disorders in the mentally retarded: Types, problems, and challenges. Am J Psychiatry 139:1297, 1982.
4. Schwartz M, Duara R, Haxby J et al: Down's syndrome in adults: Brain metabolism. Science 221:781, 1983.
5. Boshes RA: Pharmacotherapy for patients with mental retardation and mental illness. Psychiatr Ann 17: 627-632, 1987.
6. Tu J: A survey of psychotropic medication in mental retardation facilities. J Clin Psychiatry 40:125, 1979.
7. Ratey JJ, Mikkelsen EJ, Smith B, et al: Beta-blockers in the severely and profoundly mentally retarded. J Clin Psychopharmacol 6:103-107, 1986.

# Chapter 22

# The Psychotherapies

There are dozens of different psychotherapies addressing innumerable different patient problems. With the possible exception of a few specific behavioral methods applied to several very limited and discrete problems, rigorous proof of psychotherapy's effectiveness doesn't exist.[1] However, there is much nonrigorous but very compelling experience which indicates that various psychotherapies can help many patients. Unfortunately, specific indications for specific therapies generally are not available.[2-4] Some experts argue that many supposedly different psychotherapeutic methods are actually quite similar in practice.[5,6] Others suggest that trained therapists utilizing specific techniques may be less important for the patient's improvement than the therapist's personal characteristics of accurate empathy, nonpossessive warmth, and genuineness.[7]

There remain more questions than answers about the utility of and indications for psychotherapy. It is a field which has yet to reach a high level of scientific objectivity. However, it is clear that some patients benefit from such care and that an essential ingredient to that care is a good patient-therapist relationship built on trust and genuine interest.[8] Psychotherapy is an art, and a good therapist does make a difference.

<u>INDIVIDUAL THERAPY</u>

Individual treatment is the most common form of psychotherapy and comes in almost endless variations. Three of the most common types practiced in the USA are:

SUPPORTIVE THERAPY:

This is the most typical form of individual therapy provided to inpatients and outpatients.[9-11] Therapists skilled in this method include psychiatrists, clinical psychologists, and social workers. The goal is to evaluate the patient's current life situation and his strengths and weaknesses and then to help him make whatever realistic changes will allow him to be more functional. Patients usually are seen weekly (or more often) for several weeks or months (although some patients are followed infrequently for years). Also included is brief (1-3 session) crisis intervention.

The therapist deals with the patient's symptoms but works very little with the patient's unconscious processes and does not attempt major personality change. Psychological defenses are reinforced - techniques used include reassurance, suggestion, ventilation, abreaction, and environmental manipulation. The therapist must be active, interested, empathic, and warm - listen to the patient, understand his concerns, and help him find direction. Medication may be used.

Patients who are failing to cope successfully with present stress are good candidates, whether or not they have underlying psychiatric problems. Patients with serious psychiatric illnesses (eg, schizophrenia, major affective disorder) often benefit by concurrent use of biological methods and supportive psychotherapy.

PSYCHOANALYTIC PSYCHOTHERAPY:

Psychoanalysis is the classic, long-term insight oriented therapy. The goal is to make major personality changes by identifying and modifying ("working through") unconscious conflicts by means of free association, analysis of transference and resistance, and dream interpretation. An "analysis" typically takes several hundred hours. "Neurotics" and those with personality disorders are the preferred patients.

Psychoanalytic psychotherapy[12,13] is similar to supportive therapy in that the goal is removal of symptoms, yet is similar to psychoanalysis in requiring a dynamic understanding of the patient's unconscious conflicts (insight) and in utilizing analysis of the transference and dream interpretation. It is briefer than psychoanalysis and used more often.

Recently, Brief Psychotherapy has been explored as a way to impact a patient's problems while at the same time limiting both the number of therapy sessions (12-25 or more) and the number of issues addressed.[14-17] Early results appear promising.

COGNITIVE THERAPY:

Cognitive therapy attributes emotional difficulties to faulty thinking or beliefs. Psychiatric conditions presumably improve when the patient's thinking is more accurate. Thus, the cognitive therapist works with the patient to identify and correct misperceptions, one by one. Therapy is very reality based and encourages the patient to think about his thinking. Cognitive therapy has been used most successfully in the treatment of mild-to-moderate depression but is of value in a variety of other psychiatric conditions;[18] eg, anxiety disorders, substance abuse.

### BEHAVIOR THERAPY

Behavior therapy is based on <u>learning theory</u> which postulates that problem behaviors (ie, almost any of the manifestations of psychiatric conditions) are involuntarily acquired due to inappropriate learning. Therapy concentrates on changing <u>behavior</u> (behavior modification) rather than on changing unconscious or conscious thought patterns and, to that end, it is very directive (ie, patient receives much instruction and direction). Specific techniques to facilitate those changes include the following:

<u>Operant conditioning</u> - These therapeutic techniques are based on careful evaluation and modification of the antecedents and consequences of a patient's behavior. Desired behavior is encouraged by <u>positive reinforcement</u> and discouraged by <u>negative reinforcement</u>. These new ways of responding to the patient can be taught to the people who live with the patient or, for inpatients, may take the form of a <u>token economy</u>.
<u>Aversion therapy</u> - A patient is given an unpleasant, aversive stimulus (eg, electric shock, loud sound) when his behavior is undesirable. Some of these procedures have been legally discouraged. An alternate technique, <u>covert sensitization</u>, is less objectionable since it uses unpleasant thoughts as the aversive stimulus.
<u>Implosive therapy</u> - The patient with a situation-caused anxiety is directly exposed for a length of time to that situation (<u>flooding</u>) or exposed in imagination (<u>implosion</u>)
<u>Systematic desensitization</u> - The anxious or phobic patient is exposed to a gradual hierarchy of frightening situations or objects, beginning with the least worrisome. He gradually learns to handle the more frightening ones. If this is paired with relaxation (ie, an antagonistic response pattern - relaxation is incompatible with anxiety), the technique is <u>reciprocal inhibition</u>.

Common to these methods (and numerous others) is rigorous data collection. Behavior therapy relies on careful measurement of behavior. A technique is considered useful only if it is successful, and its success is determined by whether it eliminates measurable undesired behavior or increases desired behavior.

Although behavior modification has been successful in treating some kinds of conditions (eg, phobias, sexual deviance, regressed behavior), it has been criticized for not considering thought processes.[19] This has led to broader conceptualizations including Cognitive Therapy and Multimodal Behavior Therapy.

## GROUP THERAPY

Group therapy comes in many different forms - most of them derived from types of individual therapy.[20,21]

Interpersonal exploration groups - The goal is to develop self-awareness of interpersonal styles through corrective feedback from other group members. The patient is accepted and supported, thus promoting self-esteem. It is the most common type of group therapy.

Guidance-inspirational groups - Highly structured, cohesive, supportive groups which minimize the importance of insight and maximize the value of ventilation and camaraderie. Groups may be large - eg, Alcoholics Anonymous (AA), Synanon. Members often are chosen because they "have the same problem."

Psychoanalytically oriented therapy - A loosely structured group technique in which the therapist makes interpretations about a patient's unconscious conflicts and processes from observed group interactions.

Numerous other types of group therapies include behavioral therapy, Gestalt, encounter, psychodrama, transactional analysis (TA), marathon, EST, etc.

Groups may run for weeks, months,[22] or years, and usually meet weekly. They usually have 5-12 members (depending on type). Therapists from many different disciplines conduct groups - many groups run with cotherapists.

Some groups have patients with only one diagnosis (eg, schizophrenia, alcoholism) while others are mixed. It is not clear which patients will benefit (or will be harmed) by group therapy, but most patients can be treated safely in groups. Most of the success of a group appears to depend more on the experience, sensitivity, warmth, and charisma of the leader than on the group's theoretical orientation.

A group experience which is too intense or confrontive can produce anxiety, depression, or psychotic reactions in susceptible patients. Acutely psychotic patients should not be included. Paranoid individuals make poor group members.

## FAMILY THERAPY

Family therapy can be conceptualized as a variant of group therapy. There are numerous types of family therapy[23] but no "one right way." Although a family often enters therapy because one of the family members is "having problems," it is the implicit or explicit assumption of many family therapists that the system is sick, not the patient. The expectation is that improvement in unhealthy interpersonal interactions and communications will result in improvement of the identified patient.

Most (but not all) family therapists recognize that some patients bring problems to family therapy which are not due to family malfunctioning, but most therapists argue that those problems are frequently worsened by any untreated malfunctioning.

## MARITAL THERAPY

Therapy of a married couple is often called for if that is the relationship at risk. It is particularly common if there is a psychosexual problem present. Theoretical orientations and treatment techniques are diverse - none has been clearly shown to be superior. There are no clear guidelines for choosing couples likely to improve with marital therapy. Therapists may come from one of several professional disciplines (eg, psychiatry, psychology, social work, marriage and family counseling).

## MILIEU THERAPY

Milieu therapy usually takes place in an inpatient "therapeutic community." Often the entire community is geared towards support for the patient and towards helping him develop more adaptive coping skills. In a sense, all the staff members are therapists, and all the patients are likewise concerned with facilitating each other's well-being. It is a useful adjunct to other forms of therapy (eg, pharmacotherapy).

## REFERENCES

1.  Karasu TB: The psychotherapies: Benefits and limitations Am J Psychotherapy 40:324-342, 1986.

2.  Frances A, Sweeney J, Clarkin J: Do psychotherapies have specific effects? Am J Psychotherapy 39:159-174, 1985.
3.  Francis A, Clarkin J, Perry S: Differential Therapeutics in Psychiatry. New York, Brunner/Mazel Pub., 1984.
4.  Strupp HH: The nonspecific hypothesis of therapeutic effectiveness. Am J Orthopsychiatry 56:513-520, 1986.
5.  Parloff MB: Frank's "common elements" in psychotherapy. Am J Orthopsychiatry 56:521-530, 1986.
6.  Reich J, Neenan P: Principles common to different short-term psychotherapies. Am J Psychother 40:62-69, 1986.
7.  Luborsky L, Crits-Christoph P, McLellan T, et al: Do therapists vary much in their success? Am J Orthopsychiatry 56:501-512, 1986.
8.  Beutler LE: Eclectic Psychotherapy. New York, Pergamon Pr., 1983.
9.  Buckley P: A neglected treatment. Psychiatr Ann 16:515-521, 1986.
10. Conte HR, Plutchik R: Controlled research in supportive psychotherapy. Psychiatr Ann 16:530-533, 1986.
11. Winston A, Pinsker H, McCullough L: A review of supportive psychotherapy. Hosp Comm Psychiatry 37:1105, 1986.
12. Paolino TJ: Psychoanalytic Psychotherapy. New York, Brunner/Mazel Pub, 1981.
13. Wallace ER: Dynamic Psychiatry in Theory and Practice. Philadelphia, Lea & Febiger, 1983.
14. Free NK, Green BL, Grace MC, et al: Empathy and outcome in brief focal dynamic therapy. Am J Psychiatry 142:917-921, 1985.
15. Horowitz MJ, Marmar CR, Weiss DS, et al: Comprehensive analysis of change after brief dynamic psychotherapy. Am J Psychiatry 143:482-589, 1986.
16. Sifneos PE: Short-term Dynamic Psychotherapy. New York, Plenum Pub., 1987.
17. Ursano RJ, Hales RE: A review of brief individual psychotherapies. Am J Psychiatry 143:1507-1517, 1986.
18. Emery G, Hollon SD, Bedrosian RC: New Directions in Cognitive Therapy. New York, The Guilford Press, 1981.
19. Wolpe J: Misrepresentation and underemployment of behavior therapy. Compr Psychiatry 27:192-200, 1986.
20. Kaplan HI, Sadock BJ: Comprehensive Group Psychotherapy. Baltimore, Williams & Wilkins, 1983.
21. Yalom ID: The Theory and Practice of Group Psychotherapy New York, Basic Books, 1983.
22. MacKenzie KR, Livesley WJ: Outcome and process measures in brief group psychotherapy. Psychiatr Ann 16:715-720, 1986.
23. Hansen JC, L'Abate L: Approaches to Family Therapy. New York, Macmillan Pub. Co., 1982.

# Chapter 23

# Biological Therapy

## ANTIPSYCHOTICS (NEUROLEPTICS)

These are the "major tranquilizers" which revolutionized psychiatry by providing an effective treatment for large numbers of psychotic patients. Their antipsychotic effect is <u>not</u> due to sedation but to a specific action on thought and mood disorder.

### DRUGS AVAILABLE:

There are many different antipsychotics available which are divided among six chemical classes. Common examples of each class are listed below along with relative dosages (with reference to chlorpromazine).

## TRICYCLICS

| PHENOTHIAZINES | Equivalent doses (mg) |
|---|---|
| Dimethylamino-alkyl Derivatives | |
| chlorpromazine (Thorazine) | 100 |
| Piperidine-alkyl Derivatives | |
| thioridazine (Mellaril) | 100 |
| mesoridazine (Serentil) | 50 |
| Piperazine-alkyl Derivatives | |
| fluphenazine (Prolixin, Permitil) | 1-2 |
| fluphenazine decanoate (long-acting) | |
| trifluoperazine (Stelazine) | 8 |
| perphenazine (Trilafon) | 10 |

### THIOXANTHENES

| | |
|---|---|
| thiothixene (Navane) | 4 |

DIBENZOXAZEPINES

    loxapine (Loxitane)                15
    clozapine (no FDA approval - 1987)

NON-TRICYCLICS

DIHYDROINDOLONES

    molindone (Moban)                 15

BUTYROPHENONES

    haloperidol (Haldol)             1-2
    haloperidol decanoate (long-acting)

DIPHENYLBUTYLPIPERIDINES

    pimozide (Orap)                  1-2

INDICATIONS FOR USE:

Recommended for:
1. Acute schizophrenia and other acute psychoses (eg, amphetamine psychosis, psychoses with OBS). Should be used in conjunction with lithium in the acute manic attacks of bipolar disorder.
2. Chronic schizophrenia.
3. Major depression with significant psychotic features - used in conjunction with an antidepressant.
4. Gilles de la Tourette Syndrome - haloperidol is the drug most commonly used.

Other uses:
- Antipsychotics can be of temporary use in several conditions - eg, acute agitation of a nonpsychotic nature, antiemesis, etc.

MECHANISMS OF ACTION:

    The dopamine hypothesis postulates that schizophrenia is secondary to increased central dopamine activity. Antipsychotic drugs are felt to act by a postsynaptic blocking of DA receptors, thus returning a CNS DA balance. The three major CNS dopamine pathways with their associated activities are:

    Nigrostriatal - extrapyramidal actions
    Tuberoinfundibular - endocrine actions (increased pro-
        lactin)
    Mesolimbic - antipsychotic actions

The different side effect patterns of the various antipsychotic drugs are felt to be due to their different locations of primary activity. However, antipsychotics also block central noradrenergic (NE) receptors, thus we can't yet determine whether DA or NE blockage (or another mechanism entirely) is responsible for the antipsychotic effect.

PHARMACOKINETICS:

Chlorpromazine is variably absorbed from the intestine and is probably partly degraded in the mucosal wall. It is approximately 95% protein bound. Much higher blood levels are attained following IM or IV than PO administration. The half-life is 1-2[+] days but variable, with the majority of the drug stored in body fat. There is marked interindividual differences in blood levels (reasons are unclear).

Metabolism is complex (eg, chlorpromazine is degraded by sulfoxidation, hydroxylation, deamination, demethylation, etc, to form well over 100 metabolites). Some of the metabolites are active, some inactive - not completely worked out. In part because of this complexity, measured plasma levels of many antipsychotics are not clinically useful. In contrast, certain other antipsychotics (eg, Haldol, Navane) have a simple metabolism;[1] however, the measurement of their blood levels may add little to clinical dosing techniques.[2]

SIDE EFFECTS:

Side effects are common and are almost unavoidable at higher drug dosages. The particular pattern of side effects is in part determined by the chemical class of any given antipsychotic.

| Drug | Sedation | Extrapyramidal | Hypotension |
|------|----------|----------------|-------------|
| Phenothiazines | | | |
| Aliphatic | 3+ | 2+ | 3+ |
| Piperidine | 2+ | 1+ | 2+ |
| Piperazine | 1+ | 3+ | 1+ |
| Dibenzoxazepines | 2+ | 3+ | 2+ |
| Butyrophenones | 2+ | 3+ | 1+ |
| Dihydroindolones | 1+ | 2+ | 1+ |

These side effects also have marked interindividual variability.  The most common side effects of these medications include sedation, extrapyramidal and anticholinergic symptoms, hypotension, weight gain, and reduced libido, but many other side effects occur as well.  (NOTE: Several new antipsychotics are on the horizon which may have greatly reduced side effect patterns - eg, clozapine.[3])

- Sedation: Common; use a QD schedule, if possible.

- Anticholinergic symptoms:
    Dry mouth - Common.  May lead to moniliasis, parotitis, and an increase in cavities.  Consider treatment with oral water and ice, sugarless gum; also neostigmine 7.5-15 mg PO, pilocarpine 2.5 mg PO qid, or bethanechol 75 mg daily.
    Constipation - Treat with stool softeners.
    Blurred vision - Near vision.  Treat with physostigmine drops, 0.25% solution, 1 drop Q6H, if a major problem.
    Urinary hesitancy and retention - Consider using Urecholine 10-25 mg PO tid.
    Exacerbation of glaucoma
    Central anticholinergic syndrome - Occurs particularly in those patients simultaneously taking several drugs with anticholinergic properties (eg, an OD or a patient taking an antipsychotic, an antidepressant, and an antiparkinsonian).  The syndrome can vary from mild anxiety and vasodilatation to a toxic delirium or even coma.  It is much more common in the elderly.  Symptoms and signs to be looked for include:

        Anxiety, restlessness, agitation - grading into confusion, incoherence, disorientation, memory impairment, visual and auditory hallucinations-grading into seizures, stupor, and coma.
        Warm and dry skin, flushed face, dry mouth, hyperpyrexia.
        Blurred vision, dilated pupils.
        Absent bowel sounds.

    Treat an acute delirium with withdrawal of the causative agent, close medical supervision (eg, cardiac monitor), and physostigmine 1-2 mg IM or slowly IV (eg, 1 mg/min).  Repeat in 15-30 min and then every 1-2 hours, if needed.  Avoid physostigmine in patients with bowel or bladder obstruction, peptic ulcer, asthma, glaucoma, heart disease, diabetes, or hypothyroidism.  Watch for cholinergic overdosage (salivation, sweating, etc) and treat with atropine (0.5 mg for each mg of physostigmine).

- Extrapyramidal symptoms: These reactions are common, get worse with stress, disappear during sleep, and wax and wane over time.

  Acute dystonic reaction - An involuntary sustained contraction of a skeletal muscle which usually appears suddenly (over 5-60 minutes). The jaw muscles are most frequently involved (ie, "lock-jaw") but other muscle systems may also be disturbed (eg, torticollis, carpopedal spasm, oculogyric crisis, even opisthotonos). Usually occurs during the first two days of treatment (in 2-10% of patients - more common in younger patients).

  Parkinson-like syndrome - These reactions occur individually or together, usually during weeks 1-4 of treatment. They are more common in older patients.

    Tremor - An irregular tremor of the upper extremities, tongue, and jaw. It occurs with both movement and rest and is slower than the tremors produced by TCAs and lithium.
    Rigidity - A cogwheel rigidity which starts with the shoulders and spreads to the upper extremities and then throughout the body.
    Akinesia - A "zombie-like" effect with slowness, fatigue, micrographia, and little facial expression. It may occur alone and at anytime during the course of treatment and is easily mistaken for social withdrawal or depression.

  Akathisia: Common. Patients are fidgety, constantly move their hands and feet, rock from the waist, and shift from foot to foot. Easily mistaken for anxiety or agitation. Consider treating with propranolol.[4]

  Rabbit Syndrome: Involuntary chewing movements.

  Tardive dyskinesia: Slow choreiform or tic-like movements, usually of the tongue and facial muscles, but occasionally of the upper extremities or the whole body. Risk is increased in the aged, those with OBS,[5] females, high doses of medication, simultaneous use of several antipsychotics, and possibly long duration of treatment. Develops over months or years of antipsychotic use, and the more severe cases are often irreversible (perhaps 25% of affected patients).[6] Symptoms disappear with an increased dosage of antipsychotic: don't "misread" the movements as a worsening psychosis, raise the dose of medication, remove the symptom, and thus begin a vicious cycle. "Drug holidays" don't seem to prevent, and may even worsen, the development of TD.[7]     There is no acceptable treatment.     Try to discontinue the antipsychotic, if possible.

## TREATMENT OF EXTRAPYRAMIDAL SYMPTOMS

Treat with the anticholinergic <u>antiparkinsonism drugs</u>:

| Drug | Typical Dosage |
|------|----------------|
| Benztropine (Cogentin) | 1-4 mg, QD-BID, PO |
| biperiden (Akineton) | 1-2 mg, TID,QID, PO |
| procyclidine (Kemadrin) | 2-5 mg, TID-QID, PO |
| trihexyphenidyl (Artane, Tremin) | 2-5 mg, TID-QID, PO |
| diphenhydramine (Benadryl) | 25-50 mg, TID-QID, PO |

Begin at a lower dosage and raise over several days. Use for several weeks, then discontinue if possible. Try not to use for more than 2-3 months (although they may be necessary long-term in a few patients). Some studies support the use of antiparkinsonism drugs prophylactically (begun when antipsychotics are started), particularly in patients likely to be resistant. Treat acute dystonic reactions immediately (IM or IV) with (eg) Cogentin 1 mg, Benadryl 25-50 mg, or Valium 5-10 mg - then begin regular oral dose for several weeks. These drugs may be abused.[8]

- Alpha-adrenergic blocking symptoms: Orthostatic hypotension, inhibition of ejaculation (particularly thioridazine).

- Cholestatic jaundice:   Probably a sensitivity reaction. Fever and eosinophilia, usually during the first two months of treatment (in 1% of patients taking chlorpromazine).   Little cross-sensitivity with other antipsychotics.

- Agranulocytosis:   Usually in elderly females during the first four months of treatment but can occur anytime. Train patients to report persistent sore throats, infections, or fever. Rare.

- Neuroleptic Malignant Syndrome (NMS)[9]:   Rapidly developing (hrs - 1-2 days) muscular rigidity, fever, confusion, hypertension, sweating, tachycardia.[10]   In 1%+ of pts, particularly (but not exclusively) following high dose, high potency depot meds.   Often fatal if untreated. Stop meds immediately; provide medical support; consider treatment with dantrolene or bromocriptine (7.5-45 mg/day, tid[11]).   Patient may recover over 5-15 days.

- Hypothermia; hyperthermia:   Watch out for hot seclusion rooms.

- Weight gain, obesity.

- Pigmentary changes in skin:  Particularly with chlorproma-zine.  A tan, gray, or blue color.

- Retinitis Pigmentosa - Possible blindness.  Occurs with dosages of thioridazine greater than 800 mg/day.

- Photosensitivity:  Bad sunburns with Thorazine.

- Grand mal seizures:  Particularly with rapid increases in dose.

- Nonspecific skin rashes:  In 5%.

- Reduced libido in males and females.

- Increased prolactin levels:  Produces galactorrhea, ammen-orrhea, and lactation.

- EKG changes:   Particularly with thioridazine - T-wave inversions, occasionally arrhythmias.

- Appears safe during pregnancy: no known congenital abnor-malities.   Slight hypertonicity among newborns, but little effect on nursing infant.

   Suicide is difficult but possible with the antipsychot-ics - requires very large doses.


DRUG INTERACTIONS:

   Antacids - May inhibit absorption of oral antipsychotics. Tricyclic antidepressants - May inhibit antipsychotic metabolism and raise plasma levels, and vice versa.


TREATMENT PRINCIPLES:

- Drug choice:

   The primary reason to choose one drug over another is the side effect spectrum - they are all equally capable of controlling psychosis when used appropriately.  If a patient or a similarly affected family member has res-ponded well to one medication, try it.  If a patient has

a seizure disorder, use a high potency drug (eg, fluphenazine, haloperidol).

- Treatment of acute psychosis:

Sedating antipsychotics which can be given IM usually
provide the best control initially (eg, Haldol, Thorazine), although they have no long-term advantages. Give
orally if the patient is cooperative - IM if he is not.

1. If possible, give a small test dose (eg, Haldol 5 mg)
   and wait one hour to see if it is tolerated.
2. Then begin Haldol 10-15 mg/day, Thorazine 300-400
   mg/day, or the equivalent. Use tid or qid schedule
   initially, then switch to bid or qd after 1-2 wks.
   A qd schedule is usually well tolerated and helps
   insomnia. Increase 100-200 mg of Thorazine (or
   equivalent) every 3-4 days until the patient has
   improved, or side effects become limiting. Maximum
   dosages needed are variable (500 mg/day of chlorpromazine is common (15-20 mg/day of Haldol); rarely
   may be as high as 1500$^+$ mg). If side effects become
   a problem, begin antiparkinsonism drugs and/or
   reduce the dosage and increase more slowly.
3. If the patient is wild and needs immediate control,
   consider <u>rapid tranquilization</u> with antipsychotics:

   Haldol 5 mg IM every hour until calm (maximum 50
     mg in 12 hr)

   <u>NOT</u> for routine use.[12]  Monitor carefully for hypotension or oversedation. Once the patient is under
   control, switch to the preceding daily schedule.

- Disease control is cognitive as well as behavioral - the
  goal is not just to "quiet" the patient. Increasing
  socialization is an early sign of a drug response. Agitated, disruptive behavior usually improves in the first
  several days. The thought disorder disappears over wks
  or months. Antipsychotics improve the <u>positive symptoms</u>
  of psychosis (eg, hallucinations, delusions, bizarre
  behavior) but, unfortunately, they usually don't change
  the <u>negative symptoms</u> (eg, flat affect, social impairment) - a major problem. (Early reports suggest that
  pimozide may be an exception.[13])  Patients who are
  "acutely crazy" are <u>most</u> likely to respond well, as are
  those with good premorbid functioning who are having
  their first psychotic episode.

- If a patient does not respond, switch to another drug of a
  different class. However, the unimproved patient needs

at least one 2-3 week trial at a higher dose of an anti-psychotic before you conclude that he doesn't respond to medication. There is rarely a reason to use two different antipsychotics simultaneously. The most common cause for lack of response is underdosage (and noncompliance), but always be wary that the patient may have an organic psychosis.

- Once improvement has occurred, maintain drug levels over 1-2 months and then consider reducing to maintenance levels. If this is the first episode of an acute psychosis in a previously well-functioning patient, consider discontinuing the medication over another 1-2 months. If this episode is one of many, place the patient on maintenance.

- Antipsychotic maintenance therapy:

Decrease dosage slowly (over weeks - months) to one third or one quarter of the acute dose. Depending on past history, try discontinuing after 6-12 months, although some patients may need meds for many years. If a relapse develops, increase the dose. 80-90% of patients relapse (during first 24 months) without meds, 40% relapse while taking them. Teach the patient to recognize his own developing relapse so it can be caught early.

Antipsychotics are often unpleasant to take, so compliance is a major problem with outpatients[14] (particularly in those patients who are suspicious and paranoid). Pay attention to and work aggressively to control side effects (particularly akathisia). A major recent advance has been the development of long-acting depot forms of two antipsychotics: prolixin decanoate and haloperidol decanoate, given IM every 2-4 weeks. Although still being researched, the best and safest maintenance may be with low-dose depot meds[15]: eg, prolixin decanoate (12.5-25 mg IM every 2 weeks)[16] or haloperidol decanoate (50-100+ mg IM every month).[17] The relapse rate may be slightly increased at these doses, but side effects and compliance are improved as well.

A few experts recommend stopping meds altogether and restarting them for brief periods at signs of a relapse (targeted pharmacotherapy).[18]

## LITHIUM CARBONATE

### DRUGS AVAILABLE:

Lithium carbonate ($Li^+$ - atomic # 3)
Slow-release lithium (Eskalith CR; Lithobid)

### INDICATIONS FOR USE:[19]

Recommended for:

1. Acute bipolar disorder, manic.  Lithium is the drug of choice for stabilization following an acute manic attack (80% of patients return to normal) although, due to the usual 7-10 day delay in onset of clinical effect, a major tranquilizer may be needed initially as well.
2. Used with an antidepressant in acute depression in a bipolar patient to prevent "manic overshoot."
3. Long-term prophylaxis of mania in a bipolar patient. It is effective at preventing recurrences.  Be careful of chronic renal toxicity.

Possible uses:

- Prophylaxis for bipolar disorder, depressed and for major depression.
- May be an effective antidepressant for some patients with an acute bipolar depression.  It may act synergistically with tricyclic antidepressants.
- May assist or replace antipsychotics in treatment of some patients with schizophrenia or schizoaffective disorder (but lithium can make a few schizophrenics worse).
- May help control mood swings and explosive outbursts in patients with intermittent explosive disorder and emotionally unstable character disorder.
- Retarded patients with aggressiveness and/or self-mutilation.

### MECHANISMS OF ACTION:

The reasons for the clinical effects are unknown although it does increase central NE reuptake and decrease its release.

### PHARMACOKINETICS:

Lithium is quickly absorbed from the GI tract (completely absorbed in 8 hours) and develops a peak plasma level in 1-3 hr.  It is <u>not</u> protein bound or metabolized and is excreted by the kidney. The CSF concentration is 30-60% of that in plasma and equivalent to that in RBCs. It is concentrated by bone and by thyroid (4-5 x that in plasma).

Lithium can only be used safely if blood concentrations are monitored carefully (oral dosage is not an adequate measure). To obtain consistent levels, blood is routinely drawn 12 hr after the last dose (usually before breakfast). The lithium half-life is 18-36 hr (fastest in youth, slowest in elderly) - a constant oral dosage requires 5-8 days to reach steady state. Once a steady state is reached, the lithium level is proportional to the daily oral dose (and determined by the renal clearance).

## SIDE EFFECTS:

The number and severity of side effects increase with increasing or rapidly changing blood levels. A slight change in blood level (0.1-0.2 meq/l) may dramatically alter the number or intensity of the side effects. Minor side effects (tremor, thirst, anorexia, and GI distress) commonly occur at therapeutic levels (0.8-1.5 meq/l), and fatal effects (seizures, coma) may occur at only slightly higher levels (eg, as low as 2.0-2.5 meq/l but more commonly at 3-5 meq/l). Lithium has a very narrow margin of safety and is a dangerous drug in overdosage. It should be given cautiously (or not given at all) in patients who are dehydrated, febrile, have sodium depletion (kidney reabsorbs more lithium), or have major renal or cardiovascular disease. Brain damaged patients and the elderly are at risk for side effects at low blood levels.

Normal subjects administered lithium report irritability and emotional lability, anxiety, mild depression, tiredness and malaise, weakness, inability to concentrate, impaired memory, and slowed reaction time. Patients taking lithium often experience a "lithium-induced dysphoria" - 25-50% stop lithium AMA. Unlike other psychoactive medication, sedation is not a side effect.

Neurological:
  EEG - Usually shows increased amplitude and generalized slowing (in 50% of patients at therapeutic blood levels).
  Headaches, occasional slurred speech.
  Toxicity:
    Confusion, poor concentration, and clouding of consciousness; leads to delirium; leads to coma; leads to death.
    Cerebellar effects - dysarthria, ataxia, nystagmus, severe incoordination.

Basal ganglia effects - Parkinsonian symptoms, choreiform movements.
Seizures - grand mal; status epilepticus.

Neuromuscular:
Hand tremor (fine, fast) which does not respond to anticholinergics. Occurs in 50% of the patients started
on lithium but the incidence decreases with time (5%
of long-term patients). Treat with beta-blockers; eg,
30-80 mg propranolol PO/day.[20]
Muscular weakness - one third of patients during the
first week of treatment; transient.
Neuromuscular toxicity - hyperactive reflexes, fasciculations, paralysis.

Kidney[21]:
Polyuria and polydipsia - secondary to a vasopressin-
resistant, diabetes insipidus-like syndrome. Reversible and occurs in 50% of all new patients (5% of all
chronics).
Reversible oliguric renal failure with acute lithium
intoxication.
Possible irreversible nephrotoxic effect in a few chronic patients - focal interstitial cortical fibrosis
with tubular atrophy and sclerotic glomeruli. Look
for a gradually increasing blood lithium in patients
taking a constant oral dose. There is increased serum
creatinine and an increased 24 hr urine volume. Poorly characterized currently, this serious effect of
chronic lithium administration may limit the ability
to use lithium prophylactically in some.

Blood:
Leukocytosis (10,000-14,000 WBCs - neutrophilia with
lymphocytopenia). Common and reversible, it is persistent but periodic while the patient is taking
lithium.
Occasional increased ESR.

GI:
30% of patients have GI symptoms in the early weeks of
treatment - gastric irritation, nausea, anorexia,
diarrhea, bloating, abdominal pain (a switch to lithium citrate may relieve symptoms).

Heart:
T-wave flattening or inversion (common but reversible).
Unusual - myocarditis, SA block, primary AV block; ventricular irritability and perhaps sudden death (particularly in older males with cardiac pathology; more
common at toxic levels).

Thyroid:
   Lithium may produce hypothyroidism with (10% of chronic patients) or without a goiter. Measure TSH. Low dose thyroxine may help but consult an endocrinologist.

Other:
   Impaired memory
   Lithium accumulates in bone - no known harmful effects.
   Occasional maculopapular rash, acne - also (rarely) alopecia, ulceration, and exacerbation of psoriasis.[22]
   Weight gain in 10% of patients. Partly related to a Li-induced reactive hypoglycemia.
   Occasional benign, reversible exophthalmos.
   Hyperparathyroidism - increased serum calcium and parathyroid hormone, usually without other symptoms.

Most of the side effects disappear with chronic lithium administration. Persistent side effects include tremor, polyuria, leukocytosis, goiter, and elevated blood sugar.

In pregnancy[23]:

1. Lithium crosses the placenta freely and perhaps produces cardiac malformations - thus, pregnant women should not take lithium unless they absolutely must. Such infants are also at risk for nephrogenic diabetes insipidus, hypoglycemia, and euthyroid goiter.
2. Lithium in milk is 30-100% of the maternal blood level - thus, these mothers should not breast feed.
3. Lithium clearance increases 50-100% early in pregnancy and returns to normal at delivery; so a dosage which had been raised during pregnancy must be immediately reduced, or the mother will become toxic.

DRUG INTERACTIONS[24]:

Diuretics - Thiazides decrease lithium clearance and increase blood levels. Furosemide, ethacrynic acid, spironolactone, and triamterene may also. Mannitol, urea, and acetazolamide decrease blood levels. Tetracyclines, indomethacin, phenylbutazone, and methyldopa may increase lithium blood levels.
Haloperidol (and other high potency neuroleptics) - a (usually) reversible neurotoxicity may occur in some patients at higher doses of antipsychotic (confusion, disorientation, etc). Potentially life-threatening - watch for it.[25,26]
Chlorpromazine may increase the rate of lithium excretion.
Tricyclic antidepressants may act synergistically with lithium.

Aminophylline increases lithium excretion.
Lithium probably prolongs the neuromuscular blocking effect of succinylcholine.

TREATMENT PRINCIPLES[27]:

- Select appropriate patients. Screen for serious medical illness. Pre-administration laboratory evaluation should include:

    CBC, BUN, UA
    Serum creatinine.
    $T_3$, $T_4$; examine thyroid.

    Serum Na if there is reason to question the patient's electrolyte status.
    EKG if the physical or history suggest cardiac disease
    If chronic use of lithium is expected, obtain 24-hour urine volume, creatinine clearance, and protein excretion.

- Treatment of acute mania:

    The goal is to produce a therapeutic blood level (1.2-1.4 meq/l) and maintain it until a clinical effect is seen (usually 7-10 days after an appropriate level is attained). Begin lithium 300 mg PO bid-tid. Always give in divided doses (usually tid-qid; bid-tid with slow-release form). Increase by 300 mg every 2-3 days (typical effective oral dose is 1200-2400 mg/day).

    Methods to determine the appropriate steady state dose of Li based on blood levels following a single initial test dose of Li have been developed. As yet, none can be considered standard, but some appear promising[28] - they would help speed up the treatment of manic patients.

    Since the mania is not controlled by lithium for 2-3 weeks, usually also begin an antipsychotic on the first day of treatment (equivalent of chlorpromazine, 300-1200 mg/day or more, in divided doses). (Watch for possible neurotoxicity.) The antipsychotic provides rapid control of the psychomotor activity while the lithium acts more gradually but is more specific for control of the affect and ideation of mania.

    Once the mania begins to remit, the blood level may increase unless the oral dose is reduced. Maintain a therapeutic level until the mania is completely controlled (measure blood levels every 1-2 wk).

- Maintenance treatment of mania:

     If a patient has a history of recurrent mania, con-
tinue lithium after the acute attack. An effective maintenance blood level is 0.5-1.0 meq/l. When stable,
measure the blood level every 2-3 months (be aware, a
crash diet or strenuous exercise program may change the
patient's level). Unfortunately, noncompliance is common,
so work with the patient.[29]

     Teach the patient to be alert to side effects which
suggest toxicity - measure lithium level if they occur.
Lithium level increases with sodium loss so advise the
patient to be aware of changes in dietary salt intake,
sweating, and hot climates (although Li _may_ be lost more
rapidly than sodium, causing the Li level to fall).[30]

     In light of growing evidence of lithium-induced renal
toxicity, monitor renal function carefully (eg, serum
creatinine, UA, BUN, protein excretion, and 24-hour urine
volume every 6-12 months). Also monitor thyroid function
(eg, $T_3$, $T_4$, and physical exam every 6 months).

- Lithium remains effective over time. If a patient on
maintenance lithium shows early signs of developing mania,
raise the lithium to an acute therapeutic level (50%[+]
respond). If the patient develops a severe depression,
begin a tricyclic antidepressant (although a few patients
will have developed subclinical hypothyroidism $2^0$ to Li,
so consider thyroid supplementation instead).


## CARBAMAZEPINE

     Carbamazepine (Tegretol) is an anticonvulsant which
seems to be as effective as lithium for treating acute
mania[31,32] and for mania prophylaxis.[33] Moreover, it may be
of use as an antidepressant[34] and in treating certain
violent individuals.[35] Doses are 800[+] mg/day - although
dose-related side effects like sedation and dizziness are
common, watch for more serious problems of aplastic anemia
and hepatitis.


## ANTIDEPRESSANT DRUGS

     Three groups of antidepressant drugs are in common use:
tricyclic antidepressants (TCAs), newer antidepressants, and
monoamine oxidase inhibitors (MAOIs). Combinations of these
drugs are also occasionally helpful. The TCAs are generally

the first choice in treating depressions but the others have some specific indications (see below).  Lithium carbonate can improve some major depressions, and the antipsychotic drugs are essential in psychotic depression.

DRUGS AVAILABLE:    (in USA)

| TCAs | ANTICHO-LINERGIC | SEDA-TION | DOSE (MG/DAY) |
|---|---|---|---|
| imipramine (Tofranil) | 4+ | 3+ | 75-300 |
| amitriptyline (Elavil, Endep) | 5+ | 5+ | 75-300 |
| doxepin (Sinequan, Adapin) | 4+ | 5+ | 75-300 |
| desipramine (Norpramin) | 1+ | 1+ | 75-300 |
| nortriptyline (Pamelor) | 3+ | 2+ | 40-150 |
| protriptyline (Vivactil) | 3+ | 1+ | 20- 60 |
| trimipramine (Surmontil) | 3+ | 4+ | 75-200 |

NEWER ANTIDEPRESSANTS

| | | | |
|---|---|---|---|
| alprazolam (Xanax) | 1+ | 5+ | 4-8 |
| amoxapine (Asendin) | 2+ | 3+ | 200-300 |
| bupropion (Wellbutrin) | 1+ | 1+ | 200-600 |
| maprotiline (Ludiomil) | 2+ | 2+ | 50-225 |
| trazadone (Desyrel) | 1+ | 3+ | 100-800 |
| fluoxetine (Prozac) | 0-1+ | 0 | 45-90 |
| fluvoxamine | 0-1+ | 1+ | 100-300 |

MAOIs

| | | | |
|---|---|---|---|
| phenelzine (Nardil) | 1+ | 1+ | 45-90 |
| isocarboxazid (Marplan) | 1+ | 1+ | 30-60 |
| tranylcypromine (Parnate) | 1+ | 0 | 20-60 |

## TRICYCLIC ANTIDEPRESSANTS (TCAs)

INDICATIONS FOR USE:

Recommended for:

1. Major depression - particularly with vegetative symptoms and a diurnal variation (70-75% of patients respond).
2. Bipolar disorder, depressed or mixed - particularly if there are vegetative symptoms.  Lithium may be useful as well.
3. Short-term maintenance therapy in patients with resolved major depression or bipolar disease.

4. Prophylaxis in patients with severe, recurrent major depression.
5. Psychotic depression (hallucinations, delusions, paranoia, etc) - must be combined with antipsychotics (although ECT may be preferable for some).
6. Postpartum depressions which are severe.

Other uses:

- Dysthymic disorder - mild chronic depressions deserve a trial of TCAs.
- Atypical depression - patients with significant anxiety, hypochondriasis, and "neurotic" complaints- as an alternative to MAOIs.
- Panic disorder - <u>may</u> be the treatment of choice.
- Agoraphobia, with panic attacks.
- Obsessive compulsive disorder - particularly those patients who also have a depressed mood.
- Selected patients with chronic pain (with, & without, depression).
- Childhood conditions - both enuresis and school phobia may respond to low doses of a TCA.

TCAs should <u>not</u> be used routinely in the various minor depressive syndromes.

## MECHANISMS OF ACTION:

The effects of TCAs on CNS neurotransmitters are complex and vary from one tricyclic to another. Their therapeutic effects are <u>thought</u> to be related to their ability to increase the amount of CNS interneuronal norepinephrine and serotonin by blocking NE and 5-HT reuptake at the presynaptic membrane.

Although affecting both systems, <u>secondary amines</u> (desipramine, protriptyline, and nortriptyline) tend to block NE while <u>tertiary amines</u> (amitriptyline, imipramine, and doxepin) tend to block serotonin - a fact which may account for their observed interpatient response differences. Although the literature is inconclusive, it may be wise to start treatment with a $3^O$ TCA, partly because $2^O$ TCAs are generated as metabolic products of $3^O$ TCAs and partly because $3^O$ drugs may be slightly more effective.

## PHARMACOKINETICS:

TCAs are absorbed rapidly and completely from the GI tract, undergo an enterohepatic cycle, and develop peak plasma levels in 2-8 hr. TCAs are highly bound to plasma and tissue proteins and are fat-soluble - free TCA is only about 1% of the total body load. They are metabolized by

the liver and are excreted by the kidney.    The half-life
ranges from several hours to more than two days.
    Well-studied plasma blood levels are available for
imipramine, nortriptyline, desipramine, and amitriptyline.[36]
Do not measure them routinely - indications include[37]:

1. Treatment failure - Interindividual plasma levels vary
   markedly following the same oral dose (up to 30-fold
   differences), so always consider an ineffective plasma
   level when explaining a treatment failure.    Therapeutic
   range is 150-300 ng/ml for imipramine (+ its metabolite,
   desipramine), amitriptyline (+ nortriptyline), or desipramine, and 50-160 ng/ml for nortriptyline.
2. Therapeutic window - Some TCAs may have a therapeutic
   window (eg, nortriptyline and possibly desipramine)-
   the drugs are ineffective outside this range - while
   others seem to have no therapeutic upper limit (eg,
   imipramine - range limited only by side effects).
3. Suspected patient noncompliance.
4. Patients with significant side effects on a usual oral
   dose - they may have an excessively high plasma level.
5. Patients with cardiac disease - attempt to maintain a low
   (but effective) plasma level.
6. The medically unstable patient (particularly the elderly)
7. Overdose - plasma levels are mandatory.

SIDE EFFECTS:

    Side effects[38] are frequent and usually mild but they
can be serious or fatal (particularly cardiac effects in TCA
overdoses) and are more common in the elderly.

    Anticholinergic:
      Dry mouth
      Blurred vision (near vision)
      Constipation, urinary hesitancy

    Autonomic:
      Sweating
      Impotence, ejaculatory dysfunction

    Cardiac:
      In normal dosages:
        Tachycardia
        EKG changes (T-wave flattening, increased PR and QT
          interval)
      In overdose:
        PVCs, ventricular arrhythmias
        AV block and BBB
        CHF and cardiac arrest

Other:
  Orthostatic hypotension (can be severe)
  Sedation
  Restlessness, insomnia
  Rashes, allergic reactions
  Weight gain (a common cause of patient noncompliance)
  Anorexia, nausea and vomiting
  EEG changes
  Tremor (fine, rapid, usually hands and fingers)
  Confusion (in elderly)
  Seizures in patients who are predisposed

Tolerance usually develops to the anticholinergic and sedative side effects. Use cautiously in the elderly and in patients with BPH - avoid in patients with narrow-angle glaucoma. Pregnancy is not an absolute contraindication for TCA use, although there is suggestive (but not convincing) evidence of teratogenicity: avoid use in the first trimester if possible. Severe hypotension occasionally can limit drug use (it is least with nortriptyline and doxepin).

Most worrisome are the cardiac effects. There have been a few reports of sudden death from presumed arrhythmias-patients with pre-existing heart disease (particularly bundle-branch disease) and/or hypertension (eg, the elderly) are at risk for any of the cardiac side effects. Do not use following an acute MI or while in CHF. The danger is greatest with higher doses - eg, following an OD with a TCA.

There are wide differences between agents in their ability to produce some side effects, and these should be considered when choosing a drug. The presence of side effects is not a good indication that a therapeutic plasma level has been reached.

Certain psychiatric conditions may be adversely affected by TCAs.

- Schizophrenia may be made worse.
- A depressed bipolar patient may become manic.

A withdrawal syndrome occurs in some patients who have been taking high doses of TCAs (eg, imipramine 150-300 mg/day) for weeks or months. If medication is stopped abruptly, symptoms begin in 1-2 days and include anxiety, headache, myalgia, chills, malaise, and nausea. Withdraw the medication gradually (eg, 25-50 mg/wk).

DRUG INTERACTIONS:

- TCA plasma level is increased (at times dangerously) by methylphenidate, Antabuse, antipsychotics, exogenous thyroid, and guanethidine.

- TCA plasma level is decreased (<u>frequently</u> below therapeutic range) by barbiturates, alcohol, and <u>smoking</u> (may need to monitor level in heavy smokers).
- CNS depression occurs with antipsychotics, anticonvulsants hypnotic-sedatives, and alcohol.
- TCAs impair the antihypertensive effect of methyldopa, guanethidine, and bethanidine.
- There is a synergistic anticholinergic effect with other central anticholinergics - may produce a toxic psychosis
- Marked hypertension can be caused by administration of TCAs with sympathomimetic drugs (eg, isoproterenol, epinephrine, phenylephrine, amphetamines).
- TCAs may dangerously increase the half-life of anticoagulants (eg, Dicumarol) - monitor prothrombin time.

TREATMENT PRINCIPLES:

- Identify the patient likely to benefit from a TCA.
    1. Appropriate clinical presentation.
    2. Past personal history of good TCA response.
    3. Past family history of good TCA response.

- Unless side effects are likely to be a problem, begin with a tertiary TCA. They are metabolized in the liver to $2^o$ TCAs (imipramine to desipramine; amitriptyline to nortriptyline) and thus both the $3^o$ and $2^o$ TCAs are present in the body.

- Side effects may be useful (eg, consider amitriptyline or doxepin in the agitated depressive, desipramine in the elderly with anticholinergic intolerance, protriptyline if sedation is a problem, and nortriptyline if hypotension is excessive).

- One technique for treating depression with TCAs is:

    Begin imipramine 50 mg PO HS (or equivalent - less in elderly; more in the obese) and increase by 25-50 mg every 2-3 days until 150 mg is reached. If side effects interfere, slow down.
    Hold dosage at 150 mg for 1 week. If depression remains, increase to 200 mg (50 mg during the day, 150 at HS).
    Hold dosage at 200 mg for one week, then increase in 50 mg steps to 300 mg (150 mg in divided doses during the day, 150 mg at HS). Consider hospitalizing the pt for trials above 200 mg/day. Maintain at 300 mg for 2-3 weeks. It is important to do complete trials,[39] if side effect problems allow. If depression remains:
    1. Has patient been taking medication?
    2. Has a therapeutic window been passed?
    3. Measure plasma level.

If the patient is unimproved, consider:
1. A newer antidepressant or a different TCA.
2. ECT.
3. An MAOI. Allow 1-2 wks for transfer.
4. After 2-3 unsuccessful trials, reevaluate the diagnosis.

With a good response, sleep and appetite usually return first, then an improved mood. There is usually a 1-3 wk delay in the therapeutic effect, so don't stop meds prematurely.

- Never give a worrisomely depressed or seriously suicidal patient a prescription for more than 1000 mg of imipramine (or equivalent).

- If treating a psychotic depression, use a TCA and an antipsychotic simultaneously.

- If treating a depression in a bipolar patient taking lithium, continue the lithium if it has been effective prophylactically. The lithium may help prevent a manic overshoot.

- If treating a phobic-anxiety disorder, expect improvement with a lower dosage (eg, 100 mg).

- Simultaneous use of a TCA and an MAOI is currently discouraged by the FDA but is often useful.

- Maintenance care: In a successfully treated patient, maintain the medication at acute levels for 6 months. If the patient has had several recurrences of a major depression in the past, consider long-term TCA maintenance (reduces likelihood of a relapse by 50%). Consider lithium maintenance in a recurrent bipolar illness. If there is no previous history of illness, gradually withdraw the medication.

  Recognize (1) as many as one quarter of the improved patients relapse during the 1st 4 months and (2) a significant number of patients maintain a chronic, low-level depression, even though treated successfully for the acute illness ("double depression").

- TCA overdose is life-threatening and should be treated on a medical inpatient unit. Recognize that dangerously high plasma levels may continue for more than one week.

- Although generally not considered drugs of abuse, illicit use of amitriptyline by an outpatient population of narcotic abusers occurs. Watch for it.

## NEWER ANTIDEPRESSANTS[40]

The primary reason for using "newer antidepressants" is their different side effect spectrums and toxicity: they differ little from TCAs in effectiveness, disorders treated, or speed of onset.    Generally, use these drugs if a TCA trial fails.    Their mechanisms of action are diverse and poorly understood (most effect DA, NE, and/or 5-HT) although one group, the "pure serotonin reuptake inhibitors" (fluoxetine, fluvoxamine, and sertraline), have a more focused action.    The key drugs include:

**alprazolam:** a benzodiazepine that <u>may</u> be antidepressant at higher doses; few side effects except sedation and risk of <u>addiction</u>; safe in overdose.    (A "second-string" antidepressant, at best.)

**amoxapine:** a metabolite of the antipsychotic loxapine; side effects similar to TCAs; <u>may</u> be of particular use in psychotic depressions.

**bupropion:** temporarily (?) withdrawn $2^o$ to a possible production of seizures; a promising drug with few side effects and safe in overdose; can produce insomnia and sweating.

**maprotiline:** like TCAs; less cardiotoxicity in overdose.

**trazadone:** free of anticholinergic and most cardiac effects; produces orthostatic hypotension, sedation, GI distress, headaches, and (rarely) <u>priapism</u>.

**serotonin reuptake blockers**[41]: little sedation or anticholinergic effects (perhaps daytime sedation in a few); does produce GI upset, insomnia, and restlessness; recently released (flluoxetine - 1988).


## MONOAMINE OXIDASE INHIBITORS (MAOIs)

<u>INDICATIONS FOR USE</u>:

Recommended for[42]:

1. Atypical depression[43] - MAOIs should probably be the drug of choice for "atypical, neurotic depressions" (50-60% improve) - ie, patients with varying degrees of depressive and anxious affect, rejection sensitivity, irritability, emotional lability, hyperphagia, hypersomnolence, reversed diurnal variation

(worse in evening), and hypochondriasis (all with the vegetative symptoms of a major depression). If a TCA is tried first and fails, follow with a trial of an MAOI. ECT is notoriously unsuccessful with these patients.

Other uses:

- Patients with major depression or dysthymic disorder who have not improved with a trial of one or more TCAs and for whom ECT is not the obvious next choice. Has the patient or a family member responded to an MAOI in the past?
- MAOIs appear useful in panic disorder and in agoraphobia with panic attacks (particularly phenelzine).

## MECHANISMS OF ACTION:

MAOIs block MAO (and other enzymes) throughout the body (eg, blood, platelets, gut, CNS). MAO catalyzes the oxidation of the biogenic amines tyramine, 5-HT, DA, and NE. The therapeutic effect of MAOIs is <u>probably</u> related to the increase in CNS NE and 5-HT which result from the ability of MAOI to block this oxidation of intracellular catecholamines
MAO exists in two forms: MAO-A (in brain, liver, gut, and sympathetic nerves) which acts primarily on 5-HT and NE, and MAO-B (in brain, liver, and platelets) which acts on phenylethylamine. They both act on DA and tyramine. The MAOIs phenelzine, isocarboxazid, and tranylcypromine inhibit both types of MAO; clorgyline (not on the market) inhibits MAO-A; while pargyline (Eutonyl - used as an antihypertensive, not an antidepressant) and deprenyl (not on the market) inhibit MAO-B. MAO-A inhibitors may be more effective antidepressants, while MAO-B inhibitors are less prone to produce hypertensive reactions. More work remains to be done.

## PHARMACOKINETICS:

MAOIs are rapidly absorbed and are metabolized into inactive products by several means including acetylation (hydrazide MAOIs only). There may be patients who are "rapid acetylators" and who require increased oral doses of MAOI for improvement to occur. There is usually a delay of 1-4 weeks before a clinical response is seen. Measured inhibition of platelet MAO in blood samples (80-90% inhibition appears necessary) provides some indication that an effective level of CNS MAOI has been reached, although this procedure is currently primarily a research technique.

SIDE EFFECTS:

MAOIs have numerous side effects. However, they do not have the range of cardiotoxic effects of the TCAs, although some experts feel that they should be contraindicated in the elderly because of the risk of hypertensive crisis (see below) with its potentially fatal outcome in the older pt.

The most common side effects include drowsiness or stimulation (short lived), insomnia, giddiness, dizziness, dry mouth, impotence, orthostatic hypotension, constipation, and weight gain. They also can precipitate a manic or schizoaffective attack. Since occasional patients develop hepatotoxicity, patients using MAOIs long-term should have periodic examinations of liver function. They are contra-indicated in patients with liver disease, CHF, or pheo-chromocytoma.

The most serious (but infrequent) side effect is hyper-tension (hypertensive crisis, cerebrovascular bleeding) and hyperpyrexia in response to ingested tyramine (or other pressor amines). The MAO in the gut wall which usually prevents entrance of large quantities of ingested pressor amines is inhibited by MAOIs, thus allowing a generalized sympathetic effect when tyramine-containing foods are eaten. The first sign of an impending crisis is usually a sudden, severe occipital or temporal headache (also sweating, fever, neck stiffness, photophobia). Patients taking MAOIs should avoid:

Protein-containing foods which are cultured or spoiled:
  Strong cheeses (cottage, ricotta, or cream cheese are OK).
  Pickled or kippered herring; dried, salted fish.
  Chicken livers or liver pate; any slightly spoiled meat;
    ripened sausages.
  Old yogurt, chocolate.
Nondistilled alcohol - red or Chianti wine; beer.
Broad beans (Fava, Italian green, and lima beans).

A number of adrenergic drugs (see below) may also produce a hypertensive crisis. If one occurs, treat with slow admin-istration of phentolamine (Regitine, 5 mg IV). It usually resolves in a few hours. The responsible patient may carry one dose of 50 mg of Thorazine with him with instructions to take it orally when signs of a crisis appear.

DRUG INTERACTIONS:

Hypertensive crisis - can be produced by amphetamines, cocaine, and anorectics (stimulate NE release from adrenergic neurons), catecholamines (epinephrine, NE), sympathomimetic precursors (dopamine, methyldopa, levo-dopa), and sympathomimetic amines (ephedrine, phenyl-

ephrine, phenylpropanolamine, pseudoephedrine, metara-
minol, over-the-counter cold and hay fever medication).
Meperidine (Demerol) - A few patients develop severe,
immediate hypertension and sweating or hypotension and
coma. Narcotics may act similarly.
CNS depression - potentiated by alcohol, major tranquilizers, and hypnotic-sedatives.

TREATMENT PRINCIPLES:

- Instruct the patient carefully about the potential side
  effects and the drugs and foods to avoid.

- Begin phenelzine 15 mg PO bid-tid and increase by 15 mg
  weekly to 60-90 mg/day. Maintain that dosage for 4
  weeks before assuming a failure.

- Maintenance is at acute treatment doses. In some
  patients, for unknown reasons, both the antidepressant
  and antiphobic effects become ineffective after 6 months
  to one year of use.

- Allow for a 1-2 week washout before starting another drug.

- If insomnia becomes a major problem, give all doses before
  midafternoon.

- Tranylcypromine has significant stimulant properties.

- Don't give impulsive, potentially suicidal outpatients
  large prescriptions.

## ANTIDEPRESSANT DRUG COMBINATIONS

Combined drug therapy may help a patient who has failed
trials with single antidepressants. Such treatment is
empirical: proceed carefully and watch out for side effects.
Occasionally useful combinations include:

TCA and an MAOI[44] - particularly nortriptyline or amitriptyline with phenelzine; avoid imipramine and serotonin
reuptake inhibitors; do not add a TCA to an MAOI; use
lower doses than if you were using each drug alone.
Antidepressant and lithium[45] - for both unipolar and bipolar depression; adding lithium to a TCA or a MAOI[46]
occasionally produces a rapid (days) improvement.
Antidepressant and antipsychotic[47] - for psychotic depressions.
Antidepressant and thyroid[48] - occasional patients improve
(Did they have a subclinical thyroid dysfunction?).

## ANTIANXIETY AGENTS

DRUGS AVAILABLE:

There are numerous drugs available for sedation, of which only the benzodiazepines and buspirone can be recommended.

| Drug | Half-life (hrs) | Dose (mg/day) | |
|------|-----------------|---------------|---|
| alprazolam (Xanax) | 11-14 | 1-4 | |
| chlordiazepoxide (Librium) | 15-20 | 15-60 | |
| clorazepate (Tranxene) | 50-100 | 15-45 | |
| diazepam (Valium) | 30-60 | 5-40 | |
| halazepam (Paxipam) | 50-100 | 60-160 | |
| lorazepam (Ativan) | 10-20 | 2-6 | |
| oxazepam (Serax) | 5-10 | 30-120 | |
| prazepam (Centrax) | 60-70 | 20-60 | |
| [clonazepam (Klonopin)] | 30-40 | 1-15 | |
| | | | |
| flurazepam (Dalmane) | $50^+$ | 15-30 | (HS) |
| temazepam (Restoril) | 8-18 | 15-30 | (HS) |
| triazolam (Halcion) | 2-3 | 0.125-0.5 | (HS) |
| | | | |
| buspirone (Buspar) | 2-3 | 15-60 | |

INDICATIONS FOR USE:

1. Short-term treatment of restlessness and anxiety (eg, following life crises). They are sedative at low dosage and hypnotic at higher doses. They have no antipsychotic activity and thus should not be used as the exclusive treatment for psychotic disorders.
2. Generalized anxiety disorder and mild panic symptoms.
3. Alcohol withdrawal (see chapter 16); hypnotic-sedative withdrawal; psychosis due to hallucinogens.
4. Various seizure disorders.
5. Muscle relaxant (diazepam).

MECHANISMS OF ACTION AND PHARMACOKINETICS:

They enhance the inhibitory neurotransmitters (eg, GABA, glycine) and they have a specific depressant effect on the limbic system. As the dosage rises, there is generalized CNS depression.

They are well absorbed orally, are all both water and lipid soluble, and are usually metabolized by the liver but may also be excreted by the kidney. They are slowly and variably absorbed IM (faster by PO route).  There is very little hepatic enzyme induction.  Peak blood levels usually occur 1-4 hr after the oral dose (1 hr for diazepam).


## SIDE EFFECTS

In comparison to other classes of psychoactive drugs, side effects are few.

- Most common problem is CNS depression manifested by day-time sedation, decreased concentration, and poor coordination in some patients at therapeutic doses.  They are very safe drugs, although a massive OD will produce life-threatening CNS depression.
- Anterograde amnesia can occur following hypnotic-induced sleep with short-acting drugs (eg, lorazepam, triazolam).  Patients may lose memory for events which occurred during the night or during the following day.
- Tolerance and physical addiction occur, particularly with short-acting drugs[49] or when taken at high doses for several months.  The withdrawal syndrome is usually mild[50] (but may be severe) and typically occurs 3-14 days after stopping the drug.
- Untoward but infrequent psychiatric manifestations include exacerbation of schizophrenia and depression.
- There appear to be no autonomic side effects.
- Benzodiazepines seem to be safe in pregnancy.


## DRUG INTERACTIONS:

- There is an increased sedative effect when combined with CNS depressants (eg, alcohol).  Moreover, the combination with alcohol at times actually may be anxiogenic.
- Disulfiram (Antabuse) and cimetidine impair the metabolism of the long-acting benzodiazepines and thus raise the plasma levels.  The shorter-acting drugs appear less affected.
- Food, antacids, and anticholinergic drugs appear to decrease the rate but not the extent of drug absorption.


## TREATMENT PRINCIPLES:

- Use the long-acting benzodiazepines (chlordiazepoxide, diazepam, clorazepate) on an HS or bid schedule.  Use a tid-qid schedule for the shorter-acting ones (oxazepam, lorazepam).
- Recognize that the longer-acting drugs (and their active metabolites) may accumulate over days or weeks, produc-

ing increasing symptoms of sedation, etc.  Lorazepam and oxazepam have a simple metabolism and do not accumulate.
- Try to avoid use for longer than 1-3 weeks in most pts either as a sedative or a hypnotic.  Some patients may be able to use them less frequently but long-term on an "as needed" basis, but be alert for those patients prone to abuse.[51]  Reevaluate if you find that you have used meds for longer than 2-4 months.
- Use by PO route, if possible.
- Encourage the patient to avoid the simultaneous use of a benzodiazepine and alcohol or another sedative-hypnotic drug.  Do not prescribe more than a 2 weeks' supply at any one time.
- Be very careful when giving to the elderly - confusion is common.  Dosage may need to be 20% or less of the usual young adult dose.
- If the patient has been taking benzodiazepines for several months, stop meds over 2-3 weeks (particularly the long-acting drugs).
- The more sedative benzodiazepines are used primarily as hypnotics: flurazepam, temazepam, and triazolam.  Flurazepam (and, to a lesser degree, triazolam) is rapidly absorbed and is useful for sleep onset problems; temazepam and flurazepam may help frequent awakening.  Flurazepam, particularly because of its long-acting metabolite N-desalkylflurazepam, accumulates and produces a hangover in many patients.  Triazolam does not accumulate but may produce early morning insomnia and daytime anxiety.

Buspirone represents a new class of anxiolytics.  It has few side effects, produces less sedation and cognitive and psychomotor impairment than the benzodiazepines, but may be less effective as well.[52]  It may be a reasonable alternative drug.


## ELECTROCONVULSIVE THERAPY (ECT)

In spite of its notoriety, ECT is a legitimate psychiatric treatment.[53]  Although its mechanism of action is unknown, it is effective, painless, and safe, with a mortality rate less than competing therapies or the untreated state (0.01-0.03% of patients treated - mostly cardiovascular deaths).  However, because of its legal sensitivity, prior to administration always obtain:

1. Informed consent from a voluntary, competent patient.
2. Informed consent from a relative or guardian of a voluntary, incompetent patient and an independent psychiatric opinion of therapeutic need.

3. Court approval for administration to a resisting, involuntary patient who is a danger to himself or others.

Discuss the risks of amnesia, confusion, and headache with the patient and his family. Also discuss the risks of <u>not</u> receiving ECT.

<u>Indications for use</u>:

ECT is a serious procedure - use <u>only</u> in those conditions for which it is recommended.[54]  It is tempting to give ECT to any patient who is not improving - don't!

MAJOR AFFECTIVE ILLNESS:  Patients with <u>Major Depression</u> or <u>Bipolar disorder, depressed</u> respond well to ECT (80-90% recover vs 70%[+] treated with antidepressants).  Patients with marked vegetative symptoms (eg, insomnia, constipation, suicidal rumination, obsessions with guilt, anorexia and weight loss, psychomotor retardation) are particularly responsive.  ECT is much more effective than antidepressants for psychotically depressed patients - ie, vegetative symptoms and paranoid or somatic delusions.  Give antidepressants a full trial (eg, imipramine 200-300 mg/day for 4 wk), then consider ECT if there is no improvement.

Mania (<u>Bipolar Disorder, manic</u>) also responds to ECT but it should be used only if lithium carbonate (often initially coupled with an antipsychotic) fails to control the acute phase.

SCHIZOPHRENIC DISORDERS: <u>Catatonic Schizophrenia</u> of either stuporous or excited type responds well to ECT.  Try antipsychotic medication first but, if the condition is life-threatening (eg, hyperexcited delirium), go quickly to ECT.  Occasional acutely psychotic patients (particularly of the schizoaffective type) who do not respond to medication alone may improve if ECT is added, but for most schizophrenics (eg, chronics) it is of little value.

ECT is the <u>treatment of choice</u> for:

1. Actively suicidal depressed patients who may not live until antidepressants begin to work.
2. Depressed patients (particularly the elderly) whose medical condition makes administration of antidepressants risky.  Patients with both depression and OBS may do better with ECT.  ECT <u>can</u> be safely performed during pregnancy.
3. Seriously depressed patients who have had an <u>adequate</u> trial of antidepressants (60-70% recovers with ECT).

Contraindications for use:

There are no <u>absolute</u> contraindications. Always weigh the risk of the procedure against the danger incurred if the patient is untreated. Neurological disease is not a contra-indication.[55] Response improves with age - patients under 30 respond more poorly.

Very high risk:
Increased intracranial pressure (eg, brain tumor, CNS infection): ECT briefly increases CSF pressure and risks tentorial herniation. Always check for papill-edema before administration.
Recent MI: ECT frequently causes arrhythmias (vagal arrhythmias producing postictal PVCs and extravagal arrhythmias producing PVCs anytime during the proce-dure) which can be fatal if there has been recent muscle damage. Wait until enzymes and EKG have stabilized.

Moderate risk:
Severe osteoarthritis, osteoporosis, or recent fracture: Prepare thoroughly for treatment (ie, with muscle relaxants).
Cardiovascular disease (eg, hypertension, angina, aneurysm, arrhythmias): Premedicate carefully; have a cardiologist available.
Major infections, recent CVA, chronic respiratory diffi-culty, acute peptic ulcer.

TECHNIQUE OF ADMINISTRATION:

Pre-ECT Medical Workup:

Complete history and physical, concentrating on cardiac and neurological status, CBC, chemistry, UA, VDRL, chest and spine X-rays, EKG. Get EEG (and/or CT scan) if neuro-logical is abnormal.

A Typical Technique:

ECT routines vary[56] - there is no "one right way." Usually perform in a hospital and with the aid of an anes-thesiologist.

1. Prepare the patient with information and psychological support. Have him void and defecate beforehand. NPO after midnight. If markedly anxious, give 5 mg of diazepam IM 1-2 hr before treatment. Antidepressants and antipsychotics should be stopped the day before treatment. Lithium and ECT may be given concurrently if

cardiac and renal functions are good.
2. Make patient comfortable.    Remove dentures.    Hyperextend the back with a pillow.

3. When ready, premedicate with atropine (0.6-1.2 mg SC, IM, or IV).    This anticholinergic controls vagal arrhythmias and reduces GI secretions.
4. Provide 90-100% oxygen by bag when respirations are not spontaneous.
5. Give sodium methohexital (Brevital) (40-100 mg IV, rapidly).    This short-acting barbiturate anesthetic is used to produce a light coma.
6. Next quickly give enough of the muscle relaxant succinylcholine (Anectine) (30-80 mg IV, rapidly - monitor depth of relaxation by the muscle fasciculations produced) to remove all but very minor evidences of a generalized seizure (eg, plantarflexion).
7. Once relaxed, place a bite-block in the mouth and then give electroconvulsive stimulus.    Two methods are common today:

Unilateral: One electrode placed in the frontotemporal area and the other 7-10 cm away in the parietal region - both on the nondominant hemisphere (right side for right-handed persons, 60% R and 40% L for left-handers).    Unilateral ECT is commonly used because it produces less postictal confusion and amnesia but it seems to be less effective than bilateral ECT.[57]
Bilateral: Bifrontotemporal electrode placement.    This is the traditional technique - effective but produces more side effects (eg, amnesia, headache).

Effectiveness of either method depends upon producing a central generalized seizure (peripheral effects are not necessary) lasting at least 25 seconds.    Monitor this with EEG, peripheral EMG, or the tonic/clonic movement of the hand on the same side as the electrode (unilateral) which has been freed of muscle relaxant by a tight cuff applied before the administration of the succinylcholine.    If a seizure is not produced, increase the stimulus and repeat ("missed" or unilateral seizures are usually of little therapeutic value - they occur more frequently with unilateral shock, perhaps accounting for its lesser effectiveness).
8. Monitor patient carefully until stable - there is usually 15-30 minutes of postictal confusion.    These patients are at risk for prolonged apnea and a postictal delirium (5-10 mg of IV diazepam may help).

Complications of ECT:

- Amnesia (retrograde and anterograde) - variable; beginning
  after 3-4 treatments; lasting weeks to 2-3 months (but
  occasionally much longer); more severe with bilateral
  placement, increased number of treatments, and increased
  current strength.
- Headache, muscle aches, nausea.
- Dizziness, confusion - The persistence and severity of the
  confusion increases with an increasing number of treatments.
- Reserpine and ECT given concurrently have resulted in
  fatalities.
- Fractures - rare with good muscle relaxation.
- ECT anesthesia risks:
  Atropine worsens narrow angle glaucoma.
  Succinylcholine's action is prolonged in pseudocholin-
  esterase deficiency states. These conditions (malnutrition, liver disease, chronic renal dialysis, use of
  echothiophate for glaucoma) can lead to potentially
  fatal hypotonia. Procainamide, lidocaine, and quinidine can potentiate succinylcholine.
  Methohexital can precipitate an attack of acute intermittent porphyria.

Treatment Principles:

1. Usually give one treatment/day - on alternate days.
2. Depressions usually require 6-12 treatments. Mania and
   catatonia require 10-20. Expect to see improved behavior after 2-6 treatments if it is going to be effective.
   Allow the clinical response to determine the treatment
   endpoint. Be very cautious (and seek a second opinion)
   about exceeding 20 treatments during one period of illness.
3. Maintenance ECT (single treatments every 4-6 weeks during
   the months or years after recovery) may be useful, particularly with elderly depressed patients, but should be
   used only if medication is contraindicated.
4. Maintenance antidepressants, antipsychotics, and lithium
   (begin after a successful course of ECT) definitely
   forestall relapse. Without medication, the relapse rate
   is high.


## PSYCHOSURGERY

Little psychosurgery is currently performed in the USA.
Modern psychosurgeons make one of several possible small
cuts in the brain (usually in the limbic system) which can
improve a variety of psychiatric conditions and which have

few side effects (unlike the widely destructive prefrontal lobotomy of the past).

All candidates for surgery must have an intractable and devastating condition unrelieved by any other therapy. Conditions likely to respond include chronic pain with depression and severe depression alone. Improvement occurs in some patients who have severe obsessive-compulsive and anxiety states and in a few schizophrenics. The mechanism for the improvement is uncertain and a variety of different "cuts" yield similar results. Despite the lack of theoretical sophistication, there are patients for whom psychosurgery is a valid "last resort."

## REFERENCES

1.  Simpson GM, Yadalam K: Blood levels of neuroleptics. J Clin Psychiatry 46 (5, Sec.2):22-28, 1985.
2.  Zohar J, Shemesh Z, Belmaker RH: Utility of neuroleptic blood levels in the treatment of acute psychosis. J Clin Psychiatry 47:600-603, 1986.
3.  Claghorn J, Honigfeld G, Abuzzahab FS, et al: The risks and benefits of clozapine versus chlorpromazine. J Clin Psychopharmacol 7:377-384, 1987.
4.  Gelenberg AJ: Treating extrapyramidal reactions. J Clin Psychiatry 48 (9, Suppl):24-27, 1987.
5.  Waddington JL, Youssef HA: An unusual cluster of tardive dyskinesia in schizophrenia: Association with cognitive dysfunction and negative symptoms. Am J Psychiatry 143: 1162-1165, 1986.
6.  Yagi G, Itoh H: Follow-up study of 11 patients with potentially reversible tardive dyskinesia. Am J Psychiatry 144:1496-1498, 1987.
7.  Branchey M, Branchey L: Patterns of psychotropic drug use and tardive dyskinesia. J Clin Psychopharmacol 4:41, 1984.
8.  Dilsaver SC: Antimuscarinic agents as substances of abuse: A review. J Clin Psychopharmacol 8:14-22, 1988.
9.  Pearlman CA: Neuroleptic malignant syndrome: A review of the literature. J Clin Psychopharmacol 6:257-273, 1986.
10. Janicak PG, Bresnahan DB, Comaty JE: The neuroleptic malignant syndrome: A clinical update. Psychiatr Annals 17:551-555, 1987.
11. Dhib-Jalbut S, Hesselbrock R, Mouradian MM, Means ED: Bromocriptine treatment of neuroleptic malignant syndrome. J Clin Psychiatry 48:69-73, 1987.
12. Baldessarini RJ, Cohen BM, Teicher MH: Significance of neuroleptic dose and plasma level in the pharmacological treatment of psychoses. Arch Gen Psychiatry 45:79-91, 1988.

13. Meltzer HY, Sommers AA, Luchins DJ: The effect of neuro-
    leptics and other psychotropic drugs on negative symptom
    in schizophrenia. J Clin Psychopharmacol 6:329-338, 1986
14. Weiden PJ, Shaw E, Mann JJ: Causes of neuroleptic non-
    compliance. Psychiatr Ann 16:571-575, 1986.
15. Davis JM, Andriukaitis S: The natural course in schizo-
    phrenia and effective maintenance drug treatment. J Clin
    Psychopharmacol 6:2S-10S, 1986.
16. Kane JM, Woerner M, Sarantakos S: Depot neuroleptics: A
    comparative review of standard, intermediate, and low-
    dose regimens. J Clin Psychiatry 47 (5, Suppl):30-33,
    1986.
17. Kane JM: Dosage strategies with long-acting injectable
    neuroleptics, including haloperidol decanoate. J Clin
    Psychopharmacol 6:20S-23S, 1986.
18. Carpenter WT, Heinrichs DW, Hanlon TE: A comparative
    trial of pharmacologic strategies in schizophrenia. Am J
    Psychiatry 144:1466-1470, 1987.
19. Jefferson JW, Greist JH, Ackerman DL, Carroll JA: Lith-
    ium Encyclopedia for Clinical Practice. Washington, DC,
    American Psychiatric Press, 1987.
20. Carroll JA, Jefferson JW, Greist JH: Treating tremor
    induced by lithium. Hosp Comm Psychiatry 38:1280, 1987.
21. DePaulo JR, Correa EI, Sapir DG: Renal function and
    lithium. Am J Psychiatry 143:892-895, 1986.
22. Deandrea D, Walker N, Mehlmauer M, White K: Dermatologi-
    cal reactions to lithium. J Clin Psychopharmacol 2: 199-
    204, 1982.
23. Linden S, Rich CL: The use of lithium during pregnancy
    and lactation. J Clin Psychiatry 44:358-361, 1983.
24. Jefferson JW, Greist JH, Baudhuin M: Lithium: Interac-
    tions with other drugs. J Clin Psychopharmacol 1:124-
    134, 1981.
25. Miller F, Menninger J: Correlation of neuroleptic dose
    and neurotoxicity in patients given lithium and a neuro-
    leptic. Hosp Community Psychiatry 38:1219-1221, 1987.
26. Goldney RD, Spence ND: Safety of the combination of
    lithium and neuroleptic drugs. Am J Psychiatry 143:882-
    884, 1986.
27. Schou M: Lithium treatment. Br J Psychiatry 149:541-547,
    1986.
28. Rosenberg JG, Binder RL, Berlant J: Prediction of thera-
    peutic lithium dose. J Clin Psychiatry 48:284-286, 1987.
29. Shaw E: Lithium noncompliance. Psychiatr Ann 16: 583-
    587, 1986.
30. Jefferson JW, Greist JH, Clagnaz PJ, et al: Effect of
    strenuous exercise on serum lithium level in man. Am J
    Psychiatry 139:1593, 1982.
31. Lerer B, Moore N, Meyendorff E, et al: Carbamazepine vs
    lithium in mania. J Clin Psychiatry 48:89-93, 1987.

32. Placidi GF, Lenzi A, Lazzerini F, et al: The comparative efficacy and safety of carbamazepine versus lithium J Clin Psychiatry 47:490-494, 1986.
33. Fawcett J, Kravitz HM: The long-term management of bipolar disorders with lithium, carbamazepine, and antidepressants. J Clin Psychiatry 46:58-60, 1985.
34. Post RM, Uhde TW, Roy-Byrne PP, Joffe RT: Antidepressant effects of carbamazepine. Am J Psychiatry 143:29, 1986.
35. Stone JL, McDaniel KD, Hughes JR, Hermann BP: Episodic dyscontrol disorder and paroxysmal EEG abnormalities: Successful treatment with carbamazepine. Biol Psychiatry 21:208-212, 1986.
36. Preskorn SH: Tricyclic antidepressant plasma level monitoring: an improvement over the dose-response approach. J Clin Psychiatry 47 (Suppl):24-30, 1986.
37. Task Force on the Use of Laboratory Tests in Psychiatry: Tricyclic antidepressants - blood level measurements and clinical outcome. An APA Task Force Report. Am J Psychiatry 142:155-162, 1985.
38. Pollack MH, Rosenbaum JF: Management of antidepressant-induced side effects. J Clin Psychiatry 48:3-8, 1987.
39. Lydiard RB: Tricyclic-resistant depression: Treatment resistance or inadequate treatment. J Clin Psychiatry 46:412-417, 1985.
40. Johnson R, Ananth J: The newer antidepressants: Promises and realities. Compr Psychiatry 28:488-498, 1987.
41. Mendels J: Clinical experience with serotonin reuptake inhibiting antidepressants. J Clin Psychiatry 48:26-30 (Suppl), 1987.
42. Pare CMB: Monoamine oxidase inhibitors in treatment of affective disorders. Psychiatr Ann 17:309-315, 1987.
43. Liebowitz MR, Quitkin FM, Stewart JW, et al: Antidepressant specificity in atypical depression. Arch Gen Psychiatry 45:129-137, 1988.
44. White K, Simpson G: Combined MAOI-tricyclic antidepressant treatment: reevaluations. J Clin Psychopharmacol 1:264-282, 1981.
45. Price LH, Charney DS, Heninger GR: Variability of response to lithium augmentation in refractory depression. Am J Psychiatry 143:1387-1392, 1986.
46. Fein S, Paz V, Rao N, LaGrassa J: The combination of lithium carbonate and an MAOI in refractory depressions. Am J Psychiatry 145:249-250, 1988.
47. Spiker DG, Weiss JC, Dealy RS, et al: The pharmacological treatment of delusional depression. Am J Psychiatry 142:430-436, 1985.
48. Goodwin FK, Prange AJ, Post RM, et al: Potentiation of antidepressant effects by L-triiodothyronine in tricyclic nonresponders. Am J Psychiatry 139:34-38, 1982.

49. Tyrer P: Dependence as a limiting factor in the clinical use of minor tranquillizers. Pharmac Ther 36:173-188, 1988.
50. Busto U, Sellers EM, Naranjo CA, et al: Withdrawal reaction after long-term therapeutic use of benzodiazepines. NEJM 315:854-859, 1986.
51. Dominguez RA, Goldstein BJ: 25 years of benzodiazepine experience: Clinical commentary on use, abuse, and withdrawal. Hosp Formul 20:100-1014, 1985.
52. Olajide D, Lader M: A comparison of buspirone, diazepam, and placebo in patients with chronic anxiety states. J Clin Psychopharmacol 7:148-152, 1987.
53. Concensus conference: electroconvulsive therapy. JAMA 254:2103-2108, 1985.
54. Small IF, Milstein V, Miller MJ, et al: Electroconvulsive treatment - indications, benefits, and limitations. Am J Psychother 40:343-356, 1986.
55. Dubovsky SL: Using electroconvulsive therapy for patients with neurological disease. Hosp Community Psychiatry 37:819-825, 1986.
56. Glenn MD, Weiner RD: Electroconvulsive Therapy: A Programmed Text. Washington, D.C., American Psychiatric Press, 1985.
57. Sackeim HA, Decina P, Kanzler M, et al: Effects of electrode placement on the efficacy of titrated, low-dose ECT. Am J Psychiatry 144:1449-1455, 1987.

# Chapter 24

# The Elderly Patient

More than 25,000,000 Americans are over 65: 85% have a chronic illness (usually medical); 20-30% have a psychiatric illness (most common in the very old).

## EVALUATION OF THE ELDERLY

1. Assess each patient carefully - mental decline is <u>not</u> "normal" for the aged.
2. Always carefully evaluate physical condition. An impaired physical state can markedly alter the psychiatric evaluation. Make sure the patient can hear and see. Check for deficiency states (iron, folate, vitamin $B_{12}$ and D, calcium, serum proteins).
3. Interview technique: Be respectful, use surname, sit near, speak slowly and clearly, allow time for answers, be friendly and personal, pat and hug, be supportive and issue-oriented, keep interview short.
4. Collect history, do mental status - perhaps in more than one interview.
5. Identify premorbid personality - defense mechanisms and coping styles (eg, independent vs passive-dependent, rigid vs flexible, use of denial, etc).
6. Assess the major <u>risk factors</u>:
    A. Loss - of spouse, friends, physical health, job, status, independence, etc.
    B. Poverty - many elderly are poor; some are victims of crime.
    C. Social isolation - impaired mobility, few friends, etc.
    D. Sensory deprivation - poor hearing, vision, etc.
    E. Sickness - chronic pain, forced inactivity, etc.
    F. Fears - of being dependent, of being alone, of being helpless.
7. See family - assess their strengths, dynamics, support for the patient, hidden agendas.

## COMMON PSYCHIATRIC DISORDERS

Delirium[1,2]:  Common.  May be the primary presentation of:
1. CNS - Cerebral infarction (embolic or thrombotic), TIA, neoplasms.
2. Heart - MI (often without pain), arrhythmia, CHF.
3. Lungs - Pneumonia (without fever or leukocytosis), PE (without chest pain, dyspnea, tachycardia).
4. Blood - Anemia.
5. Metabolic - Diabetes, liver failure, hyper- or hypo-thyroidism, electrolyte abnormalities.
6. Psychogenic - strange surroundings, stress.
7. Infections - most kinds.
8. Other - Medication reaction, alcoholism, prescription drug misuse, dehydration, fecal impaction, "silent" appendicitis, urinary retention, UTIs, eye or ear disease, postoperative.

Treat the underlying disease process, if possible. Keep patient in a lighted room and with familiar surroundings and people.  Restrain only if essential.  If needed, use small doses of major tranquilizers (eg, thioridazine 25-50 mg, PO, often given as an HS dose; thiothixene 2-5 mg, PO, or 4 mg, IM).

Dementia[3-5]:  Most elderly have unimpaired intellectual functioning.  Dementia (20% of those 80 years old) is not "just a result of aging" - it needs an explanation.  Dementia often presents first with agitation, anxiety, depression, and/or somatic complaints - always do a mental status exam on elderly patients with these complaints but, remember, that it can also be mimicked by depression, serious physical conditions, alcoholism, and malnutrition. Dementia in the elderly frequently occurs with and is made worse by depression or delirium.  The memory loss may be unrecognized by the patient but is of major concern to the family, who ultimately insist on evaluation and treatment for it.

Most patients with a progressive and nonreversible form of dementia can be maintained at home until the late stages of the disease process.  The decision to institutionalize depends not only on what facilities are available locally (some may be very good) but also on the realistic strengths and limits of the family.  Once the cause and prognosis of the dementia is determined, the physician may most profitably spend his time helping the family adjust.

Depression[6-9]: Major Depression can develop in old age for the first time or be a recurrence of a major affective disorder.  In the elderly it may at times closely mimic a dementia (pseudodementia) - or physical symptoms, apathy, or fatigue may dominate the clinical picture. Remember that the highest suicide rate occurs among elderly males (particularly with alcoholism) so, if in doubt, hospitalize. Treat with psychotherapy and antidepressants (increase slowly; effective final daily dose may be as low as 75-100 mg). ECT may be the therapy of choice in patients with unstable cardiac status or in those patients with psychotic depression (eg, paranoia, hallucinations).

A less severe depression or depressive equivalent (listlessness, physical complaints, withdrawal) in a patient with longstanding depressive complaints may represent <u>Dysthymic Disorder</u>. Since stress and loss are so common among the elderly, <u>Adjustment Disorder with Depressed Mood</u> and <u>Uncomplicated Bereavement</u> occur frequently.

<u>Mania</u>[10]: Does occur in old age but usually with a history of bipolar disorder. Extreme agitation or manic-like behavior can be caused by delirium, dementia, schizophrenia, depression, or situational anxiety. Lithium is effective.

<u>Schizophrenia</u>: Usually there is a life-long history of schizophrenic illness but, rarely, the stresses of old age can precipitate a first episode in a predisposed individual (longstanding schizoid or borderline functioning).[11-13] Occasionally there is associated intellectual deterioration. Treat with support and antipsychotics.

<u>Paranoia</u>: Mild suspiciousness among the elderly is very common. Bizarre forms or near psychotic levels may occur with:

1. Early dementia - <u>always</u> check for intellectual loss.
2. Delirium
3. Vision or hearing problems - may resolve promptly.
4. Social isolation; chronic illness.
5. Drugs - eg, steroids, antiparkinsonians, hypnotic withdrawal.

DELUSIONAL DISORDER (DSM-III-R p 197, 297.10) often has an onset late in life (late paraphrenia).[14,15] These patients have fixed paranoid delusions and occasionally auditory hallucinations but not the loose associations, grandiosity, major hallucinations, and autistic thought of paranoid schizophrenics (although the conditions may overlap). Treat with reality-oriented psychotherapy, behavior modification, maintenance antipsychotics, and possibly ECT.

<u>Hypochondriasis</u>: The elderly are frequently ill and may develop a preoccupation with exaggerated physical complaints

and problems. This is particularly common among depressed and/or demented elderly. The physical symptoms may or may not improve with resolution of the depression.

The patient with severe hypochondriasis, whose life is dominated by ruminations about one or more physical problems, is very difficult to treat. Withdrawal and isolation are frequent. Don't expect a "cure." Develop an ongoing relationship with this patient. Be available. See every 2-3 wk for 10-20 min. Reassure that the problem may be persistent and incurable but not debilitating or fatal. Recognize that in some cases symptoms may continue because to lose them would mean to lose the reason for visiting the physician.

<u>Adjustment Disorders</u>: These are common in old age and are due to the numerous stresses (loss, physical illness, retirement, etc.) encountered. Symptoms include anxiety, depression, agitation, and physical complaints and most often occur in persons with past adjustment problems. Grief is common and may mimic a major depression but often has an obvious precipitant, is short-lived with therapy, and does not require antidepressants. Alcohol abuse is also a common response to stress in the elderly. Supportive psychotherapy, attention to concrete problems, and brief use of minor tranquilizers or low-dose antipsychotics helps.

## PSYCHOPHARMACOLOGY OF OLD AGE[16-19]

The elderly usually run higher blood levels (due to decreased hepatic metabolism and renal excretion, reduced plasma albumin and protein binding, and increased fat to lean tissue ratios), display increased receptor responsiveness, and thus require more gradual increases and <u>lower doses</u> of most psychoactive medication. They are also more susceptible to most side effects - eg, peripheral and central anticholinergic effects, sedation, hypotension, arrhythmias. They are at risk for bowel obstruction, urinary retention, BP problems (fainting, stroke), sudden death from fatal arrhythmias, glaucoma crises, delirium, and coma. Also, they are particularly likely to be taking multiple drugs, to misunderstand and fail to comply with prescribing instruction, and to have symptoms from such polypharmacy. Preferable medication may include:

Benzodiazepines: Oxazepam and lorazepam (for anxiety) are least likely to accumulate. In patients with insomnia, try relaxation or exercise first: if a medication is needed, try temazepam (less likely to accumulate than flurazepam) or one of the sedating antihistamines (eg, diphenhydramine or hydroxyzine).

Tricyclics: Nortriptyline (less cardiotoxicity and hypotension) and desipramine (few anticholinergic effects). Begin as low as 10-25 mg daily and workup. Test for glaucoma and prostatic hypertrophy first. Monitor blood levels.

MAOIs: All have little anticholinergic effect and cardiotoxicity but watch out for hypotension. They are effective antidepressants, but hypertensive crises are particularly worrisome in the elderly.

Antipsychotics: Usually choose the more potent, least sedating types (eg, haloperidol, trifluoperazine), but be guided by patient's side effects. Thioridazine is well tolerated in low doses. Be particularly careful with IM meds - use U-100 insulin syringes to assure a small dose, if necessary.

Lithium: Toxicity occurs easily, so keep on a lower maintenance level (eg, 0.6-0.7 meq/l).

## GENERAL TREATMENT PRINCIPLES

- Be supportive, respectful, sympathetic, and a "good listener." Touch the patient.
- Encourage patients to express themselves (about guilt, loneliness, helplessness) and unburden themselves (eg, grieve).
- Be directive and reality-oriented. Help in a concrete way with problems (eg, who to see about rent assistance, calling "Meals-on-Wheels," explanation of Medicare benefits). The quality of the patient's current environment is probably the single most important factor promoting recovery and continued health.
- Strengthen defenses rather than restructure them.
- Encourage self-esteem. Helping patients "review their life" (to see it as complete) can be enormously beneficial. Reminiscence is adaptive coping behavior and helps promote self-esteem.
- Encourage continued interests, friendships, socialization, activities, and self-support. Identify those things still done well and keep the patient doing them (if they can't fix the meal, maybe they can still set the table).
- Be an ongoing presence. Be available - frequent, regular, short sessions. Be reachable by telephone.
- Involve and work with the family. Teach them appropriate skills and expectation. Anger, frustrations, and resentment often develop - help them deal with these feelings.
- A psychotherapy group of elderly patients is often very helpful - locate one for the patient.
- Know and use community resources.

## REFERENCES

1. Lipowski ZJ: Transient cognitive disorders in the elderly. Am J Psychiatry 140:1426-1436, 1983.
2. Zisook S, Braff DL: Delirium: Recognition and management in the older patient. Geriatrics 41:67-78, 1986.
3. Cummings JL, Benson DF: Dementia: A Clinical Approach. Boston, Butterworths, 1983.
4. Cummings JL: Subcortical dementia. Br J Psychiatry 149: 682-697, 1986.
5. Reisberg B: Dementia: A systematic approach to identifying reversible causes. Geriatrics 41:30-46, 1986.
6. Charatan FB: Depression in the elderly. Psychiatr Ann 15:313-316, 1985.
7. Neshkes RE, Jarvik LF: Depression in the elderly: Current management concepts. Geriatrics 41:51-56, 1986.
8. Baldwin RC, Jolley DJ: The prognosis of depression in old age. Br J Psychiatry 149:574-583, 1986.
9. Blazer DG, Bachar JR, Manton KG: Suicide in late life. J Am Ger Soc 34:519-5254, 1986.
10. Rabins P: Mania in the elderly. Age & Ageing 13:210-213, 1984.
11. Bridge TP, Kleinman JE, Soldo BJ, Karoum F: Central catecholamines, cognitive impairment, and affective state in elderly schizophrenics and controls. Biol Psychiatry 22:139-147, 1987.
12. Leuchter AF: Assessment and treatment of the late-onset psychoses. Hosp Community Psychiatry 36:815-818, 1985.
13. Miller BL, Benson DF, Cummings JL, Neshkes R: Late-life paraphrenia: An organic delusional syndrome. J Clin Psychiatry 47:204-207, 1986.
14. Holden NL: Late paraphrenia or the paraphrenias? Br J Psychiatry 150:635-639, 1987.
15. Jorgensen P, Munk-Jorgensen P: Paranoid psychosis in the elderly. Acta Psychiatr Scand 72:358-363, 1985.
16. Jenike MA: Handbook of Geriatric Psychopharmacology. Littleton, MA., PSG Pub Co, 1985.
17. Richelson E: Psychotropics and the elderly. Geriatrics 39:30-42, 1984.
18. Long PP: The elderly and drug interactions. J Am Geriatr Soc 34:586-592, 1986.
19. Wieman HM: Avoiding common pitfalls of geriatric prescribing. Geriatrics 41:81-89, 1986.

# Chapter 25

# Legal Issues

The interface between psychiatry and law is in flux, partly due to recent patient's rights legislation (based on the constitutional assurance that no person shall be deprived of his liberty without "due process of law"). A psychiatrist's dealings with his patients increasingly are constrained by case law and statue. It is essential that he learn the limits to his independence.[1] Laws can differ markedly from state to state and may change with time - become familiar with those laws that apply to your area.

## CIVIL LAW

### CIVIL COMMITMENT:

All states permit civil commitment to inpatient (and, at times, outpatient[2]) psychiatric care under specific, but differing, criteria:

1. <u>Mental Illness</u>: All states require the presence of a mental illness, but definitions differ. Psychosis usually is included but personality disorder is not. Drug and/or alcohol abuse may be accepted. Mental illness alone is not sufficient for commitment but requires at least one of the following two additional conditions.

2. <u>Dangerousness</u> - to self or others: Most states require the patient to be dangerous but differ in the degree of urgency - an <u>imminent</u> danger (eg, likely to hurt himself in the next 24 hours) vs a relative danger (eg, physically deteriorating through depressive withdrawal). Two major problems with the dangerousness standard are: (1) psychiatrists have difficulty accurately predicting future dangerous behavior except in the most obvious cases,[3] and (2) it has been uncertain what level of proof the law requires - ie, the traditional lesser civil standard of "clear and convincing evidence" or the

more strict criminal standard of "beyond a reasonable doubt." This latter issue appears to have been resolved by a recent US Supreme Court decision (Addington v Texas, 1979) favoring "clear and convincing evidence."

3. Disabled and in need of treatment: Although diminished in number, some states allow commitment solely on the grounds that a person is significantly handicapped by a mental illness, is in need of treatment, and would benefit from that treatment.

Most states also have laws (usually less strict) allowing the patient to be briefly (1-14 days) held involuntarily. Committed patients who feel that they are being held illegally may obtain a hearing by a writ of habeas corpus.

Much of recent legislation defining these standards has redressed real past wrongs which occurred when commitment could result merely from a physician's OK, yet recent controversy has focused on associated losses to the patient and his family due to his exclusion from treatment because of complex, criminal-like commitment proceedings.[4] As fewer patients have been treated involuntarily, some experts have noted a shift of mental patients from the civil to the criminal system - ie, the mental illness causes them to break a law they ordinarily would not have broken, and they are then arrested. The extent of this trend has not yet been determined.

An additional impact of the changing commitment laws has been to require the release of committed patients much earlier than in the past, resulting in a marked decline in the size of state mental hospitals. An unfortunate effect of this deinstitutionalization has been to release large numbers of marginally functioning persons into communities ill-equipped to deal with them - with the resultant formation of "psychiatric ghettos" in some large cities.

## THE RIGHT TO TREATMENT[5]:

Following the classic Alabama decision of Wyatt v Stickney (1972), it has become a general standard (amazingly, it had not been before) that an involuntarily committed person must receive a level of effective treatment adequate to encourage improvement. This concept was challenged, reviewed, and supported in another well-known case - Donaldson v O'Connor (1974). Still uncertain is what to do with the patient who is unlikely to improve with any treatment.

## THE RIGHT TO REFUSE TREATMENT:

This is currently the most actively contested area of

psychiatric law, and the results of the debate remain uncertain. Involuntary commitment is not prima facie evidence that the patient is incompetent to decide what treatment he is to receive.[6] Federal court decisions set the tone but conflict: Rennie v Klein (1979) gives a patient a qualified right to refuse treatment and creates an appeal process, while Rogers v Okin (1981) allows absolute refusal but provides for treatment authorized by a guardian.[7] Presumably the U.S. Supreme Court ultimately will clarify these discrepancies, but has not done so yet. Meanwhile, be very cautious (and legal) when insisting that a patient receive ECT or medication against his will, even when he appears to need it badly. Know your local laws. The degree of a physician's liability in giving treatment to a resisting patient is likely to be clarified in the next few years.

COMPETENCY:

Psychiatrists are sometimes asked to decide if a patient is mentally competent to perform specific functions (eg, make a will, handle his finances, testify in court).[8] There are rules for some of these decisions - eg, to be judged competent to make a will, a person must know (1) that he is making a will, (2) the extent and nature of his property, and (3) to whom he is leaving his things. To be found incompetent for one task does not necessarily imply incompetence for another.


CRIMINAL LAW

COMPETENCY TO STAND TRIAL:

It is held in law that, to receive a fair trial, a person must be able to understand the nature of his charges, understand the possible penalties, understand legal issues and procedures, and work with his attorney and participate rationally in his own defense. If he can't do one or more of these, he is "incompetent to stand trial" and usually is transferred to a treatment facility until his competency is restored (eg, medication for a psychosis). Once found competent, the patient is usually returned to court to stand trial. Recently, some states have decided that if a patient's competency can't be restored in a "reasonable length of time" (eg, the length of time he probably would serve for the crime for which he has been charged), he must continue treatment in a civil facility if committable, or be released. Psychiatrists are most commonly the experts asked to help the court decide on competency (the decision is the court's).[9]

## CRIMINAL RESPONSIBILITY[10]:

The "not guilty by reason of insanity" plea is much debated by both the legal and psychiatric professions yet it continues to be used (infrequently). It is <u>not</u> widely abused. Part of the general dissatisfaction with this plea centers on whether psychiatrists (or anyone) can retrospectively determine a patient's mental functioning at the time of a crime. Just as an incompetency decision is concerned with the patient's mental state <u>at the time of the trial</u>, a responsibility decision involves the mental state <u>at the time of the crime</u>. Also in question are the criteria needed to make that judgment - several different ones are used in different states:

- The M'Naghten Rule: Did the person not <u>know</u> (1) the nature of his act and (2) that it was wrong? This is a common test (one-third of states).
- The Irresistible Impulse Test: Was he acting under an "irresistible impulse?" This test is invariably combined with other tests.
- The Durham Rule: Was his act the product of "a mental disease or defect?"
- The American Law Institute (ALI) Test: Does he have a mental disease or defect such that he "lacks <u>substantial</u> capacity either to <u>appreciate</u> the criminality of his conduct or to <u>conform</u> his conduct to the requirements of the law?" This test adds a "volitional" standard to the "cognitive" standard of the M'Naghten Rule. It is used in approximately one-half of the states and in all federal courts.

If one or more of the above conditions are met, the patient may be declared "not guilty by reason of insanity" and be freed of responsibility for his crime. If needing treatment at that point, he is usually placed in a psychiatric facility until his mental illness remits or until he is no longer felt to be a threat to the community because of mental illness.

Many states and the US Congress have considered restrictive modifications (or abolition) of the insanity defense in the wake of the public outcry following John Hinckley's "not guilty" verdict in his shooting of President Reagan. The form the insanity defense ultimately will take is not clear. Leading possibilities appear to be (1) a return to some form of the M'Naghten Rule by eliminating the "volitional" standard, and (2) a <u>guilty but mentally ill</u> verdict (thus, a person first would be judged and sentenced criminally, then treated in an appropriate setting for his mental illness).

## PERSONAL ISSUES

### MALPRACTICE:

The risk that a psychiatrist will be successfully sued for malpractice is low but climbing. Most suits involve use of ECT, improper or inadequately informed use of medication, unusual treatments, sexual involvement with patients, and successful patient suicide (suit brought by relatives).[11]

### CONFIDENTIALITY:

Physicians are ethically obligated to maintain patient confidentiality, except when voluntarily waived by the patient.[12]  General knowledge by others of details of a patient's psychiatric treatment or even awareness of psychiatric care can be damaging socially and occupationally to a patient. Unfortunately, legal protection of the physician for maintaining that confidentiality is far from complete. In some cases (eg, Tarasoff v Regents of the University of California (1976) states that a therapist has a "duty to protect" a third party threatened harm by the patient[13,14]), the psychiatrist may be liable if he does not break privacy.[15,16]  In addition, utilization review groups and third-party payers are demanding more privileged information. Become familiar with your own state's laws.

### INFORMED CONSENT:

Informed consent should be sought from all patients for all treatments, but formal (ie, written) consent should be obtained for physical procedures (eg, ECT, medication). The patient should be informed about the reasons for the treatment, it's nature, the likelihood of success, the dangers and likelihood of side effects, and any alternative treatments.

A major problem arises if the patient is "incapable of being informed" (eg, due to retardation, OBS, psychosis).[17] A guardian may need to be appointed whose duty would be to make the decision for the patient.

### REFERENCES

1.  Gutheil TG, Appelbaum PS: Clinical Handbook of Psychiatry and the Law. New York, McGraw-Hill Book Co., 1982.
2.  Bursten B: Posthospital mandatory outpatient treatment. Am J Psychiatry 143:1255-1258, 1986.

3. McNiel DE, Binder RL: Predictive validity of judgements of dangerousness in emergency civil commitment. Am J Psychiatry 144:197-200, 1987.
4. Schwartz HI, Appelbaum PS, Kaplan RD: Clinical judgements in the decision to commit. Arch Gen Psychiatry 41:811-815, 1984.
5. Appelbaum PS: Resurrecting the right to treatment. Hosp Community Psychiatry 38:703-704, 1987.
6. Hipshman L: Assessing a patient's competence to make treatment decisions. Psychiatr Ann 17:279-283, 1987.
7. Gutheil RG: Rogers v Commissioner: Denouement of an important right-to-refuse-treatment case. Am J Psychiatry 142:213-216, 1985.
8. Kern SR: Issues of competency in the aged. Psychiatr Ann 17:336-339, 1987.
9. Lamb HR: Incompetency to stand trial. Arch Gen Psychiatr 44:754-758, 1987.
10. AMA Committee on Medicolegal Problems: Insanity defense in criminal trials and limitation of psychiatric testimony. JAMA 251:2967-2981, 1984.
11. Bromberg W: The perils of psychiatry. Psychiatr Ann 13:219-236, 1983.
12. APA Committee on Confidentiality: Guidelines on confidentiality. Am J Psychiatry 144:1522-1526, 1987.
13. Gross BH, Southard MJ, Lamb HR, Weinberger LE: Assessing dangerousness and responding appropriately. J Clin Psychiatry 48:9-12, 1987.
14. Mills MJ, Sullivan G, Eth S: Protecting third parties: A decade after Tarasoff. Am J Psychiatry 144:68-74, 1987.
15. Appelbaum PS: Tarasoff and the clinician: Problems in fulfilling the duty to protect. Am J Psychiatry 142:425-429, 1985.
16. Bloom JD, Rogers JL: The duty to protect others from your patients - Tarasoff spreads to the northwest. West J Med 148:231-234, 1988.
17. Drane JF: Competency to give an informed consent. JAMA 252:925-927, 1984.